M000118128

STRAND $3.00

BROKEN SCALES

BROKEN SCALES

Race and the Crisis of Justice in a Divided America

Tom Diaz

ROWMAN & LITTLEFIELD
Lanham • Boulder • New York • London

Published by Rowman & Littlefield
An imprint of The Rowman & Littlefield Publishing Group, Inc.
4501 Forbes Boulevard, Suite 200, Lanham, Maryland 20706
www.rowman.com

6 Tinworth Street, London SE11 5AL, United Kingdom

Copyright © 2021 by The Rowman & Littlefield Publishing Group, Inc.

All rights reserved. No part of this book may be reproduced in any form or by
any electronic or mechanical means, including information storage and retrieval
systems, without written permission from the publisher, except by a reviewer
who may quote passages in a review.

British Library Cataloguing in Publication Information Available

Library of Congress Cataloging-in-Publication Data

Names: Diaz, Tom, author.
Title: Broken scales : race and the crisis of justice in a divided America / Tom Diaz.
Description: Lanham, Maryland : Rowman & Littlefield, an imprint of the Rowman & Littlefield
    Publishing Group, Inc., [2021] | Includes bibliographical references and index. | Summary: "This
    book analyzes the everyday actions of ordinary people in the context of extreme political and
    cultural polarization, distort the criminal justice system and betray the lofty ideals expressed in
    American founding documents and centuries of Anglo-American articulations of basic human
    rights"—Provided by publisher.
Identifiers: LCCN 2021011761 (print) | LCCN 2021011762 (ebook) | ISBN 9781538138502 (cloth) |
    ISBN 9781538138519 (epub)
Subjects: LCSH: Discrimination in criminal justice administration—United States. | Polarization
    (Social sciences)—United States.
Classification: LCC HV9950 .D53 2021 (print) | LCC HV9950 (ebook) | DDC 364.973089—dc23
LC record available at https://lccn.loc.gov/2021011761
LC ebook record available at https://lccn.loc.gov/2021011762

"Even if I do not commit any evil deed, if my will is to do evil, I carry the weight of sin as if I had committed that deed."
Meister Eckhart

"You have as many enemies as you have slaves."
Roman proverb

CONTENTS

I

THE LENS OF RACIAL PERCEPTION

Humans are a species that classifies. We arrange the flow of the things and events that we see and experience, place them into categories, and erect boundaries around those categories. Fruits, vegetables, apples, bananas, friends, enemies, dangerous things and dangerous people, helpful things and helpful people, and harmless things and harmless people—the categories we need simply to navigate life are endless and varied. Classification helps us make sense of the world. Without classification, our lives would be chaos.

Among the boundaries that we erect are those that we put around groups of "other" human beings. "Group boundaries are inescapable, permanent features of social life," scholar Matt Wray observed. "These may be perceived to be differences in anatomy; religious beliefs; skin color and haircut; language; economic status; mental and physical abilities; region—in short, anything at all."[1]

The history of how the ruling in-groups of societies have treated the subordinate out-groups of "others" is generally grim.[2]

The evil side of human classification of other human beings is that we sometimes create false categories of other people, as is often the case in racial, ethnic, and religious stereotypes. We assign characteristics to fictional people and erect boundaries around *empty* cells. "[B]oundaries can exist and produce social categories whether or not there are actual people inhabiting those categories."[3] In other words, some groups of others that we create may exist only in our minds and in the shared beliefs of our own group. No one in reality has the characteristics that we convince ourselves are there. Nevertheless, we resolutely act as if they did. "All of these people are criminals (or terrorists, or rapists) at heart," we think. "Therefore we need strict laws to protect *us* from *them*."

This unmindful creation of empty categories of human characteristics is what happened during two periods crucial to the construction of race in America—antebellum slavery, and the period known as Jim Crow. Through different but related classifying mechanisms, white Americans created a racial lens through which they reflexively came to perceive black Americans as a separate and inferior race (a different group), the members of which had specific characteristics—"differences in anatomy; religious beliefs; skin color and haircut; language; economic status; mental and physical abilities."

This is racism. When the term is used in this book, it refers to the widely accepted definition by scholar William Julius Wilson. "At its core, racism is an ideology of racial domination with two key features: (1) beliefs that one race is either biologically or culturally inferior to another and (2) the use of such beliefs to rationalize or prescribe the way that the 'inferior' race should be treated in this society, as well as to explain its social position as a group and its collective accomplishments."[4]

Most white Americans wear this lens unconsciously. It's not something that we deliberately take on and off. The lens is just there, virtually all of the time. It takes conscious and sustained effort to correct the distorted view of other real human beings upon whom have been projected the imagined characteristics of an empty cell.

A crucial corollary of this circumstance is that how we define race and how we act about it are the cumulative and continuing products of millions of daily interactions of ordinary people. This phenomenon has a peculiarly powerful effect in criminal law and procedure. "If we can derive one lesson from history, it is that law is not made from above," Ariela Gross observed. "Ordinary people confronted the state in local courts and administrative hearings, and those confrontations shaped the law. Race did not just happen, and law was not imposed on us. We made race, through legal institutions, and we continue to make it every day; we can also unmake it."[5]

Another important corollary is that an event may not seem "racial" on the surface. But in many cases, if one peels back a layer or two, the perceptions and constraints of the underlying racially conscious society are indeed there.

This book takes for an instructive example several things that happened after a wealthy white lawyer shot and killed his even wealthier white wife in Atlanta, Georgia, one hot night in 2016. There was nothing "racial" in the shooting itself. But peel back a few layers, and it becomes clear that the lens of racial perception, the erection of boundaries, and the classification of the "other" was there all the time. Race was very close to the heart of the incident.

WHEN TEX SHOT DIANE

It was like an earthquake. Shock waves staggered the Atlanta elite and woke the always hungry media after wealthy and politically prominent lawyer Claud Lee ("Tex") McIver, III, shot his wife Diane in the back near midnight on September 25, 2016. Sitting in the rear passenger seat of a luxury SUV, Tex somehow fired a single pistol shot that struck a mortal blow to Diane, sitting in the front passenger seat.

Diane's death could have been only one of two things.

It was either a sordid little murder, wickedly clever and spiced with a frisson of wealth and power. Or it was a tragedy, an accidental death at the hands of a husband with an adolescent fondness for reckless gun play.

A jury of Tex's peers decided that Diane's death was that fiendishly clever murder. Even so, an informed observer might to this day reasonably argue that the facts show her death to have been more probably a foolish accident. Legal guilt is different from factual guilt.

No matter. The wheels of justice having ground finely on, seventy-six-year-old Tex is now serving out a term of life imprisonment—with the possibility of parole after his one hundredth birthday—in a Georgia state prison near Jackson, about one hour south of Atlanta. The prison is roughly thirty-five miles west of the McIver's storied eighty-five-acre "ranch" in Eatonton, where the power couple lavishly entertained on weekends. Among Tex's fellow residents in the prison at Jackson are some of Georgia's most interesting inmates.

The spectacle of Tex McIver's prosecution, trial, and conviction was a polite, legalistic form of charivari, pronounced and sometimes spelled "shivaree." The charivari was one of the Old South's cultural-enforcement mechanisms, a mildly violent mob action, first cousin to the lynching. A rude means of expressing disapproval of a person's morals or actions that violated a community's cultural boundaries, the charivari's roots go back to medieval Europe, where it sometimes also took the more benign form of a boisterous wedding march. In America it most often consisted of a torch-light parade and a nighttime gathering outside of a moral offender's home. The charivari was often inspired and subtly organized by the hidden hand of the local elite, although it was apparently carried out by people from the middling and lower classes. Shouted threats, banging of pots, and the hurling of rotten vegetables and other objects made clear the community's disapproval. In extreme cases, the offender might be tarred, feathered, and paraded through town on a rail, or threatened with violent death if they did not leave the area.

Just so, news media, television documentarians, and pundits from all over the world clamored and banged during Tex's progress through the stations of the law—investigation, trial, conviction. Virtually all of that raucous media attention rolled the camera lens in tightly, panned briefly over the meager stack of direct facts about the shooting, then dwelled lovingly on a fat wad of ostensibly damning, indirect, and entirely circumstantial evidence that prosecutors threw onto the courtroom table like high-rollers going for broke in a Las Vegas casino.

It was breaking news, "true crime" at its best, breathless click-bait, and a reliable ratings driver.

But as tragic as Diane McIver's death was, the game was about much more than a simple, even-handed search for impartial justice in a courtroom. Racial tensions, a bitter lawyers' grudge match, class envy, bare-knuckle politics, and the hidden world of domestic violence all played silent roles in Tex McIver's personal and legal trials. No one took the witness stand to testify about those things. And almost no one talked or wrote about them in polite company—inside or outside the courtroom or in the news media.

I was introduced to the McIver case in 2018, when I was asked to write a book proposal on behalf of a close friend of the McIvers. Had the proposal—cast in the form of the venerable true crime genre—resulted in a book contract, I would have been ghostwriter to the principal. The book would have been very different from this one. There was a time when true crime was one of the most successful book genres, and paperbacks poured off of publishers' printing presses. The McIver homicide would have been a natural for that genre. But the true crime book market has withered, overtaken by the electronic media—television, streaming videos, podcasts. (The change may be related to another cultural phenomenon: although most other modern presidents wrote books, Donald Trump emitted tweet storms.) Alas, our proposal sank in the riptide of this changed book market. I moved on to another book project, *Tragedy in Aurora: The Culture of Mass Shootings in America* (Rowman & Littlefield, 2019).

Even while I was devoting almost all of my time and attention to *Tragedy in Aurora*, I remained fascinated by the McIver saga. The more I thought about it, the more it seemed to me that as time passed and perspective was gained, the McIver story was less interesting as true crime than as a stepping-off point for an examination of today's bitter culture war—the ongoing conflicts among America's several polarized legal, political, and social cultures—and especially the important role that our lens of race plays in that war.

The McIvers were involved in numerous ways in the cultural struggle. Their broader story is an example of how the daily thoughts, actions, and articulated desires of hundreds of millions of "ordinary people" collectively shape who we are as a nation and a culture, and how we think about race, law, and justice. The quotidian routines of these ordinary folk—how they reflexively think about and act toward each other day in and day out—have more impact on the reality of America as it is than all of the writings of academia, the wisdom of commentators, and the exhortations of professional activists about how America should be.

"The formal commands of the law emanate from social conditions, affect them, and are in turn affected by them," a leading text on criminal procedure states. "These interactions are much less governed by the intentions or aspirations of any court, legislature, or chief executive, or for that matter by the explicit terms of the formal commands themselves, than by the realities of human affairs."[6]

Among the realities of human affairs is the undeniable fact that the members of an elite stratum, empowered by wealth or station or both, are more able to shape things than most others. The McIvers were decidedly in that elect class. In addition to wealthy ideological influencers, that highest level includes elected politicians, legislators, judges, law enforcement executives, religious leaders, important business executives, and so forth. These are the people who write and enforce the laws and other social constraints that make concrete the sum of the collective's ethics, mores, desires, and demands. If the elite's enactments wander too far off

the collective rails, they can be corrected by grass roots reaction, sometimes dramatically.

What I found particularly illuminating was a racially charged excuse
that Tex's "team" floated soon after the shooting to explain why Tex had
his gun in hand during that late night trip, ensconced as he was within the
several tons of steel of an upscale Ford King Ranch SUV. It was suggested that Tex feared that the travelers—he, Diane, and a friend who was
driving—might somehow come across an improbable midnight Black
Lives Matter demonstration or, in a telling equation of perceived threats,
a carjacking. That remark was like an old-fashioned press camera's flash-
bulb. It froze Tex and the McIvers' world in a tableau, rich with context
and inviting exploration. That picture posed two threshold questions that
inform much of this book. Why is there a Black Lives Matter movement
in the first place? And why would a wealthy white man, secure in a
moving motor vehicle driving through a not particularly bad part of Atlanta, feel so threatened by its existence that he decided to draw a gun?
These two basic questions opened other corollary questions, such as:
What is "race"? What is "law"? What is "justice"?

Keying off of that incendiary remark and the questions it posed, this
book uses the persons, events, and relationships involved in Diane's homicide, and its context within the McIvers' world, as points from which to
examine past and present legal (and related cultural) issues involving
race, class, and ethnicity. (Parallel issues are involved in law, gender, and
gender identity, subjects too broad and complex to include in this text but
nonetheless as important as those treated here.)

The book's premises are that (1) systems of law and justice do not
descend from on high but are the fluid products of a society's culture,
more specifically, the collective everyday acts and convictions of "ordinary people," which propel and sometimes limit the executive actions of
more powerful elites; and (2) the United States is in a period of deep
cultural flux and conflict, much of it seen through the lens of race.

This "culture war" is affecting our legal system in the broadest sense,
including the very structure of the federal government and our understanding of the constitutional system as it relates to the relative powers of
the president, the congress, and the judiciary. I am referring here specifically to the "unitary executive theory" under which the president is conceived of having virtually dictatorial powers.[7] This is again a topic that is
related to the thrust of this book but too broad and complex to be treated

here. I note it because it is a central premise of the political and cultural phenomenon of Trumpism, and because in my opinion the theory does not get the attention it deserves in policy debates directly related to race and the legal system. The outcome of the ongoing struggle over the unitary executive theory will have major impacts on all of the issues directly discussed in this book, and most especially on the criminal justice system.

TRUMPISM AND THE MCIVERS

A major factor in America's current turmoil, including the flux in its legal system, is the political and cultural phenomenon that has come to be known as "Trumpism." A fine subject for debate is whether Donald Trump ignited today's agitation or simply exploited currents of fear and anger already roiling beneath the Obama era's deceptively tranquil fields. A corollary question is whether the former president's conduct has validated—implicitly granted grace to—ugly currents of racism and religious and ethnic intolerance. Regardless of how and when it started, Trumpism is today an undeniable reality. It is a throwback in many ways to Thomas Jefferson's and Andrew Jackson's ideal of a republic of white yeomen—libertarian and egalitarian to those *inside* its bounds, namely white males, while affirmatively and oppressively excluding those *outside*, people of color and "questionable" ethnicity.

This "inside/outside" theme is integral to Trumpism and to much of the analysis and discussion in this book. For example, the rules of personal liberty "inside" Europe in the seventeenth and eighteenth centuries were very different from the rules that Europeans applied to human beings in the "outside" world, whom they ruthlessly exploited while developing slavery on an industrial scale. In the eighteenth century, the stirring anthem "Rule, Britannia" captured the hearts of Britons, who defiantly sang that "Britons never will be slaves." Meanwhile, those same freedom-loving Britons were transporting millions of Africans to labor in the slave camps—plantations—of the so-called Sugar Revolution in the West Indies.

Even within a given society, there are "inside/outside" distinctions that result in different outcomes for the elite and the ordinary, summed up in the acidic observation of the nineteenth-century French man of letters,

Anatole France. "In its majestic equality, the law forbids rich and poor alike to sleep under bridges, to beg in the streets, and to steal their bread."[8] Tex McIver, like criminal defendants in several other Georgia cases we will explore, could afford a chauffeured ride in the leather-lined luxury limousine of expensive "inside" legal representation. But the best that many less fortunate defendants can hope for is a shared ride in a battered proletarian van—the help of an overworked public defender or a bargain basement legal hack, all under pressure to move too many cases quickly through the indifferent system of plea bargaining that has taken over America's criminal justice system and all but eliminated jury trials for "outside" defendants.

Tex and Diane McIver were "inside" people. They were truly extraordinary, accomplished, and wealthy, and they were riding the very razor's edge of a tipping point in American history. Elite, but not of elite origins, the McIvers were in the vanguard of inchoate Trumpism, "proto-Trumpists" as it were. To be sure, at the time of Diane's death in September 2016, the Trumpism of today was still considered by political insiders and pundits as a "cloud no bigger than a man's hand" on the political horizon. Yet the McIvers were among what we now know to have been a surprisingly large mass of voters who were not deterred by the smug wisdom of the pollsters and pundits predicting that Hillary Clinton would crush Donald Trump in the presidential election, which came less than two months after Diane was killed.

That small cloud became a storm. November 8, 2016, slapped a complacently progressive America in the face. Trump's election forced Americans to look into the widening chasm of polarization that divides them. Americans have sorted out and aligned themselves according to just about every difference they can see, hear, feel, touch, or imagine. Race, ethnicity, immigration status, language, social class, income, political values, and gender have all sharpened into pikes of the culture war.

The evidence of the McIvers' commitment to the principles of this rising new force can be found in things great and small in their lives. For example, death remorselessly cuts off and leaves undone things important to the unexpectedly dead—books not written, paintings not painted, love not expressed. Among the small but illuminating things left undone by Diane McIver was hanging a poster-sized photograph of her, standing beside a grinning candidate Donald Trump, taken at a political function. It was waiting in her office on the night she was killed. There is other evidence. It includes the McIvers' political contributions, Tex's pioneering political activities in voter suppression, Diane's litigation challenging Atlanta's comfortable compromise of affirmative action contract awards, and artifacts in the McIvers' sprawling "ranch" that expressed conservative cultural points of view—gun rights and support for "law and order"—that have emerged as important Trumpist memes.

THE LENS OF RACE

The questions raised by the Black Lives Matter rationale opened a window into the history of race, law, and justice in America. I have chosen to note especially two periods of that history—antebellum slavery and the combined postbellum period of Reconstruction and Jim Crow—because I believe that each separately established two different but related conditions that, taken together, created the single lens that informs every aspect of race and law in America today.

The white slave masters and other defenders of antebellum slavery constructed during the nineteenth century the "scientific" proposition that black people—slave and free alike—were of a biologically different "race" than "whites." Moreover, that black race was inherently and inescapably inferior in all the important characteristics of what it means to be human—intelligence, emotional maturity, empathy, morality, even sexuality. This doctrine of separate and inferior was the first premise, the foundational rock, of the "outside" system of law and justice imposed upon blacks in America. (The "inside" premise was that the white "race" was not merely entitled, but under a positive duty, to rule over the inferior races.) The advancement of these racist conclusions was by no means confined to the South. Some of the most influential advocates of scientific racism were scholars at Harvard and other respected Northern universities. Their conclusions were widely endorsed in literate society, in the North and South alike, including among many abolitionists.

During the second, "Jim Crow," period, from a few years after the end of the Civil War until well into the twentieth century, the dominant—which is to say, white—culture fleshed out the supposed physical, moral, and intellectual traits of the *individual* black human beings who had been consigned to the separate black "race." In a hurricane of grotesquely demeaning visual, literary, and even intellectual caricature—including but by no means limited to the popular genre known as "Sambo art"—a fantastic set of images came to define for all white Americans what black people physically looked like and how they thought and acted. In sum, blacks were portrayed as monstrously malformed in appearance, child-like, achingly and willfully ignorant, and notwithstanding everything else, always potentially dangerous—the projected characteristics of a classification of human beings, of a bounded cell, that is in reality empty of actual human beings.[9]

The volume, breadth, and duration of this torrent of racist imagery rivals the noxious stream of anti-Semitic imagery spewed by the infamous Nazi-era German publication *Der Sturmer*.[10] Not a crevice of American society escaped this deluge of dehumanization, transmuted into racial fear, hatred, and violence. Food packaging, postcards, comic books, "humorous" magazine illustrations, political cartoons, consumer product advertising, garden sculpture, amateur theater productions, church festivals, films, radio, and television, to name just a few societal transmitters, routinely portrayed black human beings in what came to be accepted as reality—something almost everyone who was white just "knew" was true.

Ordinary white people all over America, for example, celebrated vacation road trips by sending home to friends and family illustrated postcards featuring "funny" caricatures of black people, typically eating watermelon or being consumed by alligators. Perhaps the most shameful and horrific of these postcards were photographs of lynched African Americans—their bodies burned and twisted into as grotesque an indictment of crime against humanity as the emaciated corpses of Jews piled in the common yards of Hitler's Nazi extermination camps.

The combined effect of these two periods of racial definition was the creation of a distorted but universally accepted lens. Many whites—including policemen, prosecutors, and judges—could only see African Americans through that lens. When Tex McIver took out his revolver that night, he was seeing Black Lives Matter in particular but African Americans in general though that lens: dark and dangerous.

One might argue that black (or Asian, Latino, etc.) people also view white people through lenses of culturally shaped perception. This is no doubt true. The difference is that the almost limitless supremacy of white power over people of color and different ethnicities made the white lens of race powerful and oppressive throughout American history. The culturally imprinted imagery seen through that racist lens continues to be a strongly negative force in the shaping of law and the administration of justice in America.

"OUTSIDE" WHITES

The life stories of Diane McIver, and her mentor and corporate father figure—a wildly successful businessman named William ("Billy") Corey, given to taking impromptu trips in his personal jet—opens an entirely different view of race and power in America. That is the complex dimension of poor whites confined to lives "outside" of the dominant system. These are the white people sometimes currently described as "the left behind," or in the past more pejoratively as "crackers" or "poor white trash." These marginal people also suffered from biased boundary-setting and stereotypical projections, while being exploited to advance racial enmity.

Diane and Billy shared a keen business acumen. They had a crackling synergy that resulted in major business accomplishments that made them both wealthy. But neither were born into privileged circumstances, neither had the benefits of accumulated family capital or connections. Each began life on the lower rung of white society and rose to the top on their own grit, acumen, and hard work. Many of the people on the same bottom rung from which they rose share a history of exclusion, debasement, and rejection dating from colonial times in America—the results of human group classification.

Although never subjected to as much violence and brutal industrial regimentation as black slaves, the poorest of whites in America were an "outside" minority that did suffer from demeaning moral and physical exploitation. Just as the rules for black Americans were "outside" and different from the "inside" rules of the dominant white power structure, so were the rules applied to "white trash" different from and "outside" the rules for upper and middling American whites—the plantation masters and the yeoman farmers of the antebellum era, and the middling and upper classes of the century following.

Often physically connected to and competing with black people and the economics of slavery, the dismal conditions of lower-class whites constituted paradoxical evidence that—the dictates of scientific racism notwithstanding—being of the white "race" did not in fact assure "superiority" in any human dimension. In some areas, "poor white trash" were regarded by black slaves and white master alike as demonstrably inferior, subjects of open derision.

The story of these poor whites invites interesting questions, such as: Exactly what does it mean to be "white"? How have Americans historically determined at law and in society who is and who is not "white"? And what exactly has it meant to be deemed "white"?

THE CONUNDRUM OF UNLIKELY SUCCESS

The lives of Diane McIver and Billy Corey are examples one of the great conundrums of American life. How is it that some few singular individuals, of all colors and ethnicities, born into the most wretched of circumstances, are able not only to rise above the environments of their birth to respectable careers, but to reach and thrive in the thin air of the rarified top layer of American business and society? These are not the people who rise from poverty to become blue-collar technicians, data managers, or white-collar executives in a thriving business. They are rather the people who own the conglomerate that owns the corporation that owns the business.

The conventional, superficial, and thoroughly ideological explanation is that these extraordinary people are simply the logical products of the "American way." Dream big enough, work hard enough, and anyone can become anything they want to. This corollary of American "exceptionalism" serves well enough as political fodder and cultural shibboleth. But it fails to account for the many times more who do all the right things—dream big, work hard—and still cannot break the bonds of deprived circumstance, negative social and economic capital, much less rise to the heights.

This conundrum of success raises interesting questions regarding the relationships between structural and cultural forces in determining who rises and who does not in America. Sometimes expressed as the difference between "nature and nurture," these questions can be divisive among activists for the disadvantaged—even the suggestion that any given group's culture or neighborhood conditions play an important role in their plight is excoriated as "blaming the victim."

THE HISTORIES OF GEORGIA AND ATLANTA

Georgia and Atlanta are apt settings for the explorations in this book. Their histories project well onto the broader canvas of the Old South—what happened in Georgia and Atlanta generally happened everywhere else in the South—and of the United States. What happened in the South did not stay in the South. It strongly influenced and in some cases was the principal driver of events in the North and the country as a whole. [11]

Unique among all the colonies, Georgia's charter originally forbade slavery. Its founders were elite Englishmen who conceived of the colony as a place to which the lowest of England's classes—inmates of debtors' prisons, drunks, prostitutes, and impoverished idlers—could be transported at no cost to them and allowed to rise to respectable yeoman status through the virtue of hard work. The founders had neither moral nor ideological problems with slavery—some were slaveowners themselves. But they thought that the institution of slavery would erode the fundamental system for poor whites becoming productive citizens through the ethic of their own hard work, on a platform of small land-holding.

The prohibition of slavery was short-lived in Georgia. Its demise and the subsequent counterclockwise march of the plantation economy and slaveholding culture across middle Georgia to its southwest frontier is a model of the motives of greed, the means of violence, the ethnic cleansing and land grabs, and the political power that resulted in the coronation of King Cotton and the establishment of slave camp bases to cultivate the crop throughout the South. "Georgia serves as a microcosm for the development of the cotton South . . . [it] illuminates the pattern in the other states of the Deep South where cotton became king. . . . Georgia offers a model to understand the social, political, and economic transformation of the cotton South." [12]

Atlanta has a rich history as literary subject and inspiration. Best-selling novels like Margaret Mitchell's *Gone With the Wind* and Tom Wolfe's *A Man in Full*, poetry like James Dickey's "Looking for the Buckhead Boys," and dozens of other fictional works have harvested the material of Atlanta's history, its dynamic way, and its many cultural substrata.

Transportation was the very rationale for Atlanta's creation. The state's leaders saw construction of a railroad link through Tennessee and ultimately to the steamboat highway of the Mississippi River as an urgently needed way to make possible the movement of cotton from Georgia and the exchange of commodities with the West. Atlanta was originally staked out in 1837 at a place called "Terminus," meaning the "end of the line." Terminus was the railhead of a railroad that was built on the backs of slave labor. Atlanta's boosters have portrayed the city as the very model of interracial amity in something euphemistically called the "New South"—"The City Too Busy to Hate" is one of its boosters' mottos. Others speak of "the Atlanta Way," referring to political compromises through which jobs and contracts were shared with the city's black population. Atlanta has also been described as the "Black Mecca," a city singular in the opportunities for dignity and success that it has historically offered African Americans.

But not everyone agrees with this benign view of Atlanta. The city was notoriously closed to free black labor during the antebellum period. It was one of the cities in which the terror of white riots against African Americans erupted in the Jim Crow era. It was as racially segregated as anywhere else in America. And some modern critics question whether its vaunted economic compromises and opportunities ever benefited more than an elite few. These tensions have become apparent in recent years with the rise of the Black Lives Matter movement, Trumpism, and volatile demonstrations in Atlanta against police violence.

IN SUM

Looked at with the broadest lens, the story of Diane McIver's death offers many rich lines of inquiry about law, justice, and race in America. The narrative arc of this book relates the story of Tex, Diane, her death, and Tex's encounter with the justice system. The substantive arc explores the broader themes of race and the criminal justice system.

2

ALABAMA

A Notional Fiction

It was hot as hell in Auburn that day in 1958. It often was in Alabama.[1]

Somewhere nearby a song floated out of a radio and through an open screen window. The deep gravel voice of country and western star Johnny Cash sighed through his cross-over hit single, "Guess Things Happen That Way." It was the stoic lament of a man beaten down by love's rejection.

Well, you ask me if I'll forget my baby.

I guess I will, someday.

I don't like it, but I guess things happen that way.

The tears burning down Diane's cheeks and the snot bubbles pulsing in and out of her nostrils made the searing day even worse. She was outside, standing next to the mailbox in front of the modest working man's house, sobbing in uncontrollable shudders. The most important man in her life was leaving her alone, abandoning her to the emotional hell inside that house.

Diane was six years old.

"No, Daddy!" she cried. "Daddy, please! Please, Daddy, don't leave me. Please."

But Diane's daddy had had enough. Maybe he loved her. Maybe he didn't. Or maybe he didn't love her enough. Whichever it was, he just kept walking out of that little girl's life. He never looked back. He left her alone with her momma, a woman Diane would grow to detest. Her mother burned through five marriages and untold amounts of the drugs and alcohol to which she was addicted. As wretched as her tumultuous life was, Diane's mother nevertheless managed to ride her daughter just as hard and as mercilessly as the demons that tortured her. When she died years later, Diane refused to go to her funeral.

"They fought like cats and dogs," Diane's cousin said of the two women.

Diane loved country music throughout her life. But she flatly refused to accept Johnny Cash's hopeless premise that things just happen the way they do. She was damned well not going to be a victim of her father's abandonment or her mother's self-inflicted illness. Life was not going to tell her what to do. She was not going to sit at a bar, listening to the jukebox in some beer-besotted roadhouse, looking for love and feeling sorry for herself, whining about the cruel cards that life dealt her. Whatever did not kill Diane made her stronger. Somehow, she forged a steel will power on the chaotic anvil of her younger years.

Diane was determined to make things happen the way she wanted them to. She vowed to leave home the day she turned eighteen.

"She was going to make her own path in this world," her cousin recalled of her. "She wasn't going to rely on anybody. She was going to be a self-made woman."

3

MIDNIGHT MATTERS

Late in the evening of Sunday, September 25, 2016, seventy-three-year-old Tex McIver and his sixty-four-year-old wife, Diane, were driving back to their condominium in the Villa at Buckhead Heights, an eighteen-story luxury high-rise building in the elite Buckhead neighborhood of north Atlanta.

Only Tex would make it home alive.

The well-known power couple had spent the weekend relaxing on their eighty-six-acre property near the town of Eatonton in rural Putnam County, about seventy-six miles southeast of Atlanta. Others might have called the spread at 603 Pea Ridge Road Southeast a "farm" or perhaps "a gated estate." But Tex sprinkled his life with flamboyant references to his origins in the Lone Star State. He dubbed the richly appointed property his "ranch."

The weather that Sunday was as Southern as it gets. The temperature peaked at ninety-two degrees. By evening the humidity was a steaming 76 percent. Based on average weather data, the annual four-month hot season in Putnam County had ended ten days earlier. But the temperature in Eatonton that day exceeded the ninety-one-degree average temperature of the statistically hottest day of the year, July 20.

Eatonton is the county seat of Putnam County, which lies in the middle of a band of some thirty-five counties that stretches across middle Georgia from South Carolina to Alabama. That swath was known as the Old Plantation Piedmont Cotton Belt.

Under the plantation system Putnam County flourished. By 1850 . . .
the county was prosperous. The planting aristocracy was in full bloom.
The greatest wealth was among the planters. They owned plantations
of a thousand or more acres and worked a hundred or more slaves.
Their way of life was luxurious. They owned fine houses, generally of
eight rooms, each 20 feet square, which were handsomely furnished.
They had servants, and domestic life held few chores for them. They
had fine horses and excellent carriages. Their hospitality was great. [1]

It was an exceedingly good life—for the white masters. Leisure, fine
horses, and lavish sociability echo the romanticized plantation life described in Margaret Mitchell's nostalgic and perpetually best-selling novel *Gone With the Wind*. But the foundation of the pleasant living of the
"planting aristocracy" was an intricate, brutally enforced system of slavery based on rigid racial boundaries policed by remorseless violence.
Black human beings were treated as property, not unlike cattle. The white
elites' fundamental premise that black persons were of an "inferior race"
ultimately meant that there was little that a white person could not do to,
or demand of, a black person, who by definition was fit only for slavery—excepting only compromising that black person's utility as a tool, a
human cog in the industrial machinery of the plantation system.

Scientists, sociologists, and the learned of academia have long since
discredited and discarded the theory of biological racial differences. But
their impact has been far from universal. "[W]hile the belief that race is
socially constructed has gained a privileged place in contemporary scholarly debates, it has won few practical battles," historian Ira Berlin observed. "Few people believe it; fewer act on it. The new understanding of
race has changed behavior little if at all."[2]

The ethic of white racial superiority was essential to the plantation
slave camps of the South. It was also embraced by entire systems of trade
and finance in the North and in America generally, out of both commercial necessity and cultural choice.

The lives of the eight thousand black human beings enslaved on the
plantations of antebellum Putnam County at its peak in 1860 were far
from luxurious. The majority of them, the "field hands"—men, women,
and children—would have spent the long days of the hot season between
June and September stooped over, sweating under a blazing sun. These
four months were a time for hoeing weeds and trimming endless rows of
maturing cotton plants. The plants rolled like waves in an ocean of white

across fields that stretched as far as the eye could see. Depending on the weather and planting conditions of any given year, at some time in September the field hands would start the next back-breaking cycle of industrial cotton cultivation. Walking down the long rows, they picked the ripe cotton bolls from their thorny stems, stuffing them into burlap sacks slung around their necks and dragged behind. Driven by the whips of overseers and "drivers," each "hand" was expected to pick a quota of cotton by weight every day, usually about one hundred pounds. Those who failed to meet the daily quota were often punished with flesh-ripping lashes from leather whips. Those who exceeded the quota set a higher mark to meet the next day.

Reminders of the ethnic cleansing of Native Americans that preceded Georgia's slave camps still exist at two of the county's tourist sites. The colossal theft of Native American lands and the forced migration of their owners was as essential as black slavery to the rise of King Cotton and Putnam County's boom days. The Rock Eagle Effigy Mound and the Rock Hawk Effigy Mound were built by Native Americans sometime between one thousand and three thousand years ago. Each mound features thousands of pieces of quartzite assembled in the shape of a bird, several hundred feet long in each dimension. Rock Eagle and Rock Hawk are the only such effigy mounds known to exist east of the Mississippi River. The mound-builders were gone long before white settlers began relentlessly encroaching on the territory of the later-era Creek Indians. The Creeks in Georgia had a name for the English, *Ecunnaumuxuklgee*— "People greedily grasping after the lands of the Red people."[3] Some of the Creeks' land lay in what was to become Putnam County. Under pressure from the white man's greedy grasping, the Creeks ceded that land to the state of Georgia in 1802. White settlers streamed in.

Putnam County today, according to the online *New Georgia Encyclopedia*, "has become an important center of industry and recreation in Georgia. Once the land of cotton, large plantations, and great wealth, a different look is now taking hold in the county with the establishment of golf resorts, gated communities, and new businesses."[4] Part of the county's new look is its racial composition. The last census before the Civil War recorded many more black slaves living in the county than whites, about eight thousand slaves to five thousand whites.[5] Those proportions are reversed today. Of the 21,208 residents counted in the 2010 census, about 70 percent were white and 27 percent black or African American.

The elegance of the plantation aristocracy during the antebellum era lives on today in the plush real estate development around Lake Oconee. The lake was created in 1979 when the utility company Georgia Power dammed the Oconee River and created a twenty-thousand-acre reservoir. The area around the man-made lake is a complex of grandly conceived gated communities, upscale second homes, and genteel resort living for wealthy retirees. At least one antebellum mansion, Hawthorne Heights, was for a time available for tours showing the typical "life of a Southern family."[6] The development's setting of whispering pine, green fairway, and shimmering lake is said to be magnificent. A major attraction is a challenging golf course at Reynolds Lake Oconee. It was the McIvers' favorite local course.

But for all of Putnam County's new look, the ghosts of slavery and its lasting effects can be found in the works of two of the county's native authors. One is the popular late-nineteenth-century writer Joel Chandler Harris, whose apologetic view of slavery is memorialized in the Uncle Remus Museum in Eatonton. Housed in a log cabin imported from elsewhere in Georgia, the museum is one of the county's popular tourist sites.

> Uncle Remus was created by an author with a sentimental attachment to a plantation memory. Bald, bearded, bespectacled, Remus is a former slave who does odd jobs around the plantation after emancipation. He tells his stories night after night to a little white boy, son of the plantation owner, unfolding to him in grandfatherly fashion the "mysteries of plantation lore." Remus has, Harris tells us, "nothing but pleasant memories of the discipline of slavery." This fictional creation of a white Southerner was welcomed by an audience that wanted to believe Remus was a representative of his race; Uncle Remus is a cousin of those nineteenth-century minstrels who blackened their faces to entertain with jokes and songs. He is, in a way, white.[7]

Among other things, Uncle Remus opined that education was a bad thing for black folks. "Uncle Remus's rejection of book learning," writes Harvard scholar Henry Louis Gates, "was the symbolic extension of the rejection of a life in freedom. That, perhaps was the ultimate insult in the vast array of aspersions cast on the freedmen and freedwomen: had they their druthers, they'd 'druther' be slaves than free."[8]

The other author is Alice Walker, who won the 1983 Pulitzer Prize and National Book Award for her epistolary novel *The Color Purple*. Adapted into a film and stage production, the story told in *The Color Purple* offers a view of black life in 1930s Georgia that is very different from the confectionary drivel about the imaginary contentment of slave and freed person alike dispensed in Chandler's tales.

The record heat in Putnam County that Sunday did not stop Tex and Diane from playing a round of golf at the Reynolds Lake Oconee course. Diane was an avid golfer and a fierce competitor. Her handicap was considerably lower than Tex's, or for that matter, almost any man who teed up with her. She scarcely concealed her exasperation with any less-talented player who slowed things down by rooting around in the rough, looking for an errant ball.

"Diane played," one male associate remarked, "like a robot."

Putting aside the fierceness of Diane's golf game, the McIvers were a generous couple, sociable on the scale of Putnam County's antebellum planters. They often spent weekends at the ranch entertaining their many friends. The grounds included a party house that was laid out like an old-fashioned Western saloon. The wine cellar in the basement of the saloon was said to be bigger than most ordinary people's houses. Among its racks of fine wines were bottles of a privately commissioned label, McIver Meritage. Naturally enough, there were longhorn cattle and horses that Diane loved to ride. The hospitality of the Old South, the individualism of the wild west, and the folkways of the American gun culture were blended into pool parties, private country music festivals, coffee mugs labeled "Cowboy" and "Cowgirl," a pistol-ornamented chandelier, and a replica of a revolver under a sign warning, "We Don't Dial 911." Tex and Diane also had a "Blue Lives Matter" billboard erected in Eatonton—a pointed rebuttal to the Black Lives Matter demonstrations buzzing around Atlanta that year, including in Buckhead's eminence.[9]

LOOK AWAY, DIXIE LAND!

Tex bought the ranch before he met Diane. More than one observer would compare him to Charlie Croker, the protagonist of *A Man in Full*, Tom Wolfe's best-selling novel about a booming Atlanta in the 1990s. Croker, a wealthy but hapless good old boy, real estate developer, and "King of the Crackers," owned a plantation in south Georgia called Turpmtine.

> Charlie liked to think he went out shooting quail at Turpmtine just the way the most famous master of Turpmtine, a Confederate Civil War hero named Austin Roberdeau Wheat, had done it a hundred years ago, and a hundred years ago nobody on a quail hunt at Turpmtine would have been out in the sedge talking about an Atlanta whose candidates for mayor were both black. . . . When he was here at Turpmtine, he liked to shed Atlanta, even in his voice. He liked to feel earthy, Down Home, elemental; which is to say, he was no longer merely a real estate developer, he was . . . a man.[10]

For Charlie Croker, Turpmtine was more than a physical place at a certain set of geographic coordinates. The estate embodied memories—or fantasies of memories—of a way of life that connected Croker's soul and psyche to cultural phantoms wandering through the past two centuries. Those old memories provided something that Charlie felt he lacked as a modern person and fulfilled him as a man. The metaphor of Turpmtine and the values it symbolized for Charlie raise vital questions open today about America, race, and history. Have Putnam County, the state of Georgia, the broader South, and the United States at large shed the same phantom memories of the centuries-long era of white mastery? Have they positively transformed the oppressive values, norms, folkways, and mores of these years of slavery into standards more in keeping with the noble values conspicuously declared in America's foundational documents?[11]

The outcome remains uncertain.

There is no doubt that—speaking strictly in terms of regions of the United States—Atlanta, Putnam County, and the State of Georgia all fall squarely within the geographic South. But what exactly *is* "the South"? Is it Dixie, the land of the Charlie Crokers of America, or is it the progressive vision of Georgia's noted black politician Stacey Abrams? Dispute arises the instant one tries to pin down precisely what is meant by offhand reference to this larger entity. Notwithstanding the South's self-evident influence on American history and culture, contradiction and argument pop up at every turn, whether one seeks to define the South in geographic, cultural, historical, or political terms. "The South"—its boundaries, its history, what it stands for, and its legitimate denizens—is an elusive, ever-changing, always disputable thing.

Library shelves are filled with books, many by Southern authors, pondering the essence and meaning of the South. The spectrum of views is cosmic, an expanse of assertion and disputation that ranges across time, race, and ideology. William Alexander Percy's 1941 encomium to the old white Southern order, *Lanterns on the Levee: Recollections of a Planter's Son*, presents (among other things) a paternalistic view of the postbellum system of sharecropping. His benign view is very different from the description of that harsh life written from the perspective of other end of the stick in John O. Hodges' *Delta Fragments: The Recollections of a Share-cropper's Son*, published in 2013.[12] Lillian Smith's *Killers of the Dream*, originally published in 1949, challenged the assumptions of white superiority and black inferiority that are found throughout a nostalgic Southern literary genre of which Percy's book is representative. Smith's book—quite brave for the time—laid bare the savage effects of the racist order, and Southern society's collective silence about it, on the lives and minds of Southern whites, especially children.[13]

The frame of argument about the meaning of the South is not static. It changes apace with American demography and culture. Although not without its critics, W. J. Cash's psycho-cultural survey, *The Mind of the South*, originally published in 1941, has been regarded for six decades as the essential entry point for anyone seeking to understand the South as a coherent entity. In 2013 journalist Tracy Thompson critiqued Cash's observations and brought them up to date in her *The New Mind of the South*.[14] Scores of recent titles likewise reexamine scores of older writings about race and the South.

New questions are raised as time passes and analysis of the South forges on. Is any place south of the informal boundary of the Mason-Dixon Line part of the South by definition? Are twenty-first-century blue-state Virginia, progressive Maryland, or multicultural Southern Florida still part of the South? Is being a "Southerner" defined by where one was born? Or is it defined by where one lives? Or is a "real" Southerner only someone who shares a set of specific social and cultural views—within or across racial and ethnic lines, and regardless of residence?

And what about the expanding mix of ethnicities that is changing faces and politics all over the South, including Georgia? Take, for example, Piyush Jindal. Born in Baton Rouge, Louisiana, in 1971, Jindal was the son of Raj and Amar Jindal, immigrants from Punjab, India. Better known as Bobby Jindal, he was elected governor of Louisiana in 2007 and 2011, the first Indian American governor in American history.[15] Nimrata Randhawa was born in Bamberg, South Carolina, in 1972 to Punjabi immigrants Ajit Singh and Raj Kaur Randhawa. Known after her marriage as Nikki Haley, she was elected governor of South Carolina in 2010—the state's first female governor and the second Indian American governor in American history. Haley later served as United States ambassador to the United Nations in 2017 and 2018.[16] Brenda Lopez took office in 2017 as the first Latina state assembly representative in Georgia's history. But unlike Jindal and Haley, Lopez was not born in the South, nor anywhere in the United States. She was an immigrant—a native of Mexico.[17]

Whatever one might argue about the bona fides of these three politicians as "real Southerners," the indisputable fact is that they are representative faces of demographic change rolling through the geographic South. For example, Chamblee, a suburb northeast of Atlanta, is sometimes referred to as "Chambodia." The nickname reflects its multi-ethnic demographics. "With entire shopping centers full of signs in languages other than English, this—along with its neighboring community Doraville—is the epicenter of the 'international Atlanta' the local chamber of commerce is always plugging."[18]

For a variety of economic, cultural, and ideological reasons, some Southerners, like Charlie Croker, fear this change, focus on the past, and actively work to keep alive memories of the antebellum South and the Civil War—at least as they imagine them to have been. In 1993, the Georgia state assembly established the Georgia Civil War Commission, dedicated to preserving Civil War historical sites.[19] The commission and the state's tourism bureaucracy have promoted "Civil War Heritage Trails," hoping to attract tourists to visit such sites, especially those associated with Union General William Tecumseh Sherman's famous (or infamous to some Southerners) "March to the Sea." Putnam County and Eatonton have been venues for historical reenactments intended to promote them as Civil War heritage locations.[20]

For a variety of others on the ragged ideological fringe, things haven't changed much well into the twenty-first century. These are the diehards, some of whom still call the Civil War "The War Between the States" or "The War of Northern Aggression."[21] These phrases might strike one as quaintly humorous, something like verbal corncob pipes and suspenders, to be tolerated but not taken seriously. However, these dead-enders express a serious and stubborn commitment to an alternative view of the Civil War, its causes, and its meaning for contemporary America. "Such groups as the United Sons of Confederate Veterans, the United Daughters of the Confederacy, and the Southern Heritage Coalition are dedicated to the presentation of a romanticized memory of the pre-Civil War South that, if it includes slavery at all, does so in the most benign manner."[22]

Summed up in the phrase "The Lost Cause," this alternate view of American history and culture argues that slavery was benign at worse, and at best a positive good for the millions of Africans seized and transported to America as slaves. America's bloody internal war wasn't about slavery at all, but about the sacred right of the individual states to decide their own political and social order. Lost Cause advocates are determined to recreate that order. "[I]f, in the North, the war seems part of a continuum of history, here it remains a cataclysm," the *New York Times* observed in a 2011 review of Southern museums. "The war was not a continuation of Southern history; it was a break in it. And that is still, for the South, the problem."[23]

These widespread views are more than retrograde curiosities. They are not limited to grumbling racists in rocking chairs on a few porches in the South. They mark deep divisions in how Americans think about race and slavery. "How a person thinks about Negro [*sic*] slavery historically makes a great deal of difference here and now," historian Stanley Elkins wrote in 1963. "[I]t tends to locate him morally in relation to a whole range of very immediate political, social, and philosophical issues which in some way refer back to slavery."[24] Although some of Elkins's writings about the supposedly infantilizing effects of slavery are controversial, this perceptive observation is unquestionably sound.

Georgia State Representative Tommy Benton, a retired schoolteacher and Republican legislator from Jefferson County, northeast of Atlanta, is a good example of a Lost Cause adherent.

"Benton is an unapologetic supporter of Georgia's Confederate heritage," the *Atlanta Journal-Constitution* wrote in a lengthy 2016 profile. "He flatly asserts the Civil War wasn't fought over slavery, compares Confederate leaders to the Founding Fathers and is profoundly irritated with what he deems a 'cultural cleansing' of Southern history." Benton was a perennial sponsor of legislation that would protect Confederate

historical monuments from being moved or damaged. He disparaged pro-
posals to alter or remove publicly sponsored Confederate monuments and
symbols (such as the Confederate battle flag) as "no better than what ISIS
is doing, destroying museums and monuments."[25]

Benton also described the Ku Klux Klan as "not so much as racist
thing but a vigilante thing to keep law and order." The Klan as a "law and
order thing" is a common meme of the Lost Cause culture. It was roman-
tically depicted as such in Mitchell's novel *Gone With the Wind*. Benton
said that while he didn't agree with all of Klan's methods, it "made a lot
of people straighten up."

"A great majority of prominent men in the South were members of the
Klan," he said. "Should that affect their reputation to the extent that
everything else good that they did was forgotten?"

Benton further dismissed the passionate debate over public display of
the Confederate battle flag ignited by the June 2015 murder of nine
African Americans during a Bible study at the Emanuel African Metho-
dist Episcopal Church in Charleston, South Carolina. The white supremacist shooter had posted pictures of himself with the Confederate flag.
Benton argued that focusing on the flag missed the point. "Nobody said
anything about black-on-black crime, and that's about 98 percent of it."

The unreconstructed lawmaker was stripped of his chairmanship of a
Georgia legislative committee in August 2020 after he made disparaging
remarks about Congressman and civil rights icon John Lewis, shortly
after the latter died. "John Lewis, his only claim to fame was that he got
conked on the head at the (Edmund) Pettus Bridge," Benton said two
weeks after Lewis' funeral. "And he has milked that for 50 years—or he
milked it for 50 years."[26]

This view is distilled, aged, and rebottled vintage white supremacy. It
embodies the dreams of Thomas Jefferson and Andrew Jackson of a
white man's republic, a nation of white yeomen farmers, growing with
the territory of the United States as it expanded to fulfill what would
come to be called the country's "manifest destiny." In the form that the
white republic took during the antebellum years, the one that the Civil
War was fought over according to the Lost Cause myth, there were two
sets of civic rules—"inside" rules of full equality and enfranchisement for
white males, and "outside" rules that excluded and subordinated everyone
else, namely women and people of color. Assessing the effects of the
legacy of Jacksonian Democracy today, scholar Joshua A. Lynn con-

cludes that although its proponents "failed to preserve their happy republic . . . they did start conservatism on a new, populist trajectory, one in which democracy is called upon to legitimize inequality, a distinctly American conservatism that endures in our republic today."[27]

That populist trajectory of legitimized inequality finds its most recent expression in what has come to be called "Trumpism."

BUCKHEAD

The McIvers' double-wide condominium took up half of the fifteenth floor of the Villa at Buckhead Heights. The building is three blocks from the intersection of Lenox Road and Peachtree Road, the extension of Atlanta's historic Peachtree Street. Close by that intersection lies Phipps Plaza, a shopping center devoted to high-end stores, some of which could not be found within hundreds of miles of Atlanta. The upscale Lenox Square Mall is also close to the Villa.

Kingsboro Road is in the city's exclusive and mostly white Buckhead neighborhood—"the traditional Northside home of the white elite."[28] When Scarlett O'Hara, the self-absorbed heroine of *Gone With the Wind*, found a home in Atlanta in 1862, it was on Peachtree Street, "almost the last house on the north side of town."[29] In the early 1960s, a century after that bloody second year of the American Civil War, some things had not changed much in Atlanta's Northside. It was a refuge of upper-class white flight, sealed off by a genteel segregation.

> Even as they tried to pursue a new "partnership" with the ever-growing black community in city politics, the white businessmen of Buckhead would still have their own white city-within-a-city as their retreat. "It was as gracious—and segregated—a life as it had ever been," reflected one reporter. "In those north-side neighborhoods, it might as well have been 1958."[30]

Atlanta's "new partnership" in the 1960s was called "the Atlanta Way." Looking for a progressive, or at least profitable, way to come to terms with growing black political and economic power and get beyond the endemic tensions of the "color line," politicians and entrepreneurs of both races worked together to promote commercial development and jobs in forward-looking alliances across racial lines.

Although the system provided jobs and made some people wealthy on both sides of the color line, its edges were ragged. They cut both ways, sometimes leaving abrasions of resentment and perceived exploitation on both sides. Diane McIver, for example, led a determined corporate assault on the city's supposedly unfair (read, corrupt) award of airport advertising contracts to minority contractors, a major element of the Atlanta Way.

Tom Wolfe focused on this interracial partnership in *A Man in Full*. Wolfe's fictional black mayor, Wesley Dobbs ("Wes") Jordan explains the Atlanta Way by comparing it to the internal structure of a baseball, starting by removing the ball's white horsehide cover and an internal padding of white string.

> Finally, you get down to the core, which is black, a small black ball of rubber. Well, that's Atlanta. The hard core, if we're talking politics, are the 280,000 black folks in South Atlanta. They, or their votes, control the city itself. Wrapped all around them, like all that white string, are three million white people in North Atlanta and all those counties. [31]

But it was no longer 1861 or 1958 or 1994, even in the McIvers' Northside Buckhead. The urban enclave was slightly more integrated. Jeffery Lamar Williams, a black Atlanta rapper who goes by the name Young Thug, bought a $2.6 million home in Buckhead in 2016. The eleven-thousand-square-foot mansion had seven bedrooms, eleven bathrooms, an indoor pool, a bar area, a theater room, walkout patios and balconies, a "secret room," and a four-car garage. [32] Gentrification was also changing the city's overall racial balance, as young whites moved into the city and blacks moved out to the suburbs. Even so, Atlanta and Buckhead were the focus of stormy protests against white privilege and its alleged consequences in 2016, mounted primarily by local activists of the Black Lives Matter movement.

The McIver home was a combination of their two big luxury apartments, with a wall between knocked out, remodeled and combined into one mega-condo. The Villa and its occupants towered indifferently above the strident protests in America's culture war going on in Buckhead. Tex McIver was "a Republican loyalist whose money and privilege insulated him from the realities at the heart of those very protests." [33]

Diane was as well insulated as Tex. Living the American dream in that home, Diane had more control over her life and far more money than that

six-year-old crying in her little sundress in 1958 could possibly have
imagined she would ever have. Diane was a millionaire. She was the
hard-charging president of US Enterprises, a conglomerate informally
known as "the Corey Companies." She had helped shape the Corey Companies into a profitable cornucopia of entrepreneurial successes, most
recently scoring spectacular coups in the lucrative airport advertising industry. And she was the glamorous half of one of Atlanta's, indeed the
South's, most envied and respected power couples. Diane and Tex McIver, it was said, had it all. Money. Friends. Political clout.

But that elite union almost never happened.

Diane wasn't looking for romance when she bought a condominium
and moved into the Villa. Having escaped a financially draining first
marriage that her friends describe as physically and emotionally abusive,
Diane was indifferent to the prospects of another marriage.

Claud L. McIver, III, a prominent Atlanta labor lawyer and bachelor
who lived in the Villa, was smitten the first time he saw Diane. Claud
affected cowboy boots and courtly manners. He preferred to use the name
"Tex." One of Diane's closest friends quipped that if her name were
Claud, she also would have changed it to Tex. Like Diane, Tex had
survived a bitter divorce battle. It had cost him dearly financially, and he
continued to smart from its sting. Taken by Diane's vivacious beauty,
Tex let it be known around the Villa that he wanted to meet the new
resident. He slipped a note under Diane's door, welcoming her to the
condominium. Diane rebuffed Tex's probes. He persisted. Eventually
Diane relented and accepted an invitation to dinner in Tex's apartment.
Fashion-conscious Diane's choice of attire—a baseball cap and workout
clothes—evidenced her indifference to the impression she might make on
Claud, aka Tex, McIver.

Tex was not to be deterred. He mounted a dogged courtship campaign
that culminated successfully with a sixty-thousand-dollar engagement
ring for Diane. The couple were joined together till death did them part at
a lavish 2005 wedding, complete with a horse-drawn carriage for the
lovebirds to ride in, fried chicken, pralines made on the spot, and gallons
of fine wine and champagne for the hundreds of guests at Tex McIver's
ranch. It was a courtly event straight out of the romantic nostalgia of the
Old South.

But this was not a case of a woman "marrying up" into a rich man's
wealth. Diane had achieved financial and business success well before

Tex came courting. In truth, she was better off financially than Tex. And she had a track record for keeping the upper financial hand. Love was love. Business was business. When she escaped her first marriage, she made sure that her former husband paid for his sins. After Diane married Tex, she loaned him a large sum of money, secured by an interest in the ranch. That loan was strictly business. Diane made it clear. Tex would pay the loan back or forfeit his pledged interest in the ranch.

Diane took the first step on her path to the great American dream when she was just seventeen years old. She started as a part-time payroll clerk at a company in Conyers, Georgia, owned by a wildly successful businessman, William E. "Billy" Corey. Father figure and mentor to young Diane, Billy Corey had scrabbled his way out of Great Depression poverty in Cabbagetown, then one of Atlanta's most desperate neighborhoods. He became one of Atlanta's best known and inscrutably wealthy entrepreneurs. Few people knew exactly what Billy Corey was worth. But it was certainly a lot.

Corey spotted payroll clerk Diane's bigger talents and relentless drive. He took her under his wing. Business magic happened. Billy Corey spun off dozens of money-making ideas from his restless business sense. Diane became the gifted implementer and tough overseer of those ambitious ideas. When Diane was birthing a business deal for Billy Corey, it was said, she wasn't interested in a long labor. She wanted to see the baby, the completed deal—signed, sealed, delivered, and the check in the bank. She could and would inflict a withering tongue-lashing on any subordinate who failed to measure up to her high standards. "Diane could take the skin off of a skeleton," one former co-worker recalled. Yet even those who suffered Diane's scourging loved her like a sister. Diane's lash was business, not personal.

Billy and Diane got fabulously rich in the process.

Diane came to enjoy a very wealthy person's choices of sumptuous private venues and opulent accessories. There were Waterford crystal flutes for the champagne. She could choose from among her Rolex, Chanel, and Baume et Mercier watches. She could wrap herself in any of forty-four fur coats. One of them was dyed bright orange, Auburn University's school color. Diane followed the Auburn football team loyally, often traveling to important games. There were dozens of hats. Diane was rarely without a fashionable hat in public. It was her signature accessory. She could grab one of twenty-five purses from Chanel, Gucci, Louis

Vuitton, Versace, and other high-end designers. She had a treasure chest of jewelry, earrings, bracelets, and necklaces to choose from, dripping with diamonds, rubies, sapphires, opals, and pearls.

Tex McIver fancied himself a cowboy transplant from his home state of Texas, where he went to college and law school.[34] His father was a decorated aviator in the Second World War.[35] Tex himself served in the Army's judge advocate general corps in Vietnam during that bitter war.

Tex was then a partner at Fisher & Phillips, an Atlanta labor law firm. (Later on, Tex lost his partnership status as a result of his declining ability to "shake the tree" for new client fees.) He was politically connected enough to Georgia's conservative Republican establishment to have been appointed vice president of the State Election Board. His Atlanta law practice was on the management side of labor law. That put him conveniently in favor of allowing into the country the cheap immigrant labor that his clients needed for their chicken farms and carpet factories. "If we could somehow pull a switch and all of the undocumented immigrants went back to where they came from, who will eviscerate those chickens?" Tex asked *Georgia Trend Magazine*. "We were losing poultry jobs to Arkansas and other places because we couldn't find local people to do the work."[36]

Tex loved guns. He owned dozens of them. In what would turn out to be a monstrous irony, the American Bar Association had appointed Tex to its Standing Committee on Gun Violence, scarcely one month before the Sunday evening he shot Diane to death.[37] Mutual acquaintances suggest that Tex's friendship with the then-president of the bar association, his friend and fellow Buckhead resident Linda A. Klein, may have played a role in that peculiar appointment.

Tex's personality would have been called both "reserved" and "mildly flamboyant" in polite company. Within a few months, however, other adjectives would roll off of the tongues of old and new observers alike.

Everyone in Atlanta would have a strong opinion about Tex McIver.

ENTER TRUMPISM

Even as Diane and Tex were knocking golf balls around the Reynolds Lake Oconee course on that steaming September day, something new and puzzling was happening in American politics. Depending on where one

stood on the political spectrum, the 2016 presidential election campaign
was frightening, ludicrous, or inspiring. At times it was all three at once.
Reality television host Donald Trump was shaking America's political
tree like a twelve-year-old truant out on a mean-spirited lark. Old-line
conservatives from Jeb Bush to Ted Cruz were falling out of the whip-
lashed branches like over-ripe apples.

The political cognoscenti, Republicans and Democrats alike, originally dismissed Trump as little more than droll entertainment, part stunt
man, part huckster, part grifter. He would quickly fade, it was gravely
opined, when the "serious" politics started. Trump had no political experience. His views were "out of the mainstream." But by the start of 2016,
Trump was relentlessly closing in on the Republican nomination. He was
stubbornly bouncing back from body blows—sex scandals and caught-
out lies—that in the past would have promptly knocked out a more conventional candidate.

Journalists were scratching their heads. Pundits were extracting lint in
cotton-bale quantities from their confounded navels.

"I sold Trump wildly short, and his entire campaign to date has proven
it," Ross Douthat, a conservative columnist for the *New York Times* admitted in January 2016. "Of course I'm not completely humbled. Indeed,
I'm still proud enough to continue predicting, in defiance of national
polling, that there's still no way that Trump will actually be the 2016
Republican nominee."[38]

It turned out that there actually was a way. Donald Trump won the
nomination. And the presidency. But Douthat was by no means the only
pundit, journalist, or election expert to express doubt right down to the
wire about the likelihood of Trump's winning the nomination or the
presidency. Opinion polls often appeared to support that doubt, or at least
they were interpreted by an incredulous news media as if they did.

"Donald J. Trump's campaign was teetering early last month, with an
increasingly isolated candidate and a downcast staff that seemed to lurch
from crisis to crisis," the *New York Times* wrote in January 2016. "Having fired his campaign chairman and retooled his message, Mr. Trump
was still far behind Hillary Clinton in the polls, and Republicans were
running away from him."[39]

In September, the same newspaper reported that "Donald J. Trump
and Hillary Clinton are entering the final stretch of the presidential race
essentially tied," but added reassuringly that Clinton "still has the upper

hand in most of the crucial swing states, such as Pennsylvania and Florida, that will likely decide the election."[40]

Even in Georgia—a state that had not gone for a Democratic presidential candidate since Bill Clinton in 1992 and twice rebuffed Barack Obama—Donald Trump's prospects appeared to be in doubt by late summer. "As polls continue to show Hillary Clinton maintaining and steadily increasing her lead over Donald Trump in Georgia, her top surrogate in the state said it is now time for her to go for the kill," the *Atlanta Journal-Constitution* reported in early August.[41] Despite those polls, most of the state's Republican establishment was standing by Trump. Many regarded him as the lesser of two evils, the greater evil being Hillary Clinton.

"It's a choice between bad and worse—and I'm choosing bad," the *Atlanta Journal-Constitution* reported state Senator Renee Unterman as saying. "If you go on down the list, Trump was my last choice."[42]

But the last was destined to be first. America woke up on the morning of November 9, 2016, to find that it had indeed elected an inexperienced, bad boy, reality television star to be the next president of the United States of America. The swing states of Florida and Pennsylvania broke for Trump, as did Georgia.

Trumpism was born.

Writing from a stunned New York City the morning after, journalist Roger Cohen zeroed in on the "single formidable intuition" that likely accounted for Trump's slogging victory. Trump's intuition was that "American anger and uncertainty in the face of the inexorable march of globalization and technology had reached such a pitch that voters were ready for disruption at any cost."

"This is the revenge of Middle America," wrote Cohen, "above all of a white working-class America troubled by changing social and cultural mores . . . and by the shifting demographics that will make minorities the majority by midcentury."[43]

From the moment he left the starting gate at Trump Tower in New York City on June 16, 2015, Donald Trump crafted a campaign that would appeal to a base of angry white folks, the spitting-mad electorate, the plurality of Americans polled who said they got mad at least once every day at something they heard or read in the news. That was among the remarkable results of a survey conducted by *Esquire* magazine and NBC News and reported in January 2016. "White Americans are the angriest of all," the survey stated, and then revealed this fascinating nugget about "perceived disenfranchisement":

> When we cross-tabulate these feelings with reports of daily anger (which are higher among whites than nonwhites), we see the anger of perceived disenfranchisement—a sense that the majority has become a persecuted minority, the bitterness of a promise that didn't pan out—rather than actual hardship. (If anger were tied to hardship, we'd expect to see nonwhite Americans . . . who report having a harder time making ends meet than whites . . . reporting higher levels of anger. This is not the case.)[44]

Donald Trump's campaign worked "perceived disenfranchisement" like the pedals of a cathedral organ, mashing down hard on the immigration chord as a proxy for the low note of outright racism. In the process, Trump trashed the Republican party's emergent strategy of using implicit (as opposed to overt) appeals to win racist white voters. His mode was to skip implicit pretense and head directly to explicitly hostile statements. Trump set this divisive tone in his notorious campaign announcement on June 16, 2015.

> When Mexico sends its people, they're not sending their best. They're not sending you. They're not sending you. They're sending people that have lots of problems, and they're bringing those problems with us [*sic*]. They're bringing drugs. They're bringing crime. They're rapists. And some, I assume, are good people.[45]

The afterthought about good people was classic Trump. Without conceding that *any* immigrants from Mexico are in fact "good people," Trump slipped in the insipid assumption that just possibly there might be *some* good people among the drug couriers, criminals, and rapists pouring over the border. This throwaway line insulated candidate Trump from the charge of blatant racism that might have resulted had he classified *all* Mexican immigrants as degenerate racial inferiors. Over the following years Trump dropped attempts to cushion his message at the margins. Americans became numb to a new reality—a fire hose of deliberately divisive rhetoric from their president.

Trump made it clear that he was concerned not only about Mexican immigrants, but also about others of non-white complexions. "It's coming from all over South and Latin America, and it's coming probably—probably—from the Middle East."[46]

The openly racist white nationalists of the "alternative right," or "alt-right," were delighted with Trump's attack on immigrants of certain complexions. Just days before the McIvers spent their last weekend at the ranch, *Mother Jones* magazine reported that "since Trump officially announced his bid in June 2015 he has drawn effusive praise and formal backing from some of the country's most virulent neo-Nazis, white supremacists, militia supporters, and other extremist leaders."[47] The *New York Times* was optimistic about what these endorsements might mean politically, but concerned about their meaning for America's future. "There aren't enough of these people to put Mr. Trump in the White House," the newspaper editorialized. "But his candidacy has granted them the legitimacy they have craved for years. For the first time, a candidate is using a major-party megaphone to shout the ideas they once could only mutter among themselves in the shadowy fringes of national debate."[48]

The notorious white supremacist Richard B. Spencer, who coined the term "alternative right," was among those who were inspired by Trump to come out of the shadows. Spencer's National Policy Institute is "dedicated to the heritage, identity and future of people of European descent in the United States, and around the world." In May 2017 Spencer led a torch-light rally in Charlottesville, Virginia, to protest the city's plan to remove a statue of Confederate General Robert E. Lee. He was also a featured speaker at the August 2017 "Unite the Right" rally in Charlottesville that turned violent and resulted in the murder of a counter-protestor. It was in reference to this deadly August rally that Trump uttered the infamous phrase that there were "very fine people on both sides," adding, "You had a lot of people in that group that were there to innocently protest and very legally protest." Spencer hailed Trump's statement as "fair and down to earth."[49]

Several years before, Spencer had explained the racial significance of the alt-right's obsession with immigrants. "Immigration is a kind of proxy war—and maybe a last stand—for White Americans, who are undergoing a painful recognition that, unless dramatic action is taken, their grandchildren will live in a country that is alien and hostile," Mr. Spencer wrote in a National Policy Institute column.[50]

Whatever else Trumpism might prove to be, with the stalking horse of immigration it moved issues of race, and all the hate and anger they generate among many fearful white Americans, to the fore of Donald Trump's campaign, his presidency, and his legacy.

THE PROTO-TRUMPISTS

No direct evidence known to the author indicates that either Tex or Diane McIver bought into Trump's racist memes. But there is an abundance of evidence that by September 2016 they had enlisted in the ranks of an emerging and restless corps of proto-Trumpists—donors, activists, and voters—who were about to defy polls, pundits, and conventional wisdom. The McIvers were among those who enthusiastically vaulted Donald Trump into office as president of the United States of America.

Both of the McIvers had a history of contributions to the Georgia Republican party and to conservative Republican candidates in particular. According to the *Atlanta Journal-Constitution*, Tex and Diane contributed more than one hundred thousand dollars to Republicans.[51] Federal Election Commission records show that Diane and Tex both contributed to Donald Trump's campaign committee in 2016. Tex also contributed to the Trump Victory Committee, a joint Republican fundraising entity.

Like many Georgia Republicans, Diane evidenced an early preference for a Republican candidate other than Trump. In 2015 she contributed to a super PAC—CARLY for America—supporting business executive Carly Fiorina's presidential bid. But Diane's sentiments changed as the field evolved and Fiorina dropped out. Diane ended up contributing enough to the Trump effort to win a personal photo with Trump when he visited Atlanta in June 2016. That photo, enlarged to poster size, was in her office in Atlanta, waiting to be mounted. Other mementos at the ranch included a Trump coloring book, an autographed copy of Trump's ghost-written book *Crippled America*,[52] and books signed by prominent Trumpists Oliver North and Ben Carson.

The record of the McIvers' contributions does not include the many other ways in which the couple boosted conservative Republicans, such as hosting fundraising events at the ranch. Nor does the donation record touch directly on Tex's operational ties and extensive political activity within the Georgia Republican establishment, including giving advice to

Republican candidates. Tex was not only a true believer; he had the obstinate commitment to blind loyalty shown to be characteristic of Trumpism.

"In Tex's mind a candidate's conservative bona fides excused all manner of sins," *Atlanta Magazine* reported in October 2017. "When a federal grand jury indicted former Congressman Pat Swindall in 1988 on ten counts of perjury amid a money laundering investigation just weeks before he was up for reelection, McIver doubled down on his man. 'I support him more than ever and intend to give him additional money because it looks like he needs it more than ever.'"[53]

Tex was intimately involved in another theme of Trumpism—claims of widespread voting fraud that helps Democratic candidates, and the invention of formalistic restrictions on voting that critics contend are no more than clever means to continue the minority voter suppression that began in the Jim Crow era after the Civil War. Georgia has been a viral center for the dispersion of these means throughout the several states.

Tex was vice chairman of the Georgia State Election Board. From that perch he promoted a political bombshell, a controversial voter photo identification requirement. Would-be voters who did not have government identification that included a photograph, such as a driver's license or passport, were required under a law passed in 2005 to get a Georgia state identification card. Tex and the measure's Republican supporters said that the identification card was needed to stop voting fraud. Critics replied that there was hardly any voting fraud in Georgia, nor anywhere else in America for that matter.

Although informed and impartial experts agree that voter registration rolls are often an administrative shambles, there is virtually no evidence that more than a miniscule number of actual voters in any modern election vote illegally, and certainly not in big enough numbers to have affected any results. Yet the myth of "voter fraud" has been weaponized by the conservative establishment in America. The fiction of massive fraud has become a staple of Trumpist activism, spewed from the bully pulpit by the president himself.[54] This blunt club is little more than a transparent scheme to erase ethnic and racial minority voters—the base of the Democratic Party—from the voter rolls, and to make it harder for those who survive the purges to vote.[55] The identification requirement opened a raw sore in the racial politics of Georgia. It spread to other states that Republicans in power were determined to keep in the red column.[56]

DEATH DID THEM PART

When the McIvers rolled out of the ranch the evening of the shooting, Dani Jo Carter, one of the Diane's best friends, was at the wheel of their 2013 King Ranch SUV.

The massive SUV weighed nearly three tons empty at the curb—5,782 pounds. The manufacturer's sales brochure assured buyers that "should an accident occur, you and your passengers are well protected by a sturdy safety shell, side-intrusion beams, and a system of six airbags."[57] The King Ranch SUV was a rolling steel vehicular fortress. It captured the essence of Tex McIver's being. It was the top of the model line. And it was marketed by Ford in affiliation with the biggest ranch in Texas, the King Ranch, which covers 825,000 acres—more land than the state of Rhode Island.[58]

Diane was in the front passenger seat. Tex was seated behind Diane in a bucket seat in the second of the big vehicle's three leather-covered seating rows.

The three stopped to meet a friend for a dinner of steak and wine in Conyers, an Atlanta suburb about midway between the city and the ranch. Conyers was a pivotal place in the history of the Corey Companies and in Diane's life—it was where she first began working for Corey.

When the meal ended, Dani Jo—the only one of the three who did not drink—took the wheel, glided up a ramp and into the heavy end-of-weekend traffic on Interstate 20, headed for Atlanta and the McIvers' home.

Night had well fallen by then. Tex apparently fell asleep in the back seat. Dani Jo and Diane talked quietly, exchanging the humorous and intimately informed banter of two long-time, close friends. Diane, Dani Jo said, was "more like a sister than a friend." There was little that the two women did not know about each other, or could not frankly say to one another's face.

As Dani Jo maneuvered the big vehicle through the last few miles of downtown Atlanta's knot of freeways, highway maintenance work slowed traffic to a maddening crawl at a notorious choke point called The Connector. At Diane's instruction, Dani Jo took an exit off the freeway and onto a side street.

At some point shortly after they left the freeway, Tex woke up. He looked around and saw that they had left the freeway.

"This is a bad idea, girls," he said. "This is a bad area."[59]

Tex asked the women to hand him his gun, a .38 caliber Smith & Wesson Model 638 pocket revolver. The gun was wrapped in a Publix supermarket plastic bag and stuffed into the center console. Diane handed the gun to Tex. Exactly why Tex thought he needed his gun at that moment became thoroughly muddled in the coming days and weeks by his own conflicting statements. Whatever the real reason was, Tex apparently was not alarmed enough to keep him awake. He ostensibly fell back asleep—with a loaded gun in his hand.

Diane and Dani Jo continued their quiet conversation as the SUV rolled easily through light traffic along increasingly genteel blocks. At some point—perhaps ten to fifteen minutes after they had left the freeway and while stopped at a traffic light—Dani Jo heard a loud bang. Her first thought was that two other vehicles must have collided next to them. Not seeing any evidence of that, she looked back into the rear seat, simultaneously smelled the acrid bite of gun powder, and suddenly realized that the noise must have come from Tex's gun being fired. Stunned, deafened by the noise, and believing at that surreal moment that the gunshot had been a harmless accident that must at worst have left a hole in the SUV's floor, she expected to hear Diane cut loose with a classic verbal shredding aimed directly at Tex for his foolish mistake.

But after a few shocked and confused seconds, Diane turned around and said, "Tex, you shot me." Then she slumped over and began to make frightening, involuntary sounds. Danni Jo thought that Diane was in the throes of death.

A single bullet from Tex's revolver had indeed ripped through the leather of the front passenger seat, struck Diane in the back, and passed through her stomach and other organs. It had inflicted mortal wounds. Bleeding could not be stopped. She died later that morning. The blown up, poster-sized photograph of Diane and presidential candidate Donald Trump was still in her office waiting to be framed and mounted.

"Either this is an intentional homicide or a terrible accident," J. Tom Morgan, a former DeKalb County district attorney, said shortly after the shooting. A pivotal question on that point during the investigation and trial was this: Exactly why did Tex McIver—a wealthy and successful lawyer, riding in the leather comfort of a moving steel cocoon—think that he needed to have a gun in hand after the SUV left the freeway?

"A lot of people are scratching their heads on this," Morgan observed. "A lot of us have gone all over Atlanta day and night without having to pull a gun."[60]

A visitor to Atlanta who followed the exact route that the SUV took that night learned that if there were any area along that route that might be called sketchy by any reasonable urban standard, it was no more than the first block or two by the off ramp, where the route briefly passed immediately under the freeway. Just beyond that point, however, the environment quickly changes to unremarkable blocks of increasingly upscale, well-tended neighborhoods.

The first answer to that crucial question was given to the *Atlanta Journal-Constitution* five days after the shooting by Bill Crane, a family friend who was serving as Tex's spokesman. According to Crane, Tex was worried about black folks—people from a nearby homeless shelter who allegedly approached the vehicle, raising the possibility of a carjacking, and the chance of randomly coming across a midnight Black Lives Matter demonstration.[61]

The newspaper's report ignited a fury of angry response from many in Atlanta's black community. In the heat of that firestorm, Tex repeatedly asked his friend Bill Crane to withdraw the statement. Crane refused. He insisted in later court testimony that the explanation had been vetted in advance by Tex himself.[62] If Crane's account is accurate, it is strong evidence that Tex McIver was seeing things through the lens of race— what could be worse to a privileged, ultra-conservative, proto-Trumpist, aging white lawyer like Tex than coming across homeless black people or a midnight Black Lives Matter demonstration? If a tie-breaker were needed in this "he said, he said" match, it can be found in testimony about Tex's conduct in the emergency room that night. Dr. Marty Sellers testified that when Dr. Blayne Sayed—a person of color—asked Tex to sit down, in preparation for telling him that Diane had died, Tex snapped, "Don't tell me what to do, boy!"[63]

All of this assumes, of course, that Tex's explanations were not simply a dodge, a cover for his deliberate intention to shoot Diane in the back that night. In either case, as desperate as Tex was to stuff the racial genie back into the bottle, he could not. The genie he let loose not only laid bare Atlanta's racial tensions—it raised the most fundamental questions about race and justice in America.

Whatever Tex McIver might have thought, or pretended to think, there is no getting around the question of why there is a Black Lives Matter movement in the first place. How is it that America is still gridlocked in the deadly intersection of racial perception well into the twenty-first century?

4

VICTIMS

Tex McIver was not the only armed American who would feel endangered by Black Lives Matter demonstrations. On March 2, 2020, the husband of Los Angeles County district attorney Jackie Lacey threatened to shoot Black Lives Matter demonstrators gathered outside of the couple's home in Granada Hills, an affluent Los Angeles suburb in the San Fernando Valley. The timing of the confrontation was strategic. A primary election was to be held the next day in which Lacey would face a vigorous reelection challenge from several opponents encouraged by the Black Lives Matter organization.

Melina Abdullah, a professor in the department of Pan-African Studies at California State University, Los Angeles, led a group of about thirty protestors who arrived in the early morning dark and brought lawn chairs with them, intending to settle in until prosecutor Lacey met with them. Abdullah is the leader of the Black Lives Matter chapter in Los Angeles.[1] She described the crack of dawn visit to the Lacey home as the inevitable result of years of frustrated attempts to meet personally with the district attorney to complain about her failure to prosecute police officers accused of violence and her support for the death penalty, among other racially charged issues of law and order.

"We've been standing in front of her office, demanding that she meet with us for two and a half years and she refused to come out," Abdullah said. "What alternative is there?"[2]

According to news reports and a video posted online, when Abdullah knocked, David Lacey opened the front door, pointed a handgun at her and two others, and said, "Get off of my porch. I will shoot you. . . . I don't care who you are. . . . We're calling the police right now."[3]

David Lacey and his wife are both black.

Five months later, on August 3, 2020, California attorney general (and former U.S. Representative) Xavier Becerra filed three misdemeanor assault charges against David Lacey, one for each of three persons at whom he allegedly pointed his gun.[4] Abdullah scoffed at the charges, pointing out that California prosecutors usually filed more serious felony charges for firearm threats. "Had it been anyone else who pointed a gun at someone's chest, at three people in fact, and said the words, 'I will shoot you,' we know they'd be getting more than misdemeanors," Abdullah was quoted by *The Guardian* newspaper as saying. "The system is there to protect themselves."[5]

The incident poses two questions. Why is there a Black Lives Matter movement in the first place—what are its roots? And how could Jackie Lacey in particular—the first woman and first African American to serve as the Los Angeles County district attorney since the office was created in 1850—have ended up in such a volatile confrontation with the leader of the first organized local chapter of the Black Lives Matter movement?

The bitter conflict between a black woman and a black civil rights organization is especially striking when viewed in the light of a laudatory sub-headline in the October 2014 edition of the newsletter of the University of Southern California, Lacey's law school alma mater. "Even though she's a prosecutor, the USC alumna serves as the voice for victims in the courtroom."[6] The crux of this apparent paradox lies in Jackie Lacey's formative years in the gang-infested South Central Los Angeles neighborhood of Crenshaw, the rise to power of a new generation of black scholars and activists who hold views of victimhood and racial justice significantly different from that of Lacey and many others in elected office around the country, and a shift to the left in the criminal justice politics of American progressives and perhaps most Americans in general.

Not unlike U.S. Vice President Kamala Harris, a black woman who was previously the San Francisco district attorney and the attorney general of California, Lacey found herself trapped between the horns of a cultural dilemma, resulting in a "bitter irony." That irony in Harris's case was described in *The Atlantic* by writer Peter Beinart after the senator ended her campaign for the 2020 Democratic presidential nomination.

She lost, in part, because she couldn't forthrightly defend her record as a prosecutor. She couldn't forthrightly defend that record because party activists deemed it insufficiently progressive. They portrayed her as complicit in the unjust incarceration and killing of black and Latino men. . . . Yet had Harris—especially as a black woman—been the crusading criminal-justice reformer that Democrats now want to see, she would likely never have been in a position to run for president in the first place.[7]

The tough law and order stance that voters demanded of politicians in the 1980s and 1990s, when Harris and Lacey were building their careers in elected office, were swept away in the Democratic party by a remarkably sudden shift in the political winds of the second decade of the twenty-first century. Beinart's point is illustrated nicely by California congressman Adam B. Schiff's political back flip, executed with no apparent embarrassment in less than a year's time. In October 2019, Schiff issued a statement lauding Lacey. "Time and time again, Jackie Lacey has demonstrated her ability to protect the public, fight crime and ensure justice for all the people of Los Angeles County," he said.[8] But in June 2020, after an uproarious spring of Black Lives Matters protests, Schiff tweeted the withdrawal of his enthusiastic support. "This is a rare time in our nation's history. We have a responsibility to make profound changes to end systemic racism & reform criminal justice . . . and I no longer feel our endorsement of Jackie Lacey a year ago has the same meaning [and] have decided to withdraw it."[9]

To add ironic insult to injury, Kamala Harris also abandoned Lacey to twist in the shifting political winds. When Harris was attorney general of California in 2012, she endorsed Jackie Lacey in her successful run to become the first woman and first black district attorney of Los Angeles County.[10] Eight years later—after her failed run at the presidential nomination was derailed in part by her own law and order record—Harris endorsed Lacey's principal opponent in the 2020 election, Cuban American George Gascon.[11]

Lacey's election challenge and her political abandonment by former allies aptly illustrates a well-worn phrase that writer Finley Peter Dunne coined in 1895: "Politics ain't beanbag."[12] But this was much more than the routine infighting common to local politics. This was a skirmish along a major front of an ideological and cultural war in which Americans have been engaged for a good half century.[13] An actor turned conservative activist, then–National Rifle Association First Vice President Charlton Heston evoked all of the divisive, polarized resentments of this culture war in a speech before the right-wing Free Congress Foundation at its twentieth anniversary gala on December 7, 1997—which coincidentally also happened to be Pearl Harbor Day. Heston spoke at length about those whom he described collectively as the "victim of the cultural war."

> Heaven help the God-fearing, law-abiding, Caucasian, middle class, Protestant, or—even worse—evangelical Christian, Midwest, or Southern, or—even worse—rural, apparently straight, or—even worse—admittedly heterosexual, gun-owning or—even worse—NRA-card-carrying, average working stiff, or—even worse—male working stiff, because not only don't you count, you're a downright obstacle to social progress.[14]

That single paragraph sums up the cultural divide that has polarized American politics. The front in that war in which Jackie Lacey and Black Lives Matter engaged is a narrower but critical battle over the prime values and methods of America's system of law, order, and racial justice.

Like the Balkan wars of the early twentieth century,[15] alliances shift opportunistically on both sides of the cultural war. Fierce internecine guerrilla scrimmages, sparked by changing demographics and the vagaries of polling, draw political blood.[16] But the broad lines are drawn and the trenches dug. On the one side are the increasingly authoritarian nature of Trumpism and its appeal to Heston's white male "working stiff." On the other is an increasingly confrontational progressive left, a rough coalition of people of color, minority ethnics, and well-educated young people.

The outcome of the culture war lies in the future. It is unlikely to be settled by a single election.

WHO IS THE VICTIM?

There is one issue about crime and justice over which the ideological combatants in America's culture war strongly disagree—who are the victims?

To the surging progressive left, the primary victims are people of color—mostly black males—whom a racist system has victimized by policies that criminalize minor drug usage, enhance penalties for crimes committed primarily by black offenders, promote mass incarceration over large-scale programs designed to deal with the root causes of economic and social deprivations, inflict civil disabilities on convicted felons that are equivalent to the old Jim Crow laws, and rely on militarized "hyper-policing" to enforce this harsh law and order ethic.

To the reactionary right, best characterized by Trumpism, the victims are ordinary people in poor communities, innocents who suffer from the violence brought to their communities by drug-dealing criminal preda-tors, summed up in the phrase "black on black crime" that is often raised by the right. The primary vehicle for implementing this conservative view of law and order is the "War on Drugs," a term first floated by President Richard Nixon in 1971 but formally declared by President Ronald Rea-gan in 1982.[17] To these advocates, the drug war is essential to law and order, and can only be successfully pursued through a harsh collection of criminal penalties, streamlined criminal procedures, and aggressive polic-ing.

Underlying the conservative right's priorities is what Harvard profes-sor Lawrence Bobo and his colleagues have called "a modern free market or laissez-faire racist ideology."[18] The Jim Crow variety of racism was based on perceptions of racial inferiority. It was implemented by overt means, laws, and policies that never bothered in the least to conceal their racial basis (think of separate black and white drinking fountains as but one starkly simple example). Bobo and his colleagues argue that with the decline of Jim Crow racism, a new racial ideology emerged. "Under this regime, blacks are still stereotyped and blamed as the architects of their own disadvantaged status," as "a larger number of white Americans have become comfortable with as much racial inequality and segregation as a putatively nondiscriminatory polity and free market economy can pro-duce."[19] Or, as William Julius Wilson put it more simply, laissez-faire racism is "a perception that blacks are responsible for their own economic predicament and therefore undeserving of special government support."[20]

One outcome of laissez-faire racism has been the reluctance of the predominantly white power structure to address underlying structural problems that affect communities of color in general, and crime in those communities in particular. In the view of racial free market thinking, the solution to any such problems is for troubled communities of color to clean themselves up by buying into law and order ideals in the marketplace of ideas. The residents of these disadvantaged American enclaves should support tough law enforcement efforts intended to help them, and not ask for special economic programs or social consideration.

In August 2016, candidate Donald Trump indirectly summed up the laissez-faire view. Speaking to a rally of white people in a suburb of Lansing, Michigan, Trump made a pitch for black votes by posing his uniquely Trumpist description of black communities that rely on liberal social programs, such as those historically favored by the Democratic Party. "You're living in your poverty, your schools are no good, you have no jobs, 58% of your youth is unemployed, what the hell do you have to lose?"[21]

Trump more directly articulated the conservative position on crime and its victims in *The America We Deserve*, a book published under his name in 2000. "[U]nless we stand up for tough anticrime policies, they will be replaced by policies that emphasize criminals' rights over those of ordinary citizens," the book argued. "Soft criminal sentences are based on the proposition that criminals are the victims of society."[22]

Trump further argued that "the only victim of a violent crime is the person getting shot, stabbed, or raped. The perpetrator is never a victim. He's nothing more than a predator, and there can be no excuses made for killing old ladies, beating old men, or shooting adolescents."[23] He dismissed social and economic conditions, and historical mistreatment as factors generating criminal behavior. "There is a philosophy in our country that says criminals plunder because they have little or no choice; that they have been forced into crime by poverty, lack of opportunity, or early childhood mistreatment. That's an excuse? Ridiculous!"[24]

The America We Deserve also argued in favor of the death penalty, describing going to prison as a "social promotion" for violent criminals.

> I totally reject the idea that hanging these sorts of criminals is uncivilized. In fact I believe that letting them live would be totally uncivilized. They've taken an innocent life, so they should have to give theirs in return. That's the very least they can do. They don't deserve to be put into a prison where they can spend their time working out, reading, watching television, earning advanced degrees, filing bogus lawsuits, and even getting married. For this type of person, prison is a social promotion.[25]

Trump's attorneys general worked hard to make this roughshod law and order vision a reality. Jeff Sessions, the first Trump attorney general, dismissed "the false story that federal prisons are filled with low-level, nonviolent drug offenders. The truth is less than 3 percent of federal offenders sentenced to imprisonment in 2016 were convicted of simple possession, and in most of those cases the defendants were drug dealers who accepted plea bargains in return for reduced sentences." Sessions argued that minority communities are "disproportionately impacted" by violent crime and "ravaged by crime and violence." Tough anticrime policies and enforcement, he suggested, actually benefit minority communities by helping to create safe neighborhoods.[26]

Sessions was true to his word. He overturned several policies of the Obama administration that were aimed at ameliorating racial imbalances in law enforcement. For example, Sessions cut back Justice Department investigations into local police departments. These investigations helped expose police abuses and in some cases led to the imposition of monitored reforms. He revoked a Justice Department policy that directed federal prosecutors to avoid pressing charges against low-level drug offenders that might trigger lengthy mandatory minimum sentences. Sessions told prosecutors to "charge and pursue the most serious, readily provable offense" in all cases, regardless of disproportionate consequences.[27]

Michelle Alexander is a clarion voice on the other side of the criminal justice front of the American culture war. A professor of law at Ohio State University and an experienced advocate for social justice, Alexander's award-winning book *The New Jim Crow* has been praised as "the secular bible for a new social movement in early twenty-first-century America."[28] Alexander argues that the drug war has not stopped crime. On the contrary, it has created a system that imprisons disproportionate numbers of people of color in record numbers.

> The impact of the drug war has been astounding. In less than thirty years, the U.S. penal population exploded from around 300,000 to more than 2 million, with drug convictions accounting for the majority of the increase. The United States has the highest incarceration rate in the world, dwarfing the rates of nearly every developed country, even surpassing those in highly repressive regimes like Russia, China, and Iran.[29]

"The racial dimension of mass incarceration is its most striking feature," Alexander writes. "No other country in the world imprisons so many of its racial or ethnic minorities. The United States imprisons a larger percentage of its black population than South Africa did at the height of apartheid."[30]

When the men and women of color scooped up by this system are released from prison or jail, they are subject to lifelong civil disabilities that prevent their ever becoming integrated as productive and fully accepted members of society. These disabilities, Alexander argues, have in effect recreated the racially discriminatory regime of Jim Crow laws, albeit without that era's specific reference to race.

> [I]t is no longer socially permissible to use race, explicitly, as a justification for discrimination, exclusion, and social contempt. So we don't. Rather than rely on race, we use our criminal justice system to label people of color "criminals" and then engage in all the practices we supposedly left behind. . . . Once you're labeled a felon, the old forms of discrimination—employment discrimination, housing discrimination, denial of the right to vote, denial of educational opportunity, denial of food stamps and other public benefits, and exclusion from jury service—are suddenly legal. As a criminal you have scarcely more rights, and arguably less respect, than a black man living in Alabama at the height of Jim Crow.[31]

Alexander describes a three-stage process in the New Jim Crow system. The first stage is "the roundup" during which "[v]ast numbers of people are swept into the criminal justice system by the police, who conduct drug operations primarily in poor communities of color."[32] The second stage begins with the arrest, after which "defendants are generally denied meaningful legal representation and pressured to plead guilty whether they are or not." Due to "harsh sentencing laws, drug offenders in the United States spend more time under the criminal justice system's formal control—in jail or prison, on probation or parole—than drug offenders anywhere else in the world."[33]

The final stage is a period of "invisible punishment" that "operates largely outside of public view and takes effect outside the traditional sentencing framework." Its sanctions are "imposed by operation of law rather than decisions of a sentencing judge, yet they often have a greater impact on one's life course in the months or years one actually spends behind bars. . . . Unable to surmount these obstacles, most will eventually return to prison and then be released again, caught in a closed circuit of perpetual marginality."[34]

There is little room for even the most progressive prosecutor to maneuver between the front lines in this contest between different definitions of the victims of injustice and the perpetrators of their victimization. Kamala Harris, then San Francisco's district attorney, spoke to the difficulty in the preface to her 2009 book, *Smart on Crime*, arguing that "both sides of the political aisle . . . urgently need a broader vision and a willingness to innovate." For the political left that meant "getting past biases against law enforcement and recognizing that even low-income communities . . . want and deserve greater public safety resources so that they can live free from crime." For the right it meant "acknowledging that crime prevention is a key to crime fighting" and that the tools needed "are far more diverse than simply laws that make prison sentences longer."[35]

Such middle-ground voices have little traction in twenty-first-century American policy discourse. In a 2017 op-ed, legal reform activist Josie Duffy Rice raked over Lacey and other prominent and ostensibly progressive prosecutors as "faux" reformers "who get credit for changing the game while continuing draconian practices." These prosecutors "say the right things," Rice charged, while making only "bite-size improvements" and continuing "to promote the same harsh practices behind the scenes."[36]

George Gascon defeated Jackie Lacey in the November 2020 general election.[37] Kamala Harris made a remarkable comeback, winning the Democratic Party's vice presidential nomination. But even as candidate Joe Biden's running mate, advocates to the left continued to raise critical questions about her record as prosecutor and attorney general.[38] And Joe Biden himself faced skepticism about his prominent role in the passage in 1994 of a tough law and order crime bill that critics say helped drive mass incarceration.[39] Nevertheless, their team won the election.

BOYZ N THE HOOD

The 1991 coming of age drama *Boyz n the Hood* was set in and around the South Central Los Angeles neighborhood in which Jackie Lacy grew up. The film's dramatic arc traces the challenges young black men faced growing up in the area's violent gang culture. By the end of the film, most of a clique of young friends are either dead or scooped up in the grim system that Alexander describes.

Jackie Lacey emphasized her experiences as a young person in South Central during the 1960s and 1970s to justify what she sees as her advocacy for the real victims of criminal violence. "It felt like a dangerous time," she told the *New York Times*. "I can remember my parents' home getting burglarized and everything getting wiped out while they were at work. And it seems like after that they put bars on the windows and had the iron-gate door. And I really thought everybody in L.A. was doing it because all of the neighbors were doing it."[40]

Because of her early exposure to this criminal violence, Lacey was determined "to advocate for those who couldn't advocate for themselves in the criminal justice system," namely the poor victims of crime. "People who'd had their cars stolen, children who'd been molested, women who'd been beat up by their sole source of support. There are a whole lot of people that you can connect with and you can say, 'I'm going to be your voice in that courtroom.'"[41]

Kamala Harris made a supporting, corollary point in *Smart on Crime*. She argued that it is a myth that the residents of African American and Latino communities don't want the police in their neighborhoods. "In fact, the opposite is true . . . economically poor people want and support law enforcement." But the myth is perpetuated by the "extreme" ends of both sides of the American polarized divide. Partisan conservatives argue for "containment" of hopelessly crime-ridden communities, whereas partisan liberals argue that "police are an unwelcome occupation force in poor neighborhoods." Neither approach makes any sense, Harris maintained.[42]

Lacey consistently expressed her support for the death penalty. "I think the biggest fear, morally, of the death penalty is that we do not want to execute the wrong person," she said after her first election. "I think we need checks and balances in place. . . . Although I'm a prosecutor who has been on the side of seeking justice by seeking the death penalty, I believe everybody has a right to a fair trial."[43]

Lacey's discussions of the roots and nature of crime in her neighborhood brush up against one of the most charged issues of crime and race—the role of specific racial and ethnic cultures as factors in criminal behavior. That question of the impact on crime of a community's shared norms, attitudes, and behaviors is one of the "third rails" of academic and policy discourse for many experts. According to William Julius Wilson, a prominent scholar who has studied and written about the roles of social structures and culture among blacks in America, "many liberal scholars are reluctant to discuss or research the role that culture plays in the negative outcomes found in the inner city. It is possible that they fear being criticized for reinforcing the popular view that the negative social outcomes—poverty, unemployment, drug addiction, crime—of many poor people in the inner city are due to the shortcomings of the people themselves."[44] Nevertheless, Wilson argues that "cultural explanations should be part of any attempt to fully account for such behavior and outcomes. And I think it is equally important to acknowledge that recognizing the important role of cultural influences in creating different racial group outcomes does not require us to ignore or play down the role of structural factors."[45]

Harvard professor Henry Louis Gates described a similar reluctance to discuss another racial "hot-button issue"—reparations for slavery—in an interview with the *New York Times*. "[T]here are few people today who have the courage to stand up within the community and say, 'I genuinely think reparations is a mistake,'" Gates said, making it clear that was not necessarily his own position on the issue. "But I'm saying you will find nobody black standing up and criticizing reparations—it's very rare—because they're afraid that students are going to boycott them or that they'll be called an Uncle Tom. That's not right. We fall apart, particularly in the academy, when we succumb to or perpetuate that kind of intellectual bullying."[46]

Jackie Lacey won acclaim among black leaders on election night after her landmark victory in 2012.[47] But nine months earlier and twenty-five hundred miles away, the death of a young black man in Florida had already sparked the grass roots movement that would confront her at her own front door in 2020.

THE DEATH OF TRAYVON MARTIN AND THE BIRTH OF A MOVEMENT

On the rainy evening of Sunday, February 26, 2012, Trayvon Martin, a black seventeen-year-old high school junior, walked to a nearby 7-Eleven store from the home where he was staying with his father. The home was in a racially mixed gated community in Sanford, Florida. The young man bought some iced tea and Skittles candy and started walking back in the rain. He was wearing a gray hooded sweatshirt.[48]

At 7:11 p.m., George Zimmerman, a white resident of the neighborhood and a "neighborhood watch volunteer," spotted Martin. Zimmerman, armed with a Kel-Tec 9mm pistol, called the police, as he had often done in the past. "Hey, we've had some break-ins in my neighborhood, and there's a real suspicious guy," he told the 911 operator. "This guy looks like he's up to no good, or he's on drugs or something. It's raining, and he's just walking around looking about."

At about the same time, Martin noticed that he was being followed. It happened that he was talking on the phone with his girlfriend, who advised him to run. He did. At 7:13, Zimmerman told the police operator, "S—, he's running."

A beeping sound is heard at this point on the 911 tape. Zimmerman had opened the door of his vehicle. He went after Trayvon Martin on foot.

"Are you following him?" the operator asked Zimmerman.

"Yeah," he replied.

"Ok, we don't need you to do that," the operator said.

Zimmerman spent a few more minutes on the phone. First he gave the operator directions about where he would meet a police officer. Then he seemed to change his mind.

"Actually, could you have him call me, and I'll tell him where I'm at?" he said.

At 7:15, four minutes after the call began, he hung up.

What happened next is a classic case of the only survivor to a shooting death claiming self-defense. What is known for sure is that within a few more minutes, George Zimmerman shot Trayvon Martin to death. Zimmerman claimed that he had acted in self-defense after Martin attacked him. The Sanford Police Department originally declined to charge Zimmerman with any crime. But the governor appointed a special prosecutor to look into the case. Zimmerman was eventually charged with second-degree murder and manslaughter.

Trayvon Martin's homicide caused a national outcry, mostly about the racial tensions inherent in the shooting, but also about Florida's concealed carry and "Stand Your Ground" statutes, relaxed gun laws that critics argue encourage such violent confrontations. Although those laws

were not directly at issue in Zimmerman's case, prosecutors had a difficult needle to thread between the relaxed social standards on violence that
those laws embody and the murky facts of exactly how Trayvon Martin
was killed. On July 13, 2013, a Florida jury accepted Zimmerman's self-
defense claim and acquitted him of all charges. [49]

It appeared to many observers that it was okay in Florida to hunt
down, confront, and kill an unarmed black teenager who had the misfor-
tune to be out at night on an innocent errand.

Thousands of demonstrators gathered in cities across America to
protest Zimmerman's acquittal. [50] President Barack Obama said that Trayvon Martin "could have been me 35 years ago." The president spoke
eloquently about pain in the black community, underscoring that "it's
important to recognize that the African-American community is looking
at this issue through a set of experiences and a history that—that doesn't
go away." The question, Obama said, was "where do we take this? How
do we learn some lessons from this and move in a positive direction?" [51]

As President Obama spoke and thousands demonstrated, three young
women—Patrisse Cullors and Alicia Garza in Los Angeles, and Opal
Tometi in New York—decided to "take this" in a forcefully positive
direction. [52] Garza posted fourteen words on Facebook that would change
the racial discourse in America forever. "Black people. I love you. I love
us. Our lives matter. Black Lives Matter." In a *Rolling Stone* interview,
Garza described the moment. "We see black death all the time, and I
don't know what it was about this, but I know I went home and then I
woke up in the middle of the night crying. And I picked up my phone and
I started clickety-clacking, right?" [53]

Cullors saw Garza's post and added the hashtag "#blacklivesmatter."
Tometi described the impact the post had on her. "There [was] a lot of
rage, a lot of pain, a lot of cynicism. But her post resonated with me, for a
number of reasons. I think it being explicitly black, it being a message
rooted in love, and it just felt very hopeful." [54]

The three women connected over the issue and discussed how to build
a "movement not a moment." They called together a group of other
activists, including Melina Abdullah, to start that movement. [55] It was to
become a tidal wave within a few years. That wave continues to roll over
America. In the words of writer Jamil Smith, "The struggle continues to
build an America where black people can breathe, one where we do not
need white people to validate our demand to do so." [56]

In 2016, George Zimmerman auctioned off the pistol with which he had killed Trayvon Martin. He got $250,000 for the gun. In an interview with ABC News, Zimmerman promised to use some of the money "to push back against the civil rights movement Black Lives Matter."[57]

If Sanford, Florida, was the birthplace of Black Lives Matter, Ferguson, Missouri, was where it came of age. Trayvon Martin died at the hands of a private citizen. Zimmerman was one person along an ambiguous spectrum of armed private law and order enforcers who operate without much supervision at the margins of the criminal justice system. (That spectrum included Tex McIver, as we shall see in greater detail further on.)

The death of a young unarmed black man, Michael Brown, in 2014 was different. Brown was shot to death by a white policeman, a sworn officer of a government agency. The incident would focus the nation's attention on racism in the criminal justice system and police brutality in its enforcement. The nascent Black Lives Matter movement was propelled into national and enduring prominence and power.

PINOCCHIOS

"Hands up, don't shoot!"

A volatile narrative erupted like wildfire when news of eighteen-year-old Michael Brown's death raced through a neighborhood in the small town of Ferguson. It went like this: Shortly after noon on Saturday, August 9, 2014, an officer of the Ferguson Police Department had aggressively confronted Brown—often described as a "gentle giant"—and another young black male friend for jaywalking. The encounter had quickly escalated from verbal to physical. The officer, later identified as Darren Wilson, shot Brown in the back several times as he tried to flee. When the teenager turned and tried to surrender, lifting his hands up and imploring "don't shoot," Wilson shot the young man to death. The fatal round struck Brown in the top of his head as he was on his knees.

It was not a difficult narrative to believe for many.

Ferguson is a small town of about twenty-one thousand residents, one of eighty-nine municipalities in St. Louis County. It became an enforced all-white community in the 1940s when its white burghers erected a chain across the main street that connected a tiny black community to the rest of the otherwise white town. Ferguson thus became one of the "sundown towns" examined by James W. Loewen—communities all over America that excluded black residents by various means. Some towns went so far as to post signs warning African Americans to be out of the town by sundown.[58] The unstated implication was that vigilante justice would deal with any blacks found after dark, perhaps even killing them. But the facts about where such signs were located illustrate a truth that contradicts what most people think that they know about harshly segregated sundown towns, namely that such towns were a primarily a Southern phenomenon. That is certainly how they have been portrayed in films and literature. Loewen has documented that in fact, the reverse is true. For example, he discovered 472 all-white towns in Illinois alone.[59] And of the 184 towns that he identified as having had sundown warning signs, only seven were in the "traditional South." A total of 125 were in northern or western locales.[60]

Ferguson's demography has changed dramatically over recent decades. As late as 1990, 74 percent of the population was white, and 25 percent black.[61] By 2019, census data showed the ratio had flipped—24 percent were white and 70 percent were black.[62] Significantly, the town's police department was almost entirely white at the time of Michael Brown's death—of fifty-four sworn officers, only four were African American in 2015.[63] Loewen noted that all-white police forces in former sundown towns "may still be viewed by themselves and other residents as a city's first line of defense against black interlopers."[64]

The phrase "hands up, don't shoot" became a rallying cry for Ferguson residents, a powerful slogan for the Black Lives Matter movement that led weeks of demonstrations, and a universal meme for activists protesting violent mistreatment of black youths by police.[65] National Football League players raised their hands in symbolic protest. So did several members of Congress as they spoke to the issue on the floor of the U.S. House of Representatives. T-shirts and demonstrators' signs were emblazoned with the slogan.[66]

But doubts began to be raised about the facts of the incident and just how gentle a giant Michael Brown really was. Leaks from a grand jury about Officer Wilson's version of events and the prosecution's case appeared in conservative media in late October. They told a different story, one in which Officer Wilson was under physical attack from a much bigger Michael Brown and acted in self-defense.[67] On November 24,

2014, the grand jury accepted Wilson's version of events and declined to indict him.

The grand jury's decision led to more angry demonstrations and two separate federal investigations by the U.S. Department of Justice. One was a criminal investigation examining whether Officer Wilson violated federal law when he shot Brown. The other was a civil rights investigation into the operations of the Ferguson Police Department. Lengthy reports of both federal investigations were released by the Justice Department on the same day, March 4, 2015.

The criminal investigation vindicated Wilson's self-defense version of the events. Based on interviews with over one hundred witnesses, detailed records of forensic evidence including three autopsies of Brown, police communications, surveillance videos, and blood patterns at the scene, the Justice Department's eighty-six-page report firmly refuted the "hand up, don't shoot" narrative.

Pulitzer Prize winner Jonathan Capehart wrote in the *Washington Post* that the report "made me ill" and "forced me to deal with two uncomfortable truths: Brown never surrendered with his hands up, and Wilson was justified in shooting Brown."[68] Four days later, the newspaper awarded the viral Ferguson narrative four of its falsehood "Pinocchios"—the maximum for a finding of an assertion that fact-checking found to be false. "'Hands up, don't shoot' did not happen in Brown's killing," the fact-checker reported.[69] Here is what did happen that day, according to the Justice Department's report:

> Wilson was on duty and driving his department-issued Chevy Tahoe SUV westbound on Canfield Drive in Ferguson, Missouri when he saw Brown and his friend, Witness 101, walking eastbound in the middle of the street. Brown and Witness 101 had just come from Ferguson Market and Liquor ("Ferguson Market"), a nearby convenience store, where, at approximately 11:53 a.m., Brown stole several packages of cigarillos. As captured on the store's surveillance video, when the store clerk tried to stop Brown, Brown used his physical size to stand over him and forcefully shove him away. As a result, an FPD dispatch call went out over the police radio for a "stealing in progress." The dispatch recordings and Wilson's radio transmissions establish that Wilson was aware of the theft and had a description of the suspects as he encountered Brown and Witness 101.[70]

After admonishing the two young men about walking in the middle of the street, Wilson drove past them. But looking at them in his rear view mirror, he realized that these were likely the two subjects of the "stealing in progress" report.

> According to Wilson, when he backed up his SUV and attempted to get out to speak with Brown, Brown blocked him from opening the door. Brown then reached through the window and began to punch Wilson in the face, after which he reached for and gained control of Wilson's firearm by putting his hand over Wilson's hand. As Brown was struggling for the gun and pointing it into Wilson's hip, Wilson gained control of the firearm and fired it just over his lap at Brown's hand. The physical evidence corroborates Wilson's account in that the bullet was recovered from the door panel just over Wilson's lap, the base of Brown's hand displayed injuries consistent with it being within inches of the muzzle of the gun, and Wilson had injuries to his jaw consistent with being struck. Witnesses 102, 103, and 104 all state that they saw Brown with the upper portion of his body and/or arms inside the SUV as he struggled with Wilson. These witnesses have given consistent statements, and their statements are also consistent with the physical evidence.[71]

After that struggle, in which he was first shot in the hand, Brown disengaged and headed down the street, away from Wilson. The officer got out of his SUV and chased after Brown.

> Brown ran at least 180 feet away from the SUV, as verified by the location of bloodstains on the roadway, which DNA analysis confirms was Brown's blood. Brown then turned around and came back toward Wilson, falling to his death approximately 21.6 feet west of the blood in the roadway. . . . As detailed throughout this report, several witnesses stated that Brown appeared to pose a physical threat to Wilson as he moved toward Wilson. According to these witnesses, who are corroborated by blood evidence in the roadway, as Brown continued to move toward Wilson, Wilson fired at Brown in what appeared to be self-defense and stopped firing once Brown fell to the ground. Wilson stated that he feared Brown would again assault him because of Brown's conduct at the SUV and because as Brown moved toward him, Wilson saw Brown reach his right hand under his t-shirt into what appeared to be his waistband. There is no evidence upon which prose-

cutors can rely to disprove Wilson's stated subjective belief that he feared for his safety. [72]

In sum, the Justice Department's report seemed to confirm conservative columnist Rich Lowry's observation in the *National Review* magazine. "The bitter irony of the Michael Brown case is that if he had actually put his hands up and said, 'Don't shoot,' he would almost certainly be alive today." [73]

Predictably, a number of activists refuse to accept the grand jury's refusal to indict Wilson and the Justice Department's report as refutation of the Ferguson "hands up, don't shoot" narrative. In their view, the system had simply found ways to protect a violent white police officer. In any case, a series of police shootings of unarmed young black men in following years sustained the continued use of the meme in other circumstances.

If the system indeed worked to cover up wrongdoing in Ferguson, it was not yet done with its machinations. Another blow was awaiting activists who insisted that Michael Brown had been murdered.

In November 2018, four years after Michael Brown's death and three years after the Justice Department's twin reports, a young lawyer—the son of a police officer—won an election for St. Louis County prosecuting attorney. Wesley Bell's victory ended the twenty-seven-year reign of white prosecutor Robert P. McCulloch. Setting the same precedent as Jackie Lacey had in Los Angeles, Bell became the first black county prosecuting attorney in St. Louis County history when he took office in January 2019. [74] Among his first priorities, he proclaimed, would be reopening the Michael Brown case, which he soon did.

The hammer fell in July 2020 when Bell announced that after a five-month independent examination of the case, he had decided that there was not enough evidence to bring charges against Wilson. The decision angered activists, who cried betrayal and predicted a one-term tenure for Bell. [75] An editorial in the *St. Louis Post-Dispatch* newspaper proposed a different perspective on the prosecutor's decision. "Bell gave it his best shot to find some hidden piece of evidence or the hint of a smoking gun that would allow him to reopen the homicide case against former Officer Darren Wilson and score some semblance of justice for Brown's family," the paper remarked. "But the evidence simply is not there." [76]

The angry focus on finding a case against Officer Darren Wilson tended to mute public discussion of the damning conclusions of the second Justice Department report, the review by its Civil Rights Division of the overall operations of the Ferguson Police Department. That report found that—wholly aside from the shooting of Michael Brown—the police department operated as a deeply racist machine whose principal purpose was not maintaining impartial law and order, but treating the city's black residents like so many often overdrawn human ATM machines. The system imposed on and extracted from black residents accumulating fines and penalties for minor offenses, including not only traffic stops but even failing to keep one's grass cut short:

> The City's emphasis on revenue generation has a profound effect on FPD's approach to law enforcement. Patrol assignments and schedules are geared toward aggressive enforcement of Ferguson's municipal code, with insufficient thought given to whether enforcement strategies promote public safety or unnecessarily undermine community trust and cooperation. Officer evaluations and promotions depend to an inordinate degree on "productivity," meaning the number of citations issued. Partly as a consequence of City and FPD priorities, many officers appear to see some residents, especially those who live in Ferguson's predominantly African-American neighborhoods, less as constituents to be protected than as potential offenders and sources of revenue.[77]

Journalist Wesley Lowery, the *Washington Post*'s on-the-ground reporter in Ferguson, spent weeks in the community. He discovered that the Ferguson police revenue scheme was endemic throughout the greater St. Louis area. Police departments were known for stacking multiple violations onto a single traffic ticket. When tickets went unpaid, arrest warrants were issued. Warrants added additional fines and fees if the subject failed to make court appearances. Court dates were often scheduled at inconvenient times. According to Lowery, on the day that Michael Brown was killed Ferguson had "almost as many active warrants as it did residents."[78]

The Ferguson system of justice was little more than a mandatory Ponzi scheme imposed on its unwilling black residents.

Residents told Lowery stories of police misconduct that "on their face seemed unbelievable."[79] Yet the Justice Department's report made believable the claims that residents described to Lowery—"officers who pulled them over repeatedly, nights spent in jail for unpaid speeding tickets, and, most disturbing of all, shootings and other deaths at the hands of police officers about which they and the people of Ferguson still lacked answers."[80] Lowery found that the people of Ferguson had no relationship other than as victims, and accordingly did not trust the police. The police in turn "seemed to exhibit next to no humanity toward the pained residents they were charged with protecting."[81]

The municipal court through which these revenue-raising offenses were processed did not act as an independent judicial body, but as a partner in fund-raising:

> The municipal court does not act as a neutral arbiter of the law or a check on unlawful police conduct. Instead, the court primarily uses its judicial authority as the means to compel the payment of fines and fees that advance the City's financial interests. This has led to court practices that violate the Fourteenth Amendment's due process and equal protection requirements. The court's practices also impose unnecessary harm, overwhelmingly on African-American individuals, and run counter to public safety.[82]

The Justice Department found widespread evidence of racial bias in the administration of Ferguson's criminal justice system:

> Our investigation indicates that this disproportionate burden on African Americans cannot be explained by any difference in the rate at which people of different races violate the law. Rather, our investigation has revealed that these disparities occur, at least in part, because of unlawful bias against and stereotypes about African Americans. We have found substantial evidence of racial bias among police and court staff in Ferguson. For example, we discovered emails circulated by police supervisors and court staff that stereotype racial minorities as criminals, including one email that joked about an abortion by an African-American woman being a means of crime control.[83]

Within 105 pages of scathing detail, the report fleshed out these summary findings and, in effect, held up the Ferguson Police Department as a shameful case study confirming much of the Black Lives Matter movement's complaints about the structure of the American criminal justice system. The deaths of Michael Brown and scores of other young black men are symptoms of a structural sickness. So long as that illness exists, so will Black Lives Matter.

Within a year, Tex McIver and Atlanta were to find out what a powerful movement grown to maturity could do.

5

HERITAGE

The new force radiating out from Ferguson soon reached Atlanta. On the night of September 25, 2016, it struck Tex McIver's world like a bolt of lightning. The differences in polarity between the negative cultural electrons of Tex's apparent fear of black people and the positrons of the Black Lives Matter movement ignited that strike. Try as he might, Tex could not roll back the booming flash that he had fairly asked for.

A continuous chain of new cases of allegedly racist police shootings and law enforcement brutality all across America added new energy and new focal points for the umbrella of black activism that is typically described collectively as the Black Lives Matter movement.[1] Surprisingly (or not), no government agency maintains a comprehensive database of "officer-involved" shootings, much less complaints of lesser brutality. A Federal Bureau of Investigation (FBI) database relies on voluntary reports from local police agencies but only logs about half of all police shootings nationwide, according to the *Washington Post* newspaper. The paper has filled much of the void with its online database of shootings by on-duty police officers, starting in 2015. The database shows that police officers consistently shoot about one thousand people a year. Half of those shot are white. But in 2020 blacks made up only 13.4 percent of the U.S. population, compared to whites at 76.3 percent.[2] Given this gross difference in population, blacks are shot by police at a demonstrably higher rate than whites.[3]

Georgia was no different, according to a comprehensive investigation by the *Atlanta Journal-Constitution* in 2015. The newspaper reported that only sixteen of more than six hundred police agencies in Georgia reported their police shooting data to the FBI. The investigation found twice as many police shootings in Georgia than were reported to the federal agency.[4]

Database or not, names like Eric Garner, who died in July 2014 while locked in an unlawful police chokehold by a New York City police officer; Tamir Rice, a twelve-year-old boy shot to death by Cleveland police while playing with a toy gun in November 2014; and Freddie Gray, a Baltimore man who died in a police van under suspicious circumstances in April 2015, have been memorialized. No longer were stories like theirs reported only as "a small blurb in the local daily paper" that quickly faded from memory—they became "the lead story on the national news" and began to have national impact in politics and policy thinking.[5]

COMING TO ATLANTA

In the two years preceding Diane McIver's death, the network of remembrance and protest spread to Atlanta.

Georgia was fertile ground, according to two polls released by the *Atlanta Journal Constitution* newspaper in January 2015. One poll found that less than half of Georgians thought that race relations in America had improved in the thirty years since 1985. The majority was split between those who thought that things had gotten worse and those who thought they had stayed the same. There was little difference between the races in these overall views of relations between them.[6]

A more dramatic divide was revealed by the other poll, which looked at views about the criminal justice system in general and the police in particular. More than half of Georgians thought blacks and other minorities were not treated with the same dignity and respect as whites in Georgia's criminal justice system. Only a bare majority of 52 percent were confident that blacks and whites get equal treatment from police in Georgia.

The racial differences of opinion were stark regarding police treatment. A total of 85 percent of black respondents thought that the criminal justice system was not colorblind—only 36 percent of whites felt the same. And where 75 percent of black respondents thought that police didn't treat them equally with whites, 70 percent of whites thought that the opposite was true.[7]

This division in the views of blacks and whites was not unique to Georgia. A Pew Research Center report in October 2017 found that the national partisan divide in views on racial equity had grown over the past several decades. Democrats were increasingly likely to take racially liberal positions, whereas Republican views remained relatively stable. A total of 81 percent of Democrats thought the country should do more to promote equal rights for blacks, whereas only 36 percent of Republicans thought so. More than 80 percent of blacks thought more needed to be done.[8] The partisan division over issues of race and law enforcement remains a major source of deep polarization in American society and politics.

Mary Hooks, an Atlanta activist, traveled to Ferguson to join the protests after Michael Brown's death. Organizers in Ferguson urged supporters like Hooks to return to their homes and raise issues of law enforcement violence in their own communities.[9] Back in Atlanta, Brooks connected with another activist, Dre Propst. The two organized the standing-room-only inaugural meeting of the Atlanta chapter on December 17, 2015, at the Big Bethel A.M.E. church on Auburn Avenue.[10] In Hooks's view, the new movement was about more than black men being killed by police. It extended as well to the lack of affordable housing, high unemployment rates and poverty levels, and substandard public education.[11]

NOT YOUR GRANDDADDY'S MOVEMENT

The new movement was born out of a new generation with a new voice and a new way of doing things.

"This is not your granddaddy's civil rights movement," said Mary Hooks. "We're not sitting around and waiting for someone in a suit to come save us." She described the new movement as "a polarizing force in Atlanta, a group that will make people choose sides."[12]

The older generation of activists were confounded more by the confrontational attitude of the millennials of Generations X, Y, and Z, and their ways of organizing social action, than by their substantive demands. "The city of Atlanta is having a real problem when it comes to social activism and the new school leaders that are rising," journalist Mo Barnes wrote in *Rolling Out* magazine. "No longer is Atlanta seeing social movements that have roots in the Black church, but rather movements that have roots in social media, coffee shops, living rooms and the streets by young millennials."[13]

Some black leaders were outspoken in their criticism of the new movement. Andrew Young, an icon of the older generation and former mayor of Atlanta, called the new activists "brats" while speaking to members of the Atlanta Police Department.[14] Young reportedly thought that the activists of the new generation were not making any real sacrifices comparable to the ones that he and his peers made. "I knew I was gonna get beat up when I confronted the police, but they know they're gonna get away with it," Young, then eighty-four years old, was quoted as saying. "It's a cheap shot."[15] Another older generation leader, Bernard Lafayette, who was active in the Student Nonviolent Coordinating Committee, criticized the new movement's lack of a hierarchical national organization. "It's one thing to have protests," he said. "It's another thing to have a movement."[16]

The more youthful activists were just as outspoken in their criticisms of the old guard and in some cases of the "Atlanta Way" in general.

"We're tired of marching, singing 'We shall overcome,'" Atlanta chapter co-founder Dre Propst said.[17] "It's like we live in a dystopian future where all the civil rights leaders have gone wrong," said one twenty-two-year old college student. Another said, "Young people think the NAACP is a group that speaks but doesn't act."[18]

A deeper current ran through the young activists' criticisms. Some claimed that the lauded "Atlanta Way" worked only for Atlanta's black elite, who were accused of ignoring the city's black poor. "The city too busy to hate is also too busy to care about people that they've left behind," said Khalid Kamau, a Democratic national convention delegate for presidential candidate Bernie Sanders.[19]

Eventually leaders of the older generation either learned to work together under the umbrella of Black Lives Matter or were simply made irrelevant by the new wave's operational methods. "In the 1960s, organizing and informing students was likely a function of underground newspapers," wrote one analyst. "Today, a protest is just a tweet away, and social media is used to keep college students connected and engaged during school breaks."[20] Whereas old-style protests were the products of a careful process of planning meetings, training sessions, and marshals monitoring the conduct of demonstrators, the new protests were often spontaneous, fluid confrontations. "The hashtags, like #ICantBreathe and #NoJusticeNoPeace, gave the Black Lives Matter movement visibility," according to an analysis by the *Atlanta Journal-Constitution*. "People knew what to search to find out who was leading the rallies both in the streets and online."[21]

COMPARED TO WHAT—CHANGING OPINIONS

Polling showed that the opinions of Americans about police behavior and the Black Lives Matter movement were sharply divided along racial lines at the same time that the movement was taking root in Atlanta.

A PBS NewsHour/Marist Poll in September 2015 found that, when asked whether African Americans and whites have the same opportunity for equal justice under the law, 87 percent of African Americans said no and 11 percent said yes. On the other hand, 50 percent of whites said yes and 46 percent said no. Regarding Black Lives Matter specifically, 65 percent of African Americans thought it focused attention on the real issues of racial discrimination. Only 25 percent of whites agreed that the movement focused on real issues. A total of 59 percent of whites thought that Black Lives Matter distracted attention from the real issues of racial discrimination, an assessment with which only 26 percent of African Americans agreed.[22]

A *New York Times*/CBS News poll in July 2016 asked Americans whether police are more likely to use deadly force against a black person than a white person. Three-quarters of African Americans respondents answered yes. But only about half as many white people agreed. A total of 56 percent of whites thought that the race of a suspect made no difference in the use of force. Only 18 percent of black Americans said race made no difference in police treatment. Asked to rate their local police department, four out of five whites said the department was doing an excellent or good job. A majority of blacks answered that their department was doing only a fair or poor job. More than two-fifths of black people said the police made them feel more anxious than safe, while whites and Hispanics said police make them feel safer.[23]

These different views about law enforcement were reflected in answers to the same poll's questions about the aims and the approach of the

Black Lives Matter movement. A total of 70 percent of African Americans sympathized with the movement, compared with only 37 percent of whites. Among all Americans, 41 percent agreed with the movement, 25 percent disagreed, and 29 percent had no opinion either way. Support correlated directly with age. A total of 50 percent of adults younger than thirty agreed with the movement, compared to 20 percent who disagreed. Among adults forty-five and older, 36 percent agreed and 29 percent disagreed.[24]

But a significant change—perhaps driven by universal outrage over the widely publicized death of George Floyd under a policeman's knee in Minneapolis—became apparent in the spring of 2020. White opinion swung around to largely approve of the movement. One factor at work was the impact of social media, which enabled young black persons to document interactions with police that they thought were unjust. This documentation "exposed their white friends and family members to their experiences."[25] "Public opinion on race and criminal justice issues has been steadily moving left since the first protests ignited over the fatal shootings of Trayvon Martin and Michael Brown," wrote a pair of writers for the *New York Times* in June 2020. "And since the death of George Floyd in police custody on May 25, public opinion on race, criminal justice and the Black Lives Matter movement has leaped leftward."[26]

It is fairly obvious on which side of the divide in opinion Diane and Tex McIver fell, given their demographics and sponsorship of a Blue Lives Matter sign. Like Black Lives Matter, the Blue Lives Matter movement is a loosely organized national coalition. It is widely seen as "a rebuttal to Black Lives Matter . . . [insisting] that we pay more attention to killer cops than to cops killed in the line of duty."[27] A series of demonstrations in Atlanta from early July until the very day that Tex shot Diane in the back brought the Black Lives Matter movement to their door.

Black Lives Matter activists originally marched in Atlanta to protest the deaths of two African American men who were shot to death by police within two days of each other in other cities. Demonstrators would soon focus on police shootings in Georgia. In the meantime, a mass shooting of police officers in Dallas sparked angry criticism of the Black Lives Matter movement.

BRINGING IT HOME

On July 5, 2016, Alton Sterling, a thirty-seven-year-old black man, was shot dead at close range by two white police officers in Baton Rouge, Louisiana. The next day a white police officer in Falcon Heights, Minnesota, shot to death another black man, Philando Castile. On Friday, July 8, protestors took to the streets in cities across America. One of the largest protests was in Atlanta, where ten thousand were reported to have joined a march through downtown.[28]

On the same day as these demonstrations, a black gunman opened fire from a parking building on police officers who were on duty monitoring the march in Dallas. Five officers—Lorne Ahrens, Michael Krol, Michael J. Smith, Brent Thompson, and Patrick Zamarripa—were killed by the sniper. Seven other officers and two civilians were wounded. The shooter told police during an ensuing standoff that "he was upset about the recent police shootings . . . [and] wanted to kill white people, especially white officers."[29] The standoff ended when the shooter, an Army veteran, was killed by a bomb-bearing police robot.

The confluence of Black Lives Matter demonstrations and the murder of five police officers ignited a furious backlash from law enforcement officials and conservative opinion makers. Among the latter was Derryck Green, a member of a national network of black conservatives. In an op-ed in the *Atlanta Journal-Constitution* two weeks later, Green attacked the Black Lives Matter movement, declaring that "movement activists have intentionally increased its inflammatory anti-white racial hatred . . . [and] defiantly increased its anti-cop rhetoric." Black Lives Matter, Green charged, "was indeed the catalyst for [the Dallas shooter] to act on his racial anger and paranoia."[30]

The Dallas police shooting and the criticisms it generated did not stop Atlanta's activists from continuing to demonstrate throughout the next week. The new movement's eagerness for direct and uncomfortable confrontations brought them to Buckhead, where they aimed directly at the upscale lifestyle of its white elite and high-end shopping centers. "We want to be able to touch this demographic here," one activist leader said.[31] The demographic there included the McIvers.

Mayor Kasim Reed eventually agreed to meet with some of the protest leaders. The amorphous nature of Black Lives Matter leadership led to friction and criticism about the meeting from within the movement.[32]

Atlanta's police force earned praise from both the mayor and black leaders for its restraint in handling the protests.[33] Richard Rose, president of
the Atlanta branch of the NAACP, called police behavior "exemplary."[34]
Observers beamed about the Atlanta Way. "Part of the winning formula
was one employed by Police Chief George Turner in having police not
arrive in riot gear," columnist Bill Torpy wrote. "If you don't start out
antagonistic, then things are less likely to slide into chaos."[35]

(Four years later, in June 2020, things would change. Police, "most
protected by full body armor and face shields," fired tear gas and nonle-
thal projectiles to break up a demonstration in front of the state capitol.
The *Atlanta Journal-Constitution* reported that the incident was an example of "the combative tactics that law enforcement agencies have used to
suppress the uprising sparked by the killing of George Floyd by a Minneapolis police officer."[36])

By the end of September, when Tex and Diane spent their last weekend at the ranch, demonstrators in Atlanta had zeroed in on police actions
in Atlanta and were again on the march, including regular disruptive
visits to Buckhead.

There was reason enough. A study of police shootings in Georgia
published by the *Atlanta Journal-Constitution* in December 2015 found
that almost half of the 184 Georgians shot and killed by police since 2010
were unarmed or shot in the back. About three out of five blacks were
unarmed or shot in the back, compared to about two out of five whites. A
total of 78 percent of the officers who discharged their weapons were
white. And police fatally shot black residents at a rate twice that of
whites.

By no means were all of these police shootings unjustified. A majority
of the 184 shootings analyzed by the newspaper involved "dangerous
situations with people who were threatening the officers or others with
guns or other weapons. About one-quarter had discharged a firearm before or during the fatal encounter with police. But when the shooting
appeared questionable, the system always ruled in favor of the officer."[37]

There was a systematic reason embedded within Georgia's criminal
justice system that tipped the odds in favor of the rare police officer who
was charged with a crime after shooting someone. Until recently, Georgia
was the only state in the union that gave police officers the right to sit in
on the entire deliberations of any grand jury looking at their conduct.
Witnesses are not allowed to hear the testimony of other witnesses before

grand juries, to maintain the secrecy of the proceedings and to prevent their tailoring their testimony based on what they hear others say. In federal grand jury proceedings, for example, only the jurors, the prosecutor, the witness being questioned, a court reporter, and interpreter (if needed) may be in the courtroom during the hearing.[38] In Georgia practice, police officers not only had the right to sit in on other witnesses' testimony, but were privileged to give a statement at the end of the grand jury's deliberations that could not be questioned by prosecutors or grand jurors.[39]

Faced with mounting criticism about the unbalanced scale of Georgia's grand jury proceedings, the state legislature changed the rules. Today, Georgia law enforcement officers under scrutiny are no longer allowed to sit in on the testimony of others. If they choose to make a statement before the grand jury, they are now subject to the usual process of questioning by grand jurors and cross-examination by prosecutors. In the opinion of some observers, these changes "leveled the playing field."[40] A final test before the new rules went into effect was coming. An Atlanta police officer's shooting of an unarmed black man on June 22, 2016, caught the attention of Black Lives Matter activists, who warned that they were watching how the case was handled.

The basic facts were fairly simple. Police officer James R. Burns responded to a nighttime call for backup from an off-duty officer who had spotted a "suspicious person" in an apartment complex. As Burns drove into the complex, he saw a vehicle's headlights turn on. The car drove toward Burns's car. A black man, Deravis Caine Rogers, was behind the wheel. Rather than stopping when Burns flashed his blue lights, Rogers drove around Burns's vehicle. Burns shot into the moving vehicle as it passed him, without knowing who the driver was or anything about him. A bullet struck Rogers in the head, killing him.

The police department's internal affairs investigation determined that Burns had no reason to fear for his life. His shooting into Rogers's car and killing him was therefore an unnecessary, excessive use of force. Burns was fired within days of the shooting. In a move credited with defusing tensions over the police shooting death, Fulton County District Attorney Paul Howard did not wait for a grand jury to act. He charged Burns with felony murder, aggravated assault with a deadly weapon, and violation of his oath of office.[41]

A grand jury was convened at the end of August 2016. A consortium of activists including Black Lives Matter held an overnight vigil at the courthouse to draw attention to the case.[42] The grand jury was operating under the old rules, so Burns was allowed to sit in. Nevertheless, the next day the grand jury indicted Burn on five felony counts: murder, aggravated assault, two counts of violating his oath of office, and one count of making a false statement.[43] This indictment was quashed because of an evidentiary technicality before the grand jury.

Burns was promptly indicted a second time. But at this writing, four years later, his case has still not gone to trial.

SEPTEMBER'S SONG

While the McIvers were spending their last weekend at the ranch in Eatonton, protesters were raising the ante in Atlanta. Activists marched in both downtown Atlanta and Buckhead on Friday night, September 23, and Saturday, September 24. Tex shot Diane the night of Sunday, September 25.

"It is in fact an escalation," NAACP Chapter President Francys Johnson said of the Friday night downtown march. "We aren't asking anymore. We're demanding."[44] One of the organizers of the Buckhead protest complained that white police officers involved in killings of black people protected such wealthy areas and shopped in them. Police, he said, "murder us and slaughter us through the streets of our neighborhood and then they run back here to Buckhead, where they continue business as usual."[45]

The protests continued on Saturday, when entrances to the Lenox Square Mall in Buckhead were temporarily blocked.[46] On Sunday, the day the McIvers played their last round of golf together in Putnam County, the *Atlanta Journal-Constitution* published a lengthy frontpage profile of the Black Lives Matter movement and its origins.[47]

If Tex McIver was telling the truth, whatever else was on his mind, and however unreasonable his fear might be judged, he was probably aware of the weekend's demonstrations in Atlanta and Buckhead. But there was something else that informed the views of Tex McIver, most white Americans, and the nation's police forces on the Black Lives Matter phenomenon. That something else is the lens of racial perception created by centuries of slavery and by the Jim Crow era's attacks on people of color.

In its simplest articulation, police violence against black people is blamed on racial bias. Police officers are easily dismissed in this view as simply and inherently "racist." There are other strong forces at work, however. These include a universal culture of police organizations, increased militarization of law enforcement and a corollary "warrior" attitude, unrealistic expectations that policy-makers have piled on police forces' missions, networks of cultural and political support that defend police violence as necessary to keep law and order, and infiltration to some degree of law enforcement ranks by white supremacists and related vigilante groups.

POLICE CULTURE

"[T]he behavior of police only makes sense when viewed through the lens of culture," John P. Crank, a professor of sociology and criminology, wrote in *Understanding Police Culture*.[48]

There are many views of what culture is generally and what police culture is in particular. To Crank, culture is "how we act out our moral and social identities." It is not something apart from who we, including police officers, are. It is rather "a self-affirming blend of our traditions—the world past—and the world of today that we see around us and on which we act."[49] With a few moments of thought, one can easily generate a long list of subcultures that define each of us in many such ways, some of which we might move in and out of in a single day—the culture of professional athletes, an office or corporate culture, the culture of academia, the culture of a religious denomination, the cultures of ethnic and gender identities, the culture of gun enthusiasts, and so forth. These cultures help define who we are and what we do.

Police culture "covers a lot of intellectual and emotional territory," Crank writes. He summed that territory up as follows:

> Police organizational structures, policies, behaviors, arrest patterns, corruption, education, training practices, attitudes toward suspects and citizens, forms of patrol, and all other areas of police work—the whole ball of wax—are witnessed and practiced through the lens of culture. All areas of police work have meaning of some kind to cops, and as

every reformer and chief who has sought to change any organization knows, these meanings tend to bind together in sentiments and values impossible to analytically separate and individually change.[50]

Crank examines in convincing detail what he calls the component "themes" of the police culture. These themes include the patrol officers' need for territorial dominion over their beat, police use of sanctioned force, the gun culture endemic to American policing, police officers' abiding suspicion of situations and of people inherent in the ambiguous "twilight world" in which police operate, danger and anticipation of danger, the need to keep an "edge" to dominate dangerous people and control situations, police solidarity, and the moral judgments that police make about the civilian citizenry (their "other"), and other factors.

The use of force is the most emotionally charged of these themes of police culture. Crank suggests it puts the police in a difficult bind. "We want police to use force when they must, but to avoid it unless absolutely necessary," he writes. "We then ask cops to deal with our most profound social problems and to use whatever force is necessary to shelter us from the criminal and the uncivilized. We complain bitterly when police do not quickly resolve problems we ourselves cannot handle. It is a contradictory and impossible responsibility."[51]

In sum, we have criminalized and then handed to police in America a bundle of our most difficult and complex social problems—drug abuse, homelessness, untreated mental illness, domestic abuse, and illegal immigration, among others, all fairly crackling with the potential for some level of violence. We then act as if society's job is done. But the job is not done at all. The underlying structural problems still exist. When one of these problems pops out of the seams of society, we expect the police to push the problem back into the invisible underworld, with force if necessary—but not with too much force, a blurred line that we are happy to sharpen retrospectively.

Georgia police officials described the problem in the context of the July 2016 meeting of protestors with Atlanta's mayor. "Law enforcement today is not so much crime-fighter—you are a social worker with a gun," Doraville Police Chief John King said. Dunwoody Police Chief Billy Grogan echoed the thought. "Law enforcement is on the front line and it has to deal with a lot of bigger society issues, such as substance abuse and mental health issues and a lack of educational opportunities, unemployment, single-parent homes. . . . All those kinds of issues somehow or another get woven into what we have to do in our jobs."[52]

Given the scope of their charge, police and the police culture constantly interact with people of all races, ethnicities, and socio-economic status. Whether it's a burglary of our premises, being stopped for a traffic offense, or reporting the obnoxious and apparently threatening public behavior of a ranting mentally ill person, sooner or later most Americans are going to have some contact with the police, acting in one of the many roles that we have assigned them. White people also get stopped, questioned, and arrested. But race and racially sorted signals often determine how interactions with police are handled and their end results.

"Police behavior is mobilized by characteristics of dress, behavior, and attitudes," Crank observes. "These are often associated with membership in minority groups. The color of someone's skin, style of dress, or accent—symbols of cultural difference—become symbolic shorthand for identifying suspicious characters."[53]

As much as structural factors inherent in police culture help explain the attitudes of police toward blacks and ethnic minority communities, there is another, much greater force at work everywhere in America. Crank argues that effectively dealing with this problem is neither a question of sorting out "bad apples" nor one of re-educating officers who have racist or prejudiced personal attitudes (however useful these efforts may be). To come to grips with the force driving police racism we must "look at the history of police in the United States to understand how racism has been a pervasive characteristic since [police] agencies were first founded."[54]

The problem by no means ends with a review of police history and its effects. Society's rule makers today still exploit the mechanisms of law and order for their own class benefits. "The police do what we want them to do. They cannot change because we will not change."[55] We live in "a self-described free society that is unable to cope with the most consequential problems of simple human equality, lacking even a common language that would allow us to speak about shared values." We hide behind tough law enforcement to protect our economic interests and personal wealth, and to keep "dangerous" persons, real or imagined, away from us. Our politics is "too often a charade of moral righteousness and chastising zeal" through which we "justify outrageous punishments for inconsequential crimes, destroying generations of Black youth through imprisonment, and through the panopticon of a growing urban gulag in many of our largest cities."[56]

In the twenty-first century, lacking a meaningful or even civil language, our on-the-ground discourse has in its worst form become shouts and cries among baton-wielding armored police, torch-bearing rioters, and heavily armed vigilantes, increasingly punctuated by gunshots.

SLAVERY AND ITS EFFECTS

History, heritage, and legacy are curious subjects in American cultural discourse. In some contexts, we are happy to acknowledge the effects of the past on our lives today. In other contexts, we ignore or deny the same mechanism of past cause and present effect.

We are quite willing to acknowledge what we deem to be the good and noble effects of people like George Washington and events like the Revolutionary War in the historical past. We praise them as the events and the people that made America great. At the same time, we prefer to turn our faces away from the ugly events and people in our past, and their consequences for today—slave masters, ethnic cleansing, land theft, slavery, and government-imposed and -supported racial and ethnic discrimination and oppression.

Why do many American minds have so much difficulty discussing, much less acknowledging, the very real effects on today's society and culture that slavery, the systematic oppression of the Jim Crow era, and enforced segregation have had? This is a conversation that we often talk about having, usually in times of racial stress, but rarely get around to engaging in any sort of common language. On the contrary, the languages spoken on opposing sides of the trenches of a polarized America use the very same words—freedom, opportunity, fairness, and so forth—to mean very different things.

Some black minds share this aversion to our ignoble history and its effects. "[F]or some African Americans stories of slavery should be erased as well because they are shameful and better forgotten. For, they argue . . . such stories are likely to disempower contemporary generations of African Americans."[57]

In one way, this inability to talk about the unpleasant things in our national past is the inverse of the mass mind's inability to grasp the long-

term, incremental future effects of human-caused environmental degrada-
tion. Like so many dung beetles, we can seemingly only roll today's ball
of clay a few inches forward, heedless of the unpleasant horizon looming
ahead of us. Whither we are bound we know not. Nor do we much care to
know. Just so, the selectively closed mind cannot or will not look critical-
ly back at the horizon receding behind it. That mind cannot or will not
grasp that the bad things and bad people of the past have affected the
present as much as the good things and the good people. Nor can it
conceive of the possibility that the good people of the past may actually
have a mixed record and have even been downright evil in some ways.
Such a mind in denial can only belligerently insist that what's done is
done and "no one in my family ever owned a slave."

In another way, the closed mind is plainly a result of ignorance, of an
educational system that has erased the bad part of history and distorted
the good.

Even when we force ourselves to look back at slavery, the vast majority of Americans think of it as a relatively tiny historical cul-de-sac,
nestled somewhere inconsequential in the piney woods of the South,
definitely off of the great and inspiring interstate highway of American
history. "Generally, Americans believe that slavery was an exclusively
southern phenomenon. They date it from the decades immediately preceding the Civil War, and think of it as a relatively minor part of the
American story."[58] Okay, we are inclined to think, there were some
charming old plantations and life may have been tough for the slaves (or
not, for those who hold to the Lost Cause myth of slaveholder paternal-
ism). But that was just a weird agricultural side show that had nothing to
do with the dynamic engine of capitalism, liberty, and frontier grit that
swept America to greatness.

Nothing could be further from the truth. Slavery was not a cul-de-sac
off of the American mainstream. Slavery's norms and its brutal production of wealth lay at the beating heart of the great American engine of free
enterprise and free men. Slavery and cotton literally made the economy of
post-Colonial America, which was cut off from the benefits of the erst-
while mother country's system of trade. Slavery's wealth production, the
cotton trade, laid the financial foundation that made possible the brawn of
America of today. And its scars still mar the face of our society.

The roots of this ignorance of history can be found in the American
educational system. A typical public school textbook of the late 1940s

and 1950s—when many of American leaders of today and the recent past were getting their basic education—told students that "the abolition of slavery may not have been the best thing for blacks because 'slaves had snug cabins to live in, plenty of food to eat and work that was not too hard for them to do.' Then, as if to reaffirm the expected student conclusions, the text added, 'Most of the slaves seemed happy and contented.'"[59] College textbooks written by acclaimed historians were even worse. In 1950, one of the most popular college textbooks, written by Samuel Eliot Morrison and Henry Steele Commager "suggested that white abolitionists may have been more upset about slavery than were the slaves themselves. 'As for Sambo, whose wrongs moved the abolitionists to wrath and tears,' they argued, 'there is reason to believe that he suffered less than any other class in the south from the "peculiar institution."'"[60]

History education today is not much better. A total of 80 percent of the nation's colleges do not require education in American history. It is therefore not surprising that in a recent survey a majority of college students "could not identify such names as Abraham Lincoln, Thomas Jefferson, and Andrew Jackson, and many believed that George Washington was the president during the War of 1812 . . . many students in the South believe that Jefferson Davis was president of the United States during the Civil War."[61] Distortions such as these are actively promoted by such groups as the United Sons of Confederate Veterans, the United Daughters of the Confederacy, and the Southern Heritage Coalition.[62]

When historians talk about slavery and its effects, they are often charged with "presentism," that is, using twenty-first-century morality to judge the past. "Yet twenty-first-century Americans cannot excuse those of the eighteenth and nineteenth centuries with the argument that they were simply conforming to the accepted norms of their era, for many in the Revolutionary era understood the contradiction clearly and said so."[63]

THE ABSOLUTE RIGHTS OF INDIVIDUALS—TURNED INSIDE OUT

In terms of the law and law enforcement, American slavery embodied the "inside/outside" system that historian Sven Beckert described in his master work about plantation slavery and its worldwide effects, *Empire of Cotton*. Beckert contrasted the rules of law that imperial powers, such as colonial Great Britain, observed within their own countries for their native citizens, and the very different rules that they imposed for naked gain on the people that they conquered and exploited:

> The "inside" encompassed the laws, institutions, and customs of the mother country, where state-enforced order ruled. The "outside," by contrast, was characterized by imperial domination, the expropriation of vast territories, decimation of indigenous peoples, theft of their resources, enslavement, and the domination of vast tracts of land by private capitalists with little effective oversight by distant European states. In these imperial dependencies, the rules of the insider did not apply. There, masters trumped states, violence defied the law, and bold physical coercion by private actors remade markets. [64]

What were the most basic rights of the "inside" system of Great Britain, the imperial power from which the legal system of the American colonies and the United States sprang? In the mid-eighteenth century, shortly before the American Revolution, an English jurist and legal scholar, Sir William Blackstone, published a set of books titled *Commentaries on the Laws of England* in which he set out a precise and vigorous answer to that question.

American legal scholar Albert W. Alschuler called the *Commentaries* "the most influential law book in Anglo-American history."[65] The books had a major impact on the development of American common law. They are still occasionally cited by the U.S. Supreme Court in its discussions of the historical roots of modern law.[66] One thousand copies of the English edition of what is popularly known simply as "Blackstone" were sold in the American Colonies before the first American edition appeared in 1772. One year before the Declaration of Independence, Edmund Burke remarked that nearly as many copies of the *Commentaries* had been sold on the American side of the Atlantic as on the English side. Chief Justice John Marshall and President Abraham Lincoln were among the many American luminaries who read the *Commentaries* not only for their education in the law (there were no law schools in their times) but also for their general education. Historian Daniel Boorstin said that no book other than the Bible had so great an influence on the development of American institutions.

Blackstone wrote about the most fundamental rights of the English people in a powerful exposition. He declared that all individuals possess three "absolute rights, . . . vested in them by the immutable laws of nature." These were the rights of personal security ("a person's . . . enjoyment of his life, his limbs, his body, his health, and his reputation"), personal liberty, and private property. This right to personal liberty "consists in the power of . . . removing one's person to whatsoever place one's own inclination may direct without imprisonment or restraint unless by due course of law. . . . [I]t is a right strictly natural [and] the laws of England have never abridged it without sufficient cause."[67]

Notwithstanding Blackstone's influence on American legal thought, his stirring declaration of the "absolute rights" of individuals was turned inside out for black people by the mechanisms of the inside/outside system that were a central part of America's legal system for most of its history (and in the opinion of some a system still central today).

Rather than having a right to *own* private property, black slaves *were* the property of their white masters, conceptually no different from those same masters' cattle, dining room tables, or bedsteads. The rights of personal security—"the enjoyment of his life, his limbs, his body, his health, and his reputation"—and personal liberty—"removing one's person to whatsoever place one's own inclination may direct without imprisonment or restraint"—were simply erased for black slaves and free blacks.

For the most part, this perversion of the rights declared in one form or another from the Magna Carta of 1215 to the Declaration of Independence in 1776 was driven by the engine of economic greed. Slaves were essential tools of the industrial or factory system of agricultural production embodied in the plantation, and the work demanded of them—forced upon them—could not or would not be done as profitably by free persons.

But from the most ancient of times another dark, primal force drove that part of the law of slavery that dealt with the definition of crimes, the "law and order" enforcement mechanism, and state-sanctioned punishments. That force was fear. The criminal justice system for slaves has always been ultimately based on brutal and cynically instructive force inspired by the blood-cold, stomach-churning, tingling fear of the slave by the master.

EVERY SLAVE AN ENEMY

Slavery has been around since at least the beginning of recorded time. It has always been cruel, and it has always been based on physical violence. There has never been a benign slavery, except in the counterfactual narratives of Lost Cause fantasists, the narcotic dreams of generally misguided but in some case outright racist academics, and the confabulations of cynical and ignorant politicians.

The violence that sustains slavery is potential as well as kinetic.

Not every slave in history has been branded, kicked, punched, hung in excruciating pain from their thumbs or elbows, made to stand for hours under a blazing sun or in a freezing winter's cold, repeatedly raped, whipped with sticks or leather lashes, stabbed, mutilated, castrated, had their breasts cut off, been beaten to death, shot to death, starved to death, or worked to death. They didn't have to be. The horrific suffering and brutal deaths of individual slaves in all of these ways and means served well enough to forcefully evidence the master's limitless, unquestioned power over the mass of his slaves.

Even nominally free persons can be induced to endure oppression and obey unpleasant orders with only a modicum of actually imposed violence. The state's mere potential power to inflict violent pain is often enough to ensure servitude. Thus the great bulk of the good citizens of authoritarian regimes have concluded that overt resistance will only result in pain or death that they can otherwise avoid by simply going along with the state's mandates and following the herd. What happens in the bloody cellars of the secret police, or in the nominally secret but usually well-known hell of state concentration camps is best ignored for one's own good and the good of one's family.

Beyond naked power, the victims of state violence are often transformed into enemies of the people. The nation's good citizens are persuaded that the state's victims deserve every bit of pain inflicted on them—Jews, Roma people, Armenians, Kurds, homosexuals, political prisoners, undocumented aliens, black slaves, and people of color. The list is endless.

This potential for violence, whether arbitrary in an instant or calculated as a behavioral norm, is where the narrative of paternal or benevolent slavery crashes on the rocks of reality. No matter how "kind" or "benevolent" a master or mistress (and, yes, there were many female slave mistresses in the antebellum South) might have been—putting aside for the sake of argument the underlying and ineradicable brutality of involuntary servitude—a split second's anger, displeasure, drunken rage, psychopathic whim, or even the petulance of a slave master's child could and often enough did result in horrific consequences for the slaves of "benevolent" masters throughout history.

Slave masters have also always known that the potential for violence is a two-way street. Behind the mask of the slave's compliance lay a face twisted in a howl of pain and anger.

Slavery's apologetic fabulists—including the American historians discussed earlier—have spun gauzy narratives of the slave's contentment with, even grateful submission to, the fantastic benefits of human bondage. But history has proven time and again that within every slave lies the potential to strike out against the master for freedom, revenge, or simply a moment's dignity. Resistance and rebellion lay deeply coiled under every slave system. To claim otherwise, to insist that slaves actually liked being slaves—as America's smugly libertarian slaveholders ironically often did to justify their own savage inhumanity—is to deny the core premise of human dignity upon which the noble ideals of life, liberty, and the pursuit of happiness are supposedly based.

It is also to ignore evidence of slave discontent from the revolt led by the Roman slave Spartacus in 73–71 BCE, to Toussaint l'Overture's rebellion in Saint Domingue (Haiti) at the turn of the nineteenth century, to Nat Turner's Rebellion in Virginia in 1831, and to scores of other acts of organized, violent resistance throughout history and geography—not to mention the supposedly compliant slaves' subtle daily sabotage or quiet defiance and obstruction of the master's ends. Barns were burned, tools were broken, and masters were poisoned by resistors who are nameless today.

Rome's slaveholders knew and feared the self-evident fact of the potential for violent slave resistance. The wisest among them warned slaveholders that they had as many enemies as they had slaves. Cruel and collective punishments of Roman slaves were intended precisely to fend off or contain slave resistance.

FROM ATHENS TO BARBADOS

Historians of slavery caution that the nature and conditions of any system of slavery are not static over time or place. To speak of the slavery of Greece, Rome, the West Indies, or the United States is to telescope into a single discussion at least decades and more often centuries of dynamic and multi-faceted institutions that adapted to economic fortunes and misfortunes, changes in supply and demand, wars, turmoil in governments, and pandemic diseases that wiped out local labor forces. The first slaves in the American colonies in the seventeenth century were ensnared in an institution that was very different from the plantation slavery of the early nineteenth century.

Nevertheless, there are certain fundamental conditions in addition to violence with which it is possible to characterize a system of slavery, even over long periods of time and across wide stretches of geographic place. One of these is the difference between a society with slaves and a slave society.

A society with slaves is one in which slavery is permitted and common, but not central to the regime's economy. This is not to say that slaves were not integrated into the economy of a society with slaves. They might indeed have been laborers, skilled artisans, or extraordinary household or business managers as well as household servants. But even had these slaves disappeared, the social and economic life of that time and place would have gone on more or less unchanged.

In slave societies, on the other hand, the forced labor of slaves was essential to and in many cases the very foundation of that society's social and economic life. Take away slavery and that time and place would suffer catastrophic economic and cultural collapse. The plantation slavery of the United States in the nineteenth century is an example of a slave society.

Another universal measure that one can use to describe slavery is that of race. Throughout most of the history of slavery from ancient times, race was irrelevant, no more than an incidental, largely unnoticed, and unremarkable characteristic of any given slave. Human beings of all races and ethnicities were enslaved for reasons other than their race. They were often the defeated warriors and hapless masses of people made subject to conquerors. In some times and places, they were simply human units of supply in a brutal trade that connected a supply of humans with distant demands for labor or servants. The very word "slave" derives from such a traffic in white Slavs of eastern Europe.

In the slave system of British North America, however, race became the very mark of a slave. To be black was not only a marker of race. It raised the legal presumption that the person so marked was—and inescapably should be—a slave. To be white raised the contrary presumption—that person was a free person. Some of the most contentious litigation in American legal history was brought by persons seeking either to prove that they were "white" and therefore free, or to prove that another person was black and therefore a slave. Suspicions raised outside of the courtroom often plagued white social life when a person was thought not to "look" or "act" white. These divisions between black and white and suspicions about where a person belonged also informed the actions of persons charged with keeping social order, from civilian neighbors, to organized slave patrols, and eventually to police establishments.

How the American system of slavery arrived and spread into a slave society based on race is a tale driven by the rise of the industrial production of two commodities—sugar and cotton—and the demands for labor and land that production demanded. It is also a tale of the surrender and distortion of state governance and religious doctrine to the naked greed and moral disintegration of the wealthy masters of those industrial enterprises.

Sweets have been valued from the earliest days of humanity. For most of history, sweets came from the products of the humble bee—honey. The first dated reference to honeybees was in Egypt about 5500 BCE. When humanity learned to produce sugar from cane, honey was pushed to the margins.

Sugar cane is native to Polynesia. It was first refined into sugar in India, about 700 BCE. For the next two thousand years, sugar cane moved westward. By the eighth century CE, production of sugar from cane was thriving in the Mediterranean basin, where Muslims established the first plantations to produce sugar. The plantation was not a new technology but a new way of organizing work—to structure human units to efficiently make a product grown and processed in one place and transported for profit to another.

Christians pushed the Muslims out and took over the trade, moving sugar plantations further and further west, first to Spain's Canary Islands (off the coast of Morocco) and then in a great leap across the Atlantic to the New World. Sugar cane was introduced first to the island of Hispaniola (Haiti and the Dominican Republic) and then to Brazil in the 1500s. Sugar cane production required intensive labor from a large work force. Slaves purchased from Africa provided that labor. A Brazilian saying went: "Without sugar, no Brazil; without slaves, no sugar; without Angola, no slaves."

The next major leap was what was called the "Sugar Revolution" in the British West Indies. It began in Barbados, from which thousands of small British farmers were leaving. Many of them went to British North America—the Carolinas and Virginia. They and their farms were replaced by slaves and sugar plantations. Over a quarter of a million slaves were transported to Barbados—an island of only 166 square miles—in the eighteenth century. Barbados was for a time the world's greatest producer of sugar, the fountainhead of a booming and incredibly profitable world trade. Cane also produced molasses and distilled rum.

A triangular trade emerged. Goods went from Europe (and in some cases from North America) to Africa, where they were traded for slaves. The slaves were transported to the West Indies and traded for sugar and rum. The rum and sugar were then carried back to Europe. Amsterdam became a major trading port. Elite and distant owners, shipbuilders, and merchants in Great Britain became wealthy on a scale previously known only to royalty. George Washington, Alexander Hamilton, and Thomas Jefferson—among the best of the good guys we are happy to idolize in American history—all had commercial interests in the slave society of Barbados.

THE CORONATION OF COTTON

Slavery was widespread in British North America by the time the British sailing vessel *Anne* made landfall at a place that was to become Savannah, Georgia, on February 1, 1733. The ship brought the first settlers to the new colony of Georgia, the realized dream of an English noble, James Edward Oglethorpe. Georgia was to serve two aims of the British empire. The first was strategic. The Spanish and the British were sparring over the territory between South Carolina and Florida. The new colony of Georgia was to serve as a buffer to Spain's territorial ambitions. Its settlers could fight back against Spanish incursions.

The other aim was social benevolence. Unemployment, debt, and alcoholism were rampant in England's society of deeply divided classes. Georgia was intended to be a refuge for poor English workers, a place where they could start fresh and build a new life based on their own labor. Transportation to the new colony and plots of land were to be provided on reasonable terms. The new colonists could find religious salvation, virtuous living, and a comfortable life. The founders specifically forbade slavery and plantation farming, both of which it was thought would undermine the virtues of the individual's hard work on his own plot of land. Moral objections to slavery had nothing to do with it. Oglethorpe and other founders had interests in the slave-trading Royal African Company. If slavery was permitted, they thought, the settlers would soon lead immoral lives of luxury and idleness.

Within a generation, the benevolent system Oglethorpe envisioned collapsed. The small farm economy was a disaster. More importantly, plantation owners in South Carolina wanted to convert the new colony's land to plantations producing rice, which at that time was a major coastal commodity. The rules were soon changed. Rice plantations and slaves came to Georgia.

The rice trade was profitable enough for coastal slave masters. But at the turn of the nineteenth century Eli Whitney's invention of the cotton gin set off another revolution in trade and slavery. Cotton fiber was in enormous demand to feed the machines of the industrializing British textile industry. Before the invention of the cotton gin, however, separating the fiber from the plant was a slow manual process, and one not suitable for varieties of cotton that could be grown on the lands of inland North America. The gin made the production of cotton fiber efficient. Plantation farming of cotton became highly profitable and increased the demand for land and slaves.

In Georgia, the new cotton economy curled in a reverse clockwise direction from the lower coast, across the uplands and to the southwest frontier. There was plenty of land, but it belonged to Native Americans. The Indians were soon forced off of their land, many transported further west. The pattern set in Georgia repeated itself as the cotton frontier pushed further west. More land was grabbed, and more slaves were imported—several million in an internal trade from the mid-Atlantic, where demand for slave labor had lessened.

By the third decade of the nineteenth century, King Cotton com-
manded the new nation's economy and finances. The white masters of the
king's slave camps had two problems. The first was justifying the en-
slavement of millions of human beings in the face of Blackstone's "absolute rights" and a Christian doctrine founded on "brotherly love," healing
the sick, feeding the poor, etc., etc. The second was keeping those millions of black human beings under control.

POLICING THE INFERIOR RACE

Law, religion, and government policy solved the first problem by dividing the people of the world into "races." Boundaries were drawn and
people were sorted according to the shambling, ad hoc social construct of
race, dressed in the ostensibly disciplined clothing of pseudo-science. The
white race was declared to be god's favored child, destined to rule over
the other races, and most especially the black race in the immediate case
of American slavery. The black race, on the other hand, was declared to
be fit only for servitude under god's marvelous plan. Sorting human
beings into races was the first grinding of the lens through which blacks
in America came to be viewed.

Keeping control over millions of enslaved human beings was a challenge to American law and social order. The law bent to the will of the
profiteering slave masters. The England of the absolute rights of humanity had no slave law as such. Human beings might work under onerous
terms and conditions, but they were never the property of another human
being bound for life. The colonial law of North America disposed of that
inconvenience by declaring that black slaves were the property, chattels,
of their owners. The owners were free to deal with that property as they
wished for their own profit and leisure. Within certain theoretical but
rarely enforced limits, slave masters could inflict any such hardships or
punishments as they thought necessary to keep their slave force under
control. In addition to physical punishments—lashings, mutilation, tor-
ture—masters were free to break up families and "sell down the river"
any slave who proved to be uncontrollable.

In addition to the control exercised by individual masters, the community and society as a whole cooperated to enforce restrictions on the times
and places slaves might gather, to question black persons found anywhere

other than on the premises of their bondage. A primary tool for this enforcement was the "slave patrol." The terms of service in a given slave patrol varied from time to time and place to place. It might be mandatory or voluntary, subject to organized supervision or not. The slave patrol's purpose was described in the preamble to Georgia's law in 1757. "Patrols should be established under proper Regulations in the settled parts thereof, for the better keeping of Negroes and other Slaves in Order and prevention of any Cabals, Insurrections or other Irregularities amongst them."[68] Fear was realized in law. In a landmark article published in 1990, Hubert Williams and Patrick V. Murphy argued that the roots of modern policing are to be found in these slave patrols.[69]

Indeed, one can see the precursors of the nature and attitude of policing toward minority communities in the power and practices of the slave patrols, which

> had full power and authority to enter any plantation and break open Negro houses or other places when slaves were suspected of keeping arms; to punish runaways or slaves found outside their plantations without a pass; to whip any slave who should affront or abuse them in the execution of their duties; and to apprehend and take any slave suspected of stealing or other criminal offense, and bring him to the nearest magistrate.[70]

"Understandably," Williams and Murphy comment, "the actions of such patrols established an indelible impression on both the whites who implemented this system and the blacks who were the brunt of it."[71] Racism was a mirror, an institution that not only oppressed millions but also projected fear and violence into the soul of those who made and enforced its laws.

JIM CROW AND THE BLACK STEREOTYPE

The legal emancipation of slaves at the end of the Civil War presented America with a new problem. Black slaves had been the ultimate necessary condition of a large part of the country's economic and financial system. Freed blacks could no longer be forced to work as slaves. Without low-cost labor, that system would collapse. The problem was dealt with—just as slavery had been—by the imposition of both legal and cultural constraints on people of color.

The law was shaped and distorted in many different ways to force blacks down into the mass of poorly paid and wretched mass labor. This included notorious "black codes" in the South which deliberately defined and punished many of the conditions and actions that free blacks might engage in, other than working on former plantations that had been converted into fortresses of so-called sharecropping. Thus, hanging out on a street corner or even on one's own porch was turned into the notorious catch-all offense of "vagrancy." It and other deliberately crafted minor offenses served as a net to scoop up free blacks, convict them of crimes, and force them to work off their penalty in a servitude that differed from slavery in little other than name. The laws restricting and punishing free blacks were not an invention of the South. They had been developed and refined by the North for decades.

Having herded people of color into notionally inferior "races" beginning in the antebellum slave era, the dominant American culture launched a new attack on every individual member of the black "race" to justify keeping them "in their place." This was the relentless hurricane of distorted and stereotypical depiction of blacks in virtually every possible means of representation available to a developing modern society. From postcards to motion pictures, commercial advertising, books, newspaper, and magazines, even garden art, blacks were represented in the cruel and "comic" portrayals of what is sometimes called "Sambo art" as physically hideous or ludicrous, and culturally backward or dangerous.

The Jim Crow era was the second grinding of the lens of racial perception that distorts the view of many today. It was through these lens that Tex McIver viewed the world the night he drew his gun and then shot his wife to death.

6

THE ASSEMBLY LINE

Tex McIver's clever coattails were now snagged by the slowly grinding wheels of Georgia's criminal justice system. That relentless system would pull Tex into the cams, levers, chutes, and gears of the procedures of criminal law—investigation, charge, trial, a jury's verdict, and a judge's sentence. Questions would be raised early in the investigation about whether Tex was unfairly enjoying the benefits of being wealthy and white. The process would end in a legal judgment on the consequences of Tex's killing Diane. That judgment would be enforceable by the ultimate power of the state over individuals.

But what exactly is the "criminal justice system"? To say that the criminal justice system is a subset of a larger "legal system" or an embodiment of that monumental abstraction "the law" expands the scope of the question, but does not answer it. What are a legal system's essential parts? Where do laws, and specifically criminal laws, come from? What are the mechanisms, the procedures, for enforcing the laws? How do all of these processes affect different racial, ethnic, and economic groups within society? Answers to these questions are essential to understanding the relationship between race and justice in America.

Some scholars have described four essential parts of a bona fide legal system (of which the criminal justice system is half, the other half being civil law). These parts are *laws* that "define the formal rules of regulating society," *legislation* by "an agency for changing and making laws," *enforcement* in the form of "an agency for enforcing the laws," and a means for *dispute resolution*, "settling disputes between individuals" (in criminal cases, one of the individuals is the defendant, the other is the state).[1] There are other definitions, but these four elements capture the distinction between an institutionalized system with more or less predictable rules and processes and the arbitrariness of formless anarchy or capricious dictatorship.[2]

The are other means of social control outside of the criminal justice system. "Individuals in a large-scale society live a portion of their lives in various institutions, each of which may have its own methods of social control."[3] Examples among the myriad of social controls outside of the state's criminal justice system include parental "grounding" within the institution of the family, dietary and ritual rules within religious institutions, work rules imposed by employers, dress codes at restaurants, and architectural and landscaping rules of neighborhood associations. Violations of rules like these can have unpleasant consequences—including refusal of service, loss of jobs, and expensive lawsuits.

"Why even have a state criminal justice system at all?" some might ask. Why not just use other means of social control? The alternatives to state systems are vague, and one reply is obvious. "The criminal justice system exists because of crime—people behaving in unlawful and often barbarous ways toward each other," one standard scholarly text answers. "In response to crime, the state is authorized to seize and confine people, strip them of their property and liberty, and even put them to death."[4]

But what is not obvious, and remains the constant nub of social turmoil and public policy debate, is how we can ensure that the powerful state responses to crime are fair and impartial—that they dispense equal justice under law to everyone. This problem involves primarily the procedures of criminal law, although it sometimes concerns substance, the definition of crimes that impact different groups differently.

In the mid-1960s, a professor of law at Stanford University thought and wrote about criminal procedure in the context of a series of landmark decisions of the Supreme Court under the leadership of Chief Justice Earl Warren. "The innovative decisions of the Warren Court changed the law, and society," other scholars have since written.[5] These decisions collectively enhanced civil rights and decreed that these fundamental rights included certain things, such as the right to counsel in criminal cases. After thinking about the impact of the Warren Court's decisions, Herbert Packer wrote several influential law journal articles and a book in which he discussed the importance and limits of the criminal process, and what he conceived of as two basic models of criminal procedure. He called them the "Due Process Model" and the "Crime Control Model."[6] Each of Packer's models rests on different value systems.

"The value system that underlies the Crime Control Model is based on the proposition that the repression of criminal conduct is by far the most important function to be performed by the criminal process," Packer wrote. "The failure of law enforcement to bring criminal conduct under tight control is viewed as leading to the breakdown of public order and thence to the disappearance of an important condition of human freedom."[7]

The Crime Control Model, on the one hand, pays most attention to "the efficiency with which the criminal process operates to screen suspects, determine guilt, and secure appropriate dispositions of persons convicted of crime. . . . The process must not be cluttered with ceremonious rituals that do not advance the progress of a case."[8]

The Due Process Model, on the other hand, regards the "combination of stigma and loss of liberty that is embodied in the end result of the criminal process . . . as being the heaviest deprivation that government can inflict on the individual," Packer argued. "Power is always subject to abuse, sometimes subtle, other times, as in the criminal process, open and ugly. Precisely because of its potency in subjecting the individual to the coercive power of the state, the criminal process must, on this model, be subjected to controls and safeguards that prevent it from operating with maximal efficiency. According to this ideology, maximal efficiency means maximal tyranny."[9]

In sum, Packer observed, "If the Crime Control Model resembles an assembly line, the Due Process Model looks very much like an obstacle course."[10] The tension between these two models is very much evident in the explosive events of 2020, in which fundamental questions about how the criminal justice system is supposed to work and how fairly the criminal justice system treats people of color are at the fore.

But which criminal justice system are we talking about monitoring and fixing if need be? "[T]here is no 'criminal justice system' in the United States," legal scholars point out. "Rather, there are many overlapping, competing, and conflicting 'criminal justice systems' throughout the country."[11]

In 1967, President Lyndon Johnson's Commission on Law Enforcement and Criminal Justice, popularly known as the Katzenbach Commission, put it this way.

> The system of criminal justice America uses to deal with those crimes it cannot prevent and those criminals it cannot deter is not a monolithic, or even a consistent, system. It was not designed or built in one piece at one time. . . . Every village, town, county, city, and State has its own criminal justice system, and there is a Federal one as well. All of them operate somewhat alike. No two of them operate precisely alike. [12]

This stubborn fact of federalism and local control alone should give pause to any who believe that the U.S. Congress or the president can effect sweeping changes in the American criminal justice system by law or decree.

Like those of other states, the Georgia criminal justice system is distinct from and independent of the federal system (except for the ideologically variable federal oversight of constitutional protections, which has historically run hot and cold). State and local justice systems process the vast majority of crimes in America, from simple assault to murder. Although the states differ in the details of their definitions of crimes and the procedures they use to enforce their laws, their criminal justice systems are a brood of almost-identical twins.

Textbook definitions of "the law" often project the majestic image of a finely geared, well-tuned, up-to-date, rational, and objective system for dispensing even-handed justice. "No one is above the law" in the sober courts of this magnificent world. In fact, legal systems are mechanically more like hybrid engines sprung from the minds of steampunk geniuses. Subjectivity, privilege, expediency, economics, politics, and informal discretion affect each of the elements, from the creation of its parts (laws and procedure) to their daily operation (enforcement and adjudication).

Some ancient parts embedded within the machinery of the American legal system have been worn smooth over time. Many modern legal concepts and procedures were fashioned eons ago, passed through the forge of English common law, and finally shaped and blended by the peculiarities of America's history and its evolving culture. "Legal history is a story which cannot be begun at the beginning," the English legal historian Theodore Plucknett wrote a century ago. "However remote the date at which we start, it will always be necessary to admit that much of the still remoter past that lies behind it will have to be considered as directly bearing on the later history."[13] The legal systems of Greece, Assyria, Egypt, and Rome, as well as the religious codes of Judaism and Christianity, left lasting marks on the American legal system.

So did the requisites of slavery and the meanness of Jim Crow racism.

Legal systems "do not come from outer space," observed legal historian Lawrence Friedman.[14] They are the products of specific societies. "Behind the law, and above it, enveloping it, is society."[15] Laws and how they are enforced are the product of collective decisions by specific societies. They vary over time and place, responsive to cultural changes and regional differences. The antebellum legal system in America accommodated and facilitated slavery and disparate racial treatment, most extensively but not exclusively in the South. The Jim Crow legal system that followed deliberately attacked the exercise of equal rights by people of color throughout America.

These collective decisions about legal systems by societies are not made through egalitarian democracy exercised by a cheerful yeomanry. "Not everybody is part of the collective that makes the decision," Friedman observed. "When we say 'society' we really mean those who call the tunes and pay the piper. It would be worse than naive to imagine that everybody's opinion counts the same, even in a country that is supposed to be democratic."[16]

So, whose opinion counts the most? Virtually all societies are organized in a pyramid of class and power. At the narrow tip of the pyramid are the elite, at the wide bottom the least powerful, and in the bulk between the middling classes who hope to rise higher and struggle not to sink lower. "The rich and powerful, the articulate, the well positioned, have many more 'votes' on matters of definition [of crimes] than the poor, the weak, the silent."[17] In the United States, the complexion of the pyramid shades from largely white at the top to darker shades of black and brown at the bottom.[18] The societal power structure keeps the legal system conservative, slow to change, and inherently biased toward defending the comfort of the status quo as defined by the elite.

The same disparities of wealth and power are reflected in enforcement and adjudication procedures virtually every hour of every day somewhere in America. The enforcement levers of the legal system's machinery are subject to the whims and biases of the humans whose hands move them, from the police officer who decides whether to arrest to the prosecutor who decides whether to press charges. "Enforcement, of course, is *always* selective, for all sorts of reasons, the system does not, cannot, and will not enforce the norms in any total way," according to legal historian Friedman. "Unenforcement is as vital a part of the story as enforcement."[19]

Not only are the individuals who administer the system "only human" and thus subject to human flaws including racist attitudes, but the availability or lack of financial resources also plays a role. A well-funded, well-staffed, well-trained system in a wealthy jurisdiction may have the administrative space to be more deliberate and more comprehensive in its enforcement decisions than a resource-starved system in a poorer area. This will have more or less obvious implications in low-income areas with large populations of color and minority ethnicities.

Police play a unique role in the criminal justice system because "for the most part the prosecutors, the courts, and the correctional officials can deal only with those whom the police arrest."[20] Whether and whom to arrest is an individual decision. "Officers every day decide to intervene or ignore suspicious circumstances, applying broad legal standards like probable cause or reasonable suspicion, often without prior or subsequent judicial supervision. They may arrest, or choose to treat an infraction in some other way."[21]

Putting aside the discretion of police, criminal law is "much more politicized" than the civil law that deals with conflicts between individuals, such as contracts and torts. "Criminal law is enforced by politicians (the heads of most local prosecutors' offices, usually called District Attorneys, are elected officials), and the laws that they enforce are defined by other politicians (both state legislators and members of Congress are elected officials)."[22]

The handling of Tex McIver's case raised angry questions in Atlanta about these factors of discretion and political influence, and their impacts on race, justice, and disparate treatment. Depending on these gatekeepers' conclusions about the nature and severity of Tex's criminal offense, if any, he could walk away with a slap on the wrist, spend the rest of his life locked up in a Georgia prison, or suffer a lesser penalty somewhere between those two extremes.

At the most basic level, the criminal law distinguishes between less serious misdemeanor offenses and more serious felonies. What's the difference between a misdemeanor and a felony? The details vary only slightly among state criminal codes. A good rule of thumb is that any crime that calls for a punishment of imprisonment for more than a year is a felony. Crimes that call for lesser punishments, a year or less, are classified as misdemeanors (although some states classify crimes punishable with one year's imprisonment as felonies). One day of imprisonment more or less makes the difference.[23] In Georgia, misdemeanors are crimes punishable for not more than twelve months (i.e., a year or less).[24] Depending on how the police and prosecutors viewed Tex's killing of Diane, his act of homicide could be treated as a misdemeanor or as the most serious felony in the law.

Homicide is the taking of human life—killing another person. Most legal and moral authorities regard homicide as the most serious act that one human being can commit against another. But not all homicides are alike or equally serious offenses in the eyes of the criminal law. Depending on the killer's intent and the details of their act, any given homicide might range from the ultimate felony of murder, the "king of crimes,"[25] to an act not regarded as criminal at all, as in the cases of self-defense or legal exercise of state authority (executions and justifiable police shootings).[26] The felony of manslaughter is "an intermediate crime which lies half-way between the more serious crimes of murder, at the one extreme, and, at the other extreme, justifiable or excusable homicide, which is not criminal at all. Thus manslaughter constitutes a sort of catch-all category which includes homicides which are not bad enough to be murder but which are too bad to be no crime whatever."[27]

The law of homicide, even though today enacted into criminal statutes, was created by common law judges, mostly in fifteenth-century England's law courts.[28] Given their seriousness, one would think that there would be clear definitions of the range of offenses it covers, from murder to manslaughter. "Yet there may be no frequently punished offense that is so poorly, and so strangely defined."[29] The law of homicide is complicated by layers of words, laid down in centuries past attempting to define a killer's state of mind, that still play a major role in legal judgments. The meaning of words like "malice" and "intent" are unavoidably encrusted with the thoughts of ancient jurists.

In Georgia, a person "commits the offense of murder when he unlawfully and with malice aforethought, either express or implied, causes the death of another human being."[30] Malice aforethought is sometimes called "premeditation." In sum, the killer intends to kill the victim. Another type of murder is "felony murder," which is committed when the victim dies because of the actions of a perpetrator committing another felony, such as burglary or robbery. A key feature of felony murder is that all of the criminal participants acting in concert may be held liable for a homicide committed by only one of them. If three men go in to rob a store and one of them shoots and kills a clerk, all three may be held liable for felony murder. At the other end of the scale is involuntary manslaughter, committed when a person "causes the death of another human being without any intention to do so by the commission of an unlawful act other than a felony."[31]

SLEEPING SCORPIONS

There was almost no direct evidence to explain what Tex had done or why he had done it.

No one saw how Tex was holding the gun. Was he pointing it directly at Diane? Or was it dangling from his hands, maybe loosely cradled in his lap? No one saw Tex pull the trigger, an act that could have been either an easy finger flick or a hard pull, depending on whether the hammer had been cocked. Cocking a revolver's hammer requires a deliberate downward pull with the thumb. A revolver's cocked hammer results in what is popularly known as a "hair trigger." It is an act of preparation that indicates that the shooter probably intends to fire the gun. If the hammer were cocked, only about two pounds of finger pressure would have been enough to pull the trigger. If the hammer were not cocked, considerably more pressure would have been required—about twelve pounds.

Tex's fate would have to be decided by circumstantial evidence— indirect evidence from which everyone in the chain of Tex's fate, from police to prosecutors to jurors, would have to infer what Tex had done in those fatal seconds, and most importantly why he had done it.

Circumstantial evidence in a criminal trial is like a nest of scorpions lurking under a carpet of leaves in a forest. In the absence of witnesses and clear direct physical evidence, the scorpions of indirect circumstance determine guilt or innocence. When a prosecutor sweeps off the leaves, the scorpions scramble into action. Usually they sting the defendant. But sometimes they sting the prosecutor.

Law professors, lawyers, and judges will explain patiently that there are two basic kinds of evidence—direct and circumstantial. [32] Direct evidence is in and of itself proof of a fact. Circumstantial evidence is proof of one fact from which one must make a logical inference to accept the truth of another fact. Legal experts insist that both types of evidence are equally valid. There is nothing inferior about circumstantial evidence. Both are ways to establish facts from which the jury in a criminal trial can conclude beyond a reasonable doubt that the defendant committed the crime with which he or she is charged. Criminal convictions can be, and regularly are, based almost entirely on circumstantial evidence.

An example that is often used to illustrate this difference between direct and circumstantial evidence is deciding whether it is raining. If you can look out the window and see the rain coming down, that's direct evidence that it's raining. If someone you trust comes in and says, "It's raining," that testimony is also direct evidence. In either case, you can accept what you see, or what you hear from a credible witness, as conclusive evidence that it is raining.

But suppose you are in an interior room and you can't see outside. Someone comes into the room directly from outside. Their clothes are wet, and they are folding up a dripping umbrella. That's circumstantial evidence. They don't have to say anything. The person is wet, has recently used an umbrella, and has just come in from outside. These are facts from which one can apply logic and reasonably infer the additional fact that it must be raining outside. Even so, some jurors will insist that all this evidence of the weather outside is "just circumstantial."

Beyond that, and despite what judges instruct and lawyers argue, some jurors stubbornly demand direct evidence of a specific type—laboratory or "forensic" evidence, such as DNA. This demand is popularly known as the "CSI syndrome," a reference to a television series in which laboratory evidence played a crucial role in criminal trials. But many criminal cases simply don't need laboratory evidence. "The problem today is that citizen jurors expect to be dazzled when selected and seated for jury duty, waiting to be overwhelmed and over-impressed when the prosecution produces tons of forensic evidence and related scientific whiz-bang devices," explained retired Federal Bureau of Investigation expert Clint Van Zandt. "When these 'toys for boys' are not introduced, it's like, well, 'Where's the beef?' Enter the CSI Syndrome." [33] This is one reason why the scorpions sometimes sting the prosecutor who stirred them up.

Throughout American legal history, the middle step of inference between direct evidence and factual conclusion has also been a crude imple-
ment of race-based discrimination. Police, prosecutors, and jurors have
regularly made different inferences about the conclusions to be drawn
from the circumstance of a dead body and a gun in a suspect's hand,
depending upon the races of the victim and the alleged offender.

During the Jim Crow era, these cases were more blatant, or perhaps
just less hidden, than they are today. Because of the unwritten law of
racial bias, for example, antilynching laws "were nothing more than
words on paper."[34] In the rare cases in which members of a lynch mob
were indicted, "they were rarely convicted . . . conviction of a lyncher—
any conviction of any lyncher—occurred in less than 1 percent of the
lynchings in the United States after 1900."[35] When a grand jury was
impaneled in Georgia's Cobb County to consider the notorious case of
the lynching of a white Jew, Leo Frank, seven members of the lynch mob
were on the jury. "There was also immunity for men who, for whatever
reason, were accused of committing *any* sort of crime against an African-
American. White juries simply acquitted these men."[36]

The failed 1995 California prosecution of O.J. Simpson on charges of
murdering his ex-wife, Nicole Brown Simpson, and her friend, Ron Gold-
man, is often cited as a high-profile case in which the scorpions stung the
prosecutors. Another is the unsuccessful 2011 Florida prosecution of Casey Marie Anthony for the alleged murder of her two-year-old daughter,
Caylee. Although other factors may also have strongly influenced the
successful defenses in those cases, both prosecutions were based almost
entirely on circumstantial evidence.[37]

Georgia was home to a famous cases of repeatedly stung prosecutors
during the 1980s—the four trials and three successful appeals from conviction of James Arthur Williams, a fifty-year-old man accused of murdering in his Savannah home his twenty-one-year-old former male lover,
Danny Lewis Hansford. Shortly after Williams was finally acquitted once
and for all, he dropped dead in his home. Author John Berendt's best-
selling novel *Midnight in the Garden of Good and Evil*[38] and the block-
buster movie of the same name starring Kevin Spacey were loosely based
on Williams's story. (The tendrils of criminal justice in Georgia are as
entwined as the suffocating sprawl of the infamous kudzu vine. Don
Samuel—a heavyweight Atlanta criminal defense lawyer who would help
slug it out for Tex McIver—represented Williams during one of his four

trials. Samuel was accused of using high-level political influence to wire one of Williams' appeals before the Georgia Supreme Court. The accusation never resulted in any decision or sanctions.)

The scorpion's sting is not always fatal. It might even be thought to have been a good thing for Dep Kirkland, the first of several prosecutors to take the Williams murder case to trial. Kirkland abandoned the practice of law, left Georgia for Hollywood, and became a successful writer and actor. His book *Lawyer Games—After Midnight in the Garden of Good and Evil*[39] is a skeptically wry treatise on the factual underbelly of the Williams case and the games that lawyers play. It is a not very delicate rebuttal to Berendt's cosmetic treatment of the story.

DEATH IN A HOT CAR

At about the same time that suspicious prosecutors in the Fulton County district attorney's office were raking the leaves around the shooting of Diane McIver, a sensational trial was making headlines in Georgia and across the world. It involved another death in an SUV, also claimed to be accidental, but eventually treated as felony murder. The case was entirely circumstantial. The media scramble, the public outrage, the prosecution, trial, and outcome would be an instructive template for the thousand stings that were coming for Tex McIver.

Justin Ross Harris was arrested and charged with murder after he left his twenty-two-month-old toddler son, Cooper Harris, all day in a car seat in a closed SUV on June 18, 2014. It was a hot and sunny day. Cooper died before noon, suffering from the intense heat that built up in the SUV—clinically called "pediatric vehicular heatstroke." Cooper would have suffered through several hellish stages—nausea, headache, dehydration, diarrhea, and convulsions. The boy's body had marks where he had scratched himself, crying, struggling, trying to get out of the car seat.

Harris (who went by the name "Ross") insisted that he had simply forgotten that Cooper was in the car. It was a story that was not incredible on its face. On average, thirty-seven children die in hot cars in the United States every year. A study of 742 such deaths over almost twenty years found that 54 percent of the young victims were inadvertently forgotten by their parents or other caregivers, just as Ross Harris claimed he had done. The next largest category was children who got into cars on their own, accounting for 27 percent of the deaths. And by no means were all of the 18 percent who were intentionally left in a car and died deliberately murdered—some adults who left unattended children in a vehicle were using their car as a surrogate babysitter. They mistakenly thought that cracking the windows would be enough, or did not grasp how quickly a vehicle can heat up and kill a child even in the course of the parents' brief errands.

There was little direct evidence to counter Ross Harris' claim that he simply forgot to drop his son off at a daycare center. But prosecutors found stunning circumstantial evidence that they thought pointed to a deliberate plan to get rid of Cooper. It turned out that Justin Ross Harris was a serial and constant adulterer. "I cheat a lot," he texted one of his female liaisons. "I know it's not right, but I'm addicted to sex." Harris was constantly at it, sexting hookups through an online app, even from inside his church on Sundays. This was not mere fantasy play. Ross met and had illicit sex with many women. Some of them were underage, a fact that added the charge of sexual exploitation of a minor.

On June 18, the day that Cooper died, Harris exchanged texts with at least six women. In one of them, sent ten minutes before he left Cooper locked in the car, he wrote, "I love my son and all, but we both need escapes."

Shortly after lunch that day, Ross exchanged explicit texts with one of his paramours.

"Can I see your tits?" he asked her. She obliged with a photo, to which Ross replied, "Mmmmm."

"I asked if he wanted to play with them," the woman testified. "He said, 'Fuck yes, I do.'"

To prosecutors, this addictive conduct provided the motive for intentionally murdering his own son. He simply wanted to get Cooper out of the way. And he thought he could get away with the murder by playing the guilt-ravaged father who made a horrible mistake.

The trial was held in the coastal Georgia town of Brunswick, a city we'll visit again later in this book. In November 2016, a jury found Ross Harris guilty of malice murder. He was sentenced to life in prison without any possibility of parole. As of this writing, he is seeking a new trial.

The circumstantial evidence that prosecutors stirred up in Tex's case was less lurid. It focused on the details of the McIvers' relative financial positions—Diane's wealth was going up, Tex's was sliding down, particularly because he had lost partnership status at his law firm. This imbalance would allow prosecutors to argue, and jurors to infer, that Tex had a classic motive for killing Diane—greed.

Circumstances other than the circumstantial evidence of the courtroom also affect the outcomes of all sorts of encounters with the criminal justice system—the scorpions of race and class, for example. The circumstance of being poor or a person of color is often treated as different from the circumstance of being wealthy and white, whether in a routine traffic stop or the final vote in a jury room. Color and ethnicity are in themselves circumstantial evidence in America. Driving while black, jogging while black, even working as a deliveryman while black or banking while black have had serious, sometimes fatal, outcomes in incidents that likely would never have happened were the "person of interest" white.

From the moment he arrived at the hospital with a mortally wounded Diane, Tex began a Texas two-step dance to avoid criminal liability for his actions. Even as Diane was bleeding to death in a surgical suite only yards away, Tex was huddling in a hallway, arms over shoulders with a hastily assembled team that included his lawyer and public relations adviser. He also attempted to persuade Dani Jo Carter to change her story about what happened, specifically to erase the fact that she was driving the SUV.

"I don't trust these guys, Dani Jo," he said, referring to the police. "I hate to see you get wrapped up in this. I've seen how these things can go down. You just need to tell them that you're down here as a friend of the family."[40]

Dani Jo refused to go along with Tex's curious fiction.

"Tex, I just drove you into the emergency room," she replied.

"He looked at me and said, 'Well, they don't know that,'" Carter later testified. "That took my breath away. I said, 'I can't lie.'"[41]

"What kind of idiot would I look like?" she asked in an interview with the author, noting that the lie that she had not been in the SUV and driving would have been easily and quickly exposed.

Only a month later would it be clear how, more than two decades before that fatal night in 2016, Tex had indeed acquired firsthand experience in seeing "how these things can go down."

THE GUN JUST WENT OFF DEFENSE

The core question when a bullet fired by one person strikes another person revolves around the shooter's intention—if indeed they had any intention at all—when the trigger was pulled. How believable could it be that a person could unintentionally—unconsciously or reflexively—pull the trigger of a given handgun and fire a bullet into someone's back? In Tex's case, the question boiled down to only two possibilities: either a hapless Tex had blundered into a tragic act of negligence and accidentally shot his wife, or a cynically calculating Tex had deliberately murdered her and tried to make it look like an accident. Opinion divided almost immediately among casual and informed observers alike. Most of Diane's friends and colleagues at the Corey Companies were suspicious of Tex and skeptical of his meandering narrative.

Tex's camp fell back on the unintentional discharge, or "the gun just went off" defense. Tex insisted that he had no recollection of pulling the trigger. He maintained that he was asleep. He must have been startled and reflexively fired the stubby revolver, either as he woke up or as he drowsed in a semi-conscious state. "The gun just went off" defense is not uncommon when one person shoots and kills another person and there is no clear evidence as to motive and intent. It has variable success.

The defense worked for Jose Ines Garcia Zarate, a Mexican national in the United Sates illegally. Garcia Zarate was charged with murder in the shooting of Kathryn Steinle, a San Francisco Bay area resident. Steinle was shot in the back in July 2015 as she walked with her father on San Francisco's Pier 14. Garcia Zarate's lawyers successfully argued that he had found the stolen gun and that it accidentally fired while he was handling it. In short, the gun had "just gone off." The undocumented immigrant was acquitted of murder and manslaughter charges after trial in November 2017.[42] The verdict infuriated President Trump, who seized on the case from its beginning as an example of the problem of "illegal immigration" from Mexico. On the evening the jury's verdict was returned, Trump tweeted that it was "disgraceful." The next day he renewed his call for a wall to be built along the border with Mexico.[43] Garcia Zarate was eventually deported.

On the other hand, the same defense did not work for rookie New York City Police Department cop Peter Liang, charged with homicide after a bullet he fired in a darkened stairwell struck and killed an innocent black resident. Liang insisted in his testimony that his gun "just went off." But the jury found him guilty of manslaughter. Liang was sentenced to probation and community service and served no jail time.[44]

The prosecution of Peter Liang sparked an eruption among Asian Americans. Activists pointed out that "Liang's conviction [was] a glaring anomaly among cops who have killed unarmed civilians, the vast majority of whom don't face criminal charges."[45] Thousands demonstrated on Liang's behalf. They claimed that Liang was "a minority scapegoat . . . sacrificed to a nation incensed by officers killing black men." The *New York Daily News* had reported before the Liang episode that in fifteen years, and in at least 179 New York City Police Department officer-involved deaths, only three officers had ever been indicted.[46]

WOKE SCORPIONS

Would "the gun just went off" defense work for Tex McIver? It might have had Tex not dragged the Black Lives Matter movement into the equation. The instant he did, everything changed. The first step of Tex's clever dance planted his feet in the middle of legal and cultural scorpion nests.

Tex woke the scorpions himself.

"The mention of Black Lives Matter catapulted what seemed to be a tragic mistake into a worldwide media feeding frenzy," observed *Atlanta Journal-Constitution* columnist Bill Torpy. "The backlash came hard and loud—here was a racially insensitive and well-connected white lawyer blaming his wife's killing on a fear of black people, and he was being treated with kid gloves by investigators."[47]

In assessing Tex's claim that he felt in peril, it must be noted that there had indeed been an apparent spike in carjackings in and around Atlanta over the preceding year.[48] (The increase is "apparent" because carjackings—the armed seizure of a motor vehicle—are not reported separately in vehicle theft data gathered by Georgia and published annually in the Federal Bureau of Investigation's national crime report. The evidence is only anecdotal.) In the year before Diane's fatal shooting, the Atlanta news media reported a number of violent carjacking incidents.[49] It is possible that Tex was aware of these carjackings.

Two carjackings were reported in Buckhead, the McIvers' wealthy neighborhood. In August 2015 a man armed with a box cutter forced a woman out of her SUV in the parking lot of a Whole Foods store in Buckhead.[50] An even more troubling incident occurred in June 2016 in the parking lot of the OK Cafe, a popular Southern-style restaurant noted for its upscale clientele. A woman was about to strap her one-year-old into a car seat when two men, one armed with a gun, ordered her out and stole her new 2016 Mercedes Benz.[51]

Even if the carjackings were on Tex's mind, the question is whether it was reasonable for him to pull out a gun. Most of the reported carjackings happened when the stolen vehicle was stopped and the driver had gotten out, at gas stations or parking lots. And another scorpion reflecting on Tex's behavior was lurking in the leaves—it would surface with the stunning revelation that this was not Tex's first armed rodeo. He had been indicted on five felony counts in another shooting incident in 1990. That inconvenient incident had been settled, hushed up, and sent to the limbo of dusty case files until the media broke the story scarcely one month after Diane's death.

Tex's alleged fear of running across a midnight Black Lives Matter demonstration was of an entirely different order.

"This was downtown Atlanta, near Georgia State University—not crack-infested streets near the projects circa 1989," wrote Bill Torpy. "But it's hard to overcome a mindset in some quarters: Atlanta is dangerous! Grab your gun and get ready to defend yourself!"[52]

Whether Tex actually said that he took out his gun because he feared Black Lives Matter demonstrators hardly mattered. The racially charged excuse was out there. Its destructive force was as invisible as nuclear radiation. Buildings did not topple. Atlanta did not grind to a halt. Aside from a few newspaper articles and media emissions, the legal business of life and death went on without apparent change. But cultural and legal seismographs in Atlanta and America at large registered the tremors radiating from an expression of fear and loathing that was a nearly perfect encapsulation of the American dynamic of race and justice.

SLOW-WALKING JUSTICE

The original investigation of Diane McIver's violent death was conducted at a leisurely, and some thought biased, pace by the Atlanta Police Department. In an unusual demonstration of a prosecutor's lack of confidence in the police, the Fulton County district attorney's office started its own independent investigation. It took over the case several months later, an example of another reality of America's many criminal justice systems. "Even within any particular 'system,' various components may be more in tension with each other than working smoothly toward uniform goals."[53]

During Tex's later criminal trial, Clint Rucker, the county's lead prosecutor, flayed the police department's prime investigator, Detective Darrin Smith. Rucker grilled Smith with a day of scathing questions about delay and missed opportunities in the police investigation. For example, he asked, why had Smith not interviewed Tex until three days after the shooting, even though Tex was still at the hospital after the driver, Dani Jo Carter, had been interviewed on the first night? Why had Tex not been asked in his interview whether the revolver's hammer was cocked? Why had the detective suggested to Dani Jo that "accidents happen," implying that he had already reached a benign conclusion? Why had the detective not more closely examined the relative financial conditions of Diane and Tex McIver? The police interview of Tex itself, shown to jurors at the trial, appeared perfunctory. After first talking alone to Tex's two lawyers, the detective then asked Tex only general questions. The implication Prosecutor Rucker left was that the police department had made up its mind early. It had merely shambled through a sloppy, pro forma investigation.[54]

For whatever reasons, Tex was not charged by police until three months after the shooting. The police treated Diane's death as the result of an avoidable accident, charging Tex only with reckless conduct and involuntary manslaughter.[55] The cops bought Tex's theory that the gun had just gone off. "After an extensive investigation . . . I determined that Claud McIver was holding the gun in a careless and reckless manner, that if [discharged] would cause significant injury or death if anyone was directly in front of said gun," wrote Detective Smith.[56]

The district attorney had another view of where Diane's death might fall on the scale of homicide. A grand jury was impaneled to consider more serious charges against Tex.

THE CIRCUMSTANCE OF RACE

Meanwhile, Atlanta's black citizenry were watching, and they didn't like what they saw. Viewed through the prism of race, it looked as if a prominent, affluent, and politically influential white lawyer was being handled with deference and benefiting from assumptions based on his race and class. Activists argued that had Diane and Tex been black, the case would have been handled more aggressively with very different assumptions.

One of the activists was Joe Beasley, well known in the Atlanta civil rights community. Among other things, Beasley served as the Southern Regional Director of the National Rainbow/PUSH Coalition, founded by the Rev. Jesse Jackson Sr., and as the president of African Ascension, an organization he formed to develop economic and political ties throughout Africa and the African Diaspora. He was the Georgia Deputy Director for Jesse Jackson's 1984 and 1988 presidential campaigns, and he worked on redistricting Georgia's congressional boundaries to increase African American representation in the U.S. Congress.[57]

"I just think we're seeing a double standard of justice," Beasley said in October 2016, one month after the shooting. "I'm worried [Tex] is getting special treatment."[58]

Others focused directly on Tex's Black Lives Matter excuse, describing it as a "blame a black man" defense.

"If I as a black man had given an explanation like that, I would be arrested and there would be calls for a murder indictment by the DA," said Derrick Boazman, an outspoken radio talk show host, former Atlanta City Council member, and businessman.[59]

The impression that Tex McIver was enjoying the special treatment accorded an influential white man was underscored by the stunning revelation in mid-October 2016 that in 1990 he had fired several shots at a moving car occupied by three white teenagers. This was the event when Tex got his firsthand experience in how shootings "go down" with the police. He was indicted on five felony counts. Some twenty-five years later it was a fair question whether a black man who shot at a moving car full of teenagers of any race would have emerged with his arrest, indict-ment, and court records buried from public view, and his life and career untouched.[60] The story of that shooting also provides insight into Tex's penchant for reckless gun slinging, a factor probably not known to the American Bar Association when it appointed Tex to its Standing Com-mittee on Gun Violence.

On February 27, 1990, Tex and his first wife lived at 2946 Cravey Trail, a cul-de-sac in suburban northeast Atlanta. Late that evening, three teenagers were sitting in a red Ford Mustang parked near the end of the cul-de-sac, about three hundred feet from the McIver residence. The teens were toasting a friend going off to Marine Corps boot camp, drinking beer, and, among other things, talking about cars. There is no evidence in the record that they were boisterous or otherwise disturbing the neighbor-hood. One of the teens knew McIver's son and testified at a hearing that Tex had once told him that he had no problem with the teens coming to that location, as long as they did not leave empty beer cans.[61] If that were true, something about that night flipped Tex's volatile switch.

Some time around 11:00 p.m. Tex arrived home, parked in the drive-way, and went inside. A few minutes later he came back out. He un-leashed a large dog which ran barking toward the car. The driver opened his door and barked back, apparently cowing the dog. Tex then fired several shots into the air with a handgun. Alarmed, the driver backed the Mustang away. Tex then stepped into the street and pointed his handgun at the car. He apparently asked no questions and spoke no warning. The teenagers then decided that they had no choice but to leave. That would require them to exit the cul-de-sac by driving past Tex. As the moving car approached, Tex jumped out of the way, then fired two shots into the car as it passed him.

The driver immediately reported the incident to the police. The re-sponding officer found several expended handgun shells in the roadway. Tex told the investigating officer that the presence of the parked Mustang scared his wife, and that he was concerned about unspecified burglary and vandalism in the area. He claimed that he had chased the car on foot but repeatedly and adamantly denied that he had fired a gun. Tex's ac-tions were in the rough Southern tradition of enforcing criminal laws by private persons, the pinnacle of which is the so-called citizen's arrest. Allowed in Georgia law since 1863, rooted in control over slaves in the middle of the Civil War, citizen's arrests have been at the core of several fatal white-on-black incidents in modern Georgia.

Tex's story did not wash, belied by the direct evidence of the three teenagers' statements and the physical evidence of the expended shells in the road and the bullet holes in the Mustang. On March 27, Tex was arrested on a charge of criminal assault, booked, and released. Three weeks later, on May 18, a grand jury returned an indictment in the case of *The State vs. Claud Lee McIver, III*, charging him with five felonies— three counts of aggravated assault and one count each of damage to property in the first degree and possession of a firearm during the com- mission of a crime.

The case never went to trial. At least one of the teens' families was friendly with the McIvers. Behind-the-scene negotiations went on. Ac- commodations were made. On November 28, 1990, the district attorney agreed not to prosecute the case, informing the court that "the victims do not want to prosecute" and "have decided to settle the matter through civil litigation."

The decision to drop the case was within the bounds of prosecutorial discretion set out in standards published both by the American Bar Asso- ciation and the National District Attorneys Association.[62] In deciding whether to press charges, prosecutors may consider (although they are not bound by) the wishes of the victim and the availability of suitable civil remedies. Tex paid twenty-nine hundred dollars for the repair of damage to the car. The court consigned his closed case to the "dead-docket," a legal graveyard where the story of Tex's felonious gun slinging was buried from public view. As far as Tex's career went, it was as if the incident never happened. It is a fair question to ask whether a black man who had fired at a carload of teenagers of any race would have enjoyed the same degree of solicitous discretion by a prosecutor.

Aside from the cozy disposal of a multiple felony indictment that Tex enjoyed, the episode illustrates aspects of the white South's singular cul- ture of honor—an unwritten code for male conduct that was central to the antebellum South and survives in many quarters today.

A variety of explanations have been offered to account for the South- ern culture of honor and its link to historically high levels of violence in the South. Psychology professors Richard E. Nisbett and Dov Cohen argue that "the Southern preference for violence stems from the fact that much of the South was a lawless, frontier region settled by people whose economy was originally based on herding."[63] The authors further explain, "Herdsmen constantly face the possibility of loss of their entire wealth—through loss of their herds. Thus a stance of aggressiveness and willingness to kill or commit mayhem is useful in announcing their determination to protect their animals at all costs."[64]

Others find the source of Southern honor in codes of ethical conduct handed down through many societies from ancient times. "Southern whites believed . . . that they conducted their lives by the highest ethical standards," Bertram Wyatt-Brown wrote in his book *Southern Honor*. "Above all else, white Southerners adhered to a moral code that may be summarized as the rule of honor."[65] That code made its peculiarly defined "honor" a possession of white men and white men alone. Questioning the morality of a code that perpetuated racial and class distinctions, Wyatt-Brown noted that "white man's honor and black man's slavery became in the public mind of the South practically indistinguishable."[66] Without the honor code and its elevation of white male privilege, he argues, "slavery would scarcely have lasted a moment."[67]

One aspect of the code is the expectation that an honorable man handles threats on his own, violently if he thinks it necessary, rather than calling on state authority. "To go to the law for help amounts to a public confession of weakness in the face of an admitted wrong."[68] Tex could have called on police to handle the matter from inside his home. Instead, he chose to go outside and confront the teenagers himself, armed with a gun. It was as if Tex were swaggering around the Old South, where for white men it was "a matter of personal reputation to prove oneself a master of events to one's family and household, as well as to the world at large."[69]

A corollary point of Southern honor was the requirement that an honorable white man protect and personally defend the female members of his family against any threat to their reputation or safety. "To attack his wife, mother, or sister was to assault the man himself," according to Wyatt-Brown. "Outsider violence against family dependents, particularly females, was a breach not to be ignored without risk of ignominy. An impotence to deal with such wrongs carried all the weight of shame that archaic society could muster."[70]

As Tex's gun-slinging actions in both 1990 and 2016 illustrate, aspects of the honor code are still influential to some in twenty-first-century Southern culture. "There is no longer any economic reason for southern males to show their physical toughness, yet they believe they will suffer loss if they do not," Nisbett and Cohen wrote. "For individuals, it may be socially beneficial to continue with culture-of-honor norms."[71] After Tex shot Diane, Atlanta media consultant Grayson Daughters offered a withering commentary on this vestigial cultural worldview and its influence on Tex. Her commentary touched on the theme of white privilege but hammered the outmoded demands of white Southern honor.

"Here's this bumbling old geezer who sees a black person and has to get his gun out to protect the ladies," said Daughters. "He can't handle the fact that he's lost his [law] partnership, that his wife makes more than him so he gets into this horrible mess and thinks he can spin this thing, he can manage this thing. It's his last gasp to exert control while they still have it. He thinks he can run this game but learns it's not his game anymore."[72]

The old "game" was still being "run" in some quarters. Three years to the day after Diane's shooting, Wednesday, September 25, 2019, Joe Beasley suffered precisely the kind of treatment at the hands of the police that he and other activists argued that Tex would have gotten in either shooting incident had he been a black man. On that day officers of the Atlanta Police Department were serving a narcotics warrant on a street down which Beasley was coincidentally driving at the same time. A police officer stopped Beasley. The officer drew his gun for no apparent reason and directed eighty-two-year-old Beasley to turn his car around. The incident crackled with a current of profiling. The police department issued an immediate apology. "The officer drew his service weapon while directing Mr. Beasley to turn around," police spokesman Carlos Campos said. "The drawing of the weapon is not consistent with APD's training and we will be addressing that internally, along with expressing our apologies to Mr. Beasley for the stress that this undoubtedly caused him."[73]

One is left to wonder whether the police department would have been as quick to apologize had Beasley been just another black man driving while black at the wrong time and the wrong place.

DIFFERENT STROKES FOR DIFFERENT FOLKS

Was Tex's homicide case really being handled differently and preferentially? As in many matters in the administration of justice, the answer lies in the question, compared to what?

If Tex's case is compared to two notorious accidental shooting incidents in Georgia that happened at about the same time, and in which senior law enforcement officials were the potential defendants, his treatment appears to be business as usual. But a different picture emerges when Tex's case is compared to the stream of instances—in Georgia and throughout America—in which ordinary black people bumped up against the criminal justice system. Some were suspected of committing crimes. Others were like Joe Beasley, coincidentally and innocently at the dangerous intersection of law and racial perception.

First take the case of the chief of police of Peachtree City, William McCollom.

Peachtree City lies about thirty miles southwest of downtown Atlanta. It is noted for a web of paths that enable residents to get almost anywhere in town riding in a golf cart. The police department conducts some of its patrols in golf carts as well.

In the early morning of New Year's Day, January 1, 2015, McCollom, who is white, shot his former wife (also white, and with whom he had resumed relations) in the back while both were in bed. Margaret McCollom was sleeping when she was shot. The chief may or may not have been sleeping—his story changed over time. In his call to 911 for help, Chief McCollom said that as he was putting his pistol on the night table beside the bed, the gun somehow just went off. He later settled on a different story, remarkably similar to the account that Tex would give of his shooting Diane some months later. In his later version, William McCollom was holding the Glock 17 9mm pistol in his hand as he slept. He claimed that he was jarred awake by the sound of the gun firing— precisely what Tex said happened when he shot Diane. Margaret McCollom survived, but she was paralyzed for life.

The question, of course, was why in the world would the chief, or any sane person for that matter, go to bed and sleep with a loaded pistol in his hand? McCollom explained that after having a few drinks, he took an over-the-counter sleep aid, went to bed, and fell asleep. The sound of barking dogs woke him. He got out of bed, took his pistol from a holster on a dresser, and checked around the house. He then returned to bed and fell asleep, with Margaret and the gun in hand between the sheets with him.

The shooting proved to be little more than an embarrassing inconvenience for Chief McCollom over the next several months. The Georgia Bureau of Investigation was called in to handle the case. McCollom was neither arrested nor booked with a mug shot. The city manager placed him on paid administrative leave. Opinion was divided about whether the chief was getting special treatment.

Several legal experts interviewed by the *Atlanta Journal-Constitution* newspaper agreed that McCollom's journey through the legal system was uncommon.

"Somebody else would probably be arrested, put in jail," said one of them, Michael Mears, an associate professor at Atlanta's John Marshall Law School. "They would have to be bailed out and get a lawyer up front. He probably would have lost his job. He would have gotten a mug shot and it would be on TV and in the press."[74]

Mears suggested that McCollom was being given the "gift of time." As time passed, emotions would be quelled and the case would be seen as less serious.

But J. Tom Morgan (a former DeKalb County district attorney who would later comment skeptically on Diane's shooting) argued that McCollom's treatment was reasonable, given his position. "There's not been a travesty of justice," Morgan said. "Everyone is just being cautious going after a public official."[75]

The discrepancy in Chief McCollom's story—was he putting the gun on the night table or was it between the sheets, sleeping with him and Margaret?—evaporated. The final version was that he was sleeping with gun in hand. McCollom resigned in March 2015. In August he pleaded guilty to a misdemeanor charge of reckless conduct. He was sentenced to twelve months of unsupervised probation and ordered to pay a one thousand dollar fine.[76]

All in all, not a bad outcome for shooting one's mate in the back.

Meanwhile, another senior Georgia law enforcement officer was embroiled in another remarkable accidental shooting. On May 3, 2015, Clayton County Sheriff Victor Hill shot a female friend, Gwenevere McCord, in the stomach. According to Sheriff Hill's account, he and McCord were practicing "police tactics" in a vacant model home in neighboring Gwinnett County, where McCord was working as a real estate broker, when the "tragic accident" happened.

Hill was the first black sheriff elected to office in Clayton County—the site of Margaret Mitchell's fictional plantation, Tara, and home to a museum memorializing her book, *Gone With the Wind*, and the plantation life. He has a reputation for being tough on crime and an enthusiast of tactical training and the forceful display of police power.

"The legal, hypothetical question is: Is it a reasonable exercise to run police tactics in an open model home on a Sunday afternoon?" Gwinnett County District Attorney Danny Porter told the *Los Angeles Times* newspaper. "There are things that make me question the reasonableness of practicing police tactics in a business open to the public."[77]

Hill was in no hurry to answer that question or to provide details about the shooting. When Gwinnett County detectives arrived at the model home, they found that several members of Hill's Clayton County command staff had beaten them to the scene. It was a verbal standoff. Neither Sheriff Hill nor his staff were willing to answer the detectives' questions. Three days after the shooting, Hill turned himself in but still declined to talk to investigators. He was released on bond and continued to serve as sheriff. McCord recovered from her wounds.

Sheriff Hill's case was closed in August 2016 after he took a negotiated "no contest" plea to a misdemeanor charge of reckless conduct. Under the terms of the plea deal and Georgia's First Offender Act, Hill's criminal record from the incident was erased. "It's like it never happened," Hill's attorney said.[78]

If the procedure followed in these two cases—one white, one black defendant—is taken to be the standard, Tex's case was not unusual. In both instances, investigators took their time and in Hill's case faced a wall of silence. In both cases, the shooter was charged with reckless conduct, a misdemeanor, the same as one of the two offenses with which the police charged Tex. Because both victims survived, neither of the two senior law enforcement officers were charged with the felony of involuntary manslaughter, as was Tex in his first round with the police. (Police officials suggested that Hill likely would have been so charged had Gwenevere McCord died.)

If, however, one broadens the scope and looks at a myriad of instances in which blacks interacting with law enforcement suffered frightening treatment and death, the argument raised by Atlanta's black activists is persuasive. Whether statistical or anecdotal in analysis, scholarly or legal-istic in form, evidence abounds that when black persons cross the path of the justice system in the United States, they are quite likely to be treated far less cordially than was Tex McIver.

"SEARCH AND DESTROY MODE"

Georgia is an instructive historical exemplar. But the criminal justice system's lens of racial perception—seeing black persons and especially black men as dangerous—is not restricted to any state or region of the United States. It is universal. On January 21, 2020, for example, attorneys for a young college student filed a lawsuit against several police officers in northern Illinois. The first searing paragraph graphically sums up the systemic problem at the intersection of race, justice, and policing in America:

> Plaintiff Jaylan Butler has always known that he could be targeted by police officers because he is Black. Mr. Butler's father taught him at a young age how to maximize his chances of surviving an encounter with law enforcement—stop instantly, put your hands up, drop any-thing you are holding, and drop to your knees. Mr. Butler hoped he would never have to use his father's advice. His hope was shattered on February 24, 2019 when, within minutes, Mr. Butler went from riding on a bus with his college swim team returning from a conference championship swim meet, to being forcefully held on the ground by police officers with a handgun pressed into his forehead while a police officer threatened to "blow [his] fucking head off" if he moved. Even once the police officers realized that this was a case of mistaken iden-tity and that Mr. Butler had committed no crime, they continued with his detention and arrest.[79]

Jaylan Butler was nineteen years old on the cold winter's night of February 24, 2019.[80] He and his fellow teammates on the Eastern Illinois University swim team were on a bus, returning to Charleston, Illinois, from a regional swim competition in South Dakota. When the bus pulled into a rest stop along Interstate 80 at about 8:00 p.m. for a break, Jaylan and his teammates got out and stretched their legs. A coach suggested that Butler take a photo of a nearby road sign that warned "Buckle Up. It's the

Law." The young athlete took a smiling selfie photo and headed back to the bus. Before he could get there, he was suddenly swarmed by at least six law enforcement officers from several jurisdictions arriving in a kaleidoscope of flashing lights. Officers jumped out of their vehicles with guns drawn.

The officers, the bus driver said, "were in a search-and-destroy mode."[81]

"When Mr. Butler saw the law enforcement vehicles pull up, he was surprised and confused, but he knew what to do. He instantly stopped, put his hands up, dropped the cell phone that was in his hand, and dropped to his knees."[82]

Jaylan's instant compliance did him little good. The police forced Butler to lie face down on the snowy ground. One shoved his knee into the young athlete's back. Another pressed his knee against Jaylan's neck—a precursor of another incident that would convulse America and the world. A third put his pistol against the youth's forehead and said, "If you keep moving, I'm going to blow your fucking head off."[83]

It soon became apparent that the police had the wrong man. They were looking for a suspect in a shooting incident whose only physical similarity to Butler was the fact that he was black. The man they were after was over six feet tall and weighed 230 pounds. Butler was five feet, ten inches tall and weighed 160 pounds. Moreover, the bus driver and Jaylan's coaches quickly explained to the police who the young man was and why they were there. Despite all of this, the officers forced the handcuffed Butler into the back of a squad car, where he was held for a long and entirely unexplained time.

Eventually, Jaylan Butler was allowed to get his school ID from the bus and rejoin his teammates. But the officers refused to identify themselves and failed to file paperwork required under Illinois law, intended to collect data to study racial bias in such incidents. When the American Civil Liberties Union filed its lawsuit on behalf of Butler, the law enforcement community shifted into a familiar tactic—smearing the victim, raising allegations of what might be called "contributory badness." In the face of multiple contrary witness stories, the officers and their lawyers claimed that the young swimmer had resisted their requests and become unruly.

Much worse was to come in the year following. (Similar events cascaded even as this book was being written.) Among the most explosive were the killings of two black men that were recorded on video—Ah-maud Arbery in Georgia and George Floyd in Minneapolis. These and other videos of other black and brown men being killed were widely viewed in social and news media. They set off months of intense public protest, vows from politicians to reform the system, and continuing conflict with the long-established social and political norms of white America. The ultimate outcome is yet to be seen, but we will likely see decades of reshaping race and justice in America.

7

THROUGH A LENS DARKLY

Packer's due process "obstacle course" was on Tex McIver's side when the Atlanta Police Department finally decided to charge him. The scholar's description of the criminal process with which Tex was now engaged is a classic:

> People who commit crimes appear to share the prevalent impression that punishment is an unpleasantness that is best avoided. They ordinarily take care to avoid being caught. If arrested, they ordinarily deny their guilt and otherwise try not to cooperate with the police. If brought to trial, they do whatever their resources permit to resist being convicted. And even after they have been convicted and sent to prison, their efforts to secure their freedom do not cease. It is a struggle from start to finish. [1]

Tex's ample financial resources permitted him to put up a struggle, to resist being convicted, from start to finish. Among the arrows in his defensive quiver were two foundational premises of the American system of criminal justice.

The first arrow was his entitlement to be represented by counsel, mandated by the Sixth Amendment of the Constitution, which states "In all criminal prosecutions, the accused shall enjoy the right . . . to have the Assistance of Counsel for his defense." A standard text on criminal procedure states that one of the defining characteristics of the American system is that a criminal defendant "is entitled to the assistance of counsel and, if indigent, to have one appointed at public expense if incarceration will result from conviction."[2]

One of the first things that Tex did after he shot Diane was to take advantage of his right to counsel. An emergency room nurse testified at Tex's trial that there was something odd going on that fatal late night. While the medical staff were struggling to revive the injured woman and save her life, an older guy in a red polo shirt was conferring quietly with two other men in a nearby corridor. One of them was scribbling on a legal pad. The men had their arms on each other's shoulders, like a football team in a huddle.

"This is what you're going to tell them," the nurse heard one of the men say.

"I had the impression," she said, "of a plan being enacted."

The older man in the red shirt was Tex. The man with the legal pad was his lawyer, and the third man was a friend who acted as his public affairs adviser. If the plan centered on Tex's fear of Black Lives Matter excuse, it blew up in his face.

As the district attorney's office got involved and Tex's criminal exposure got significantly worse, he was able to afford the luxury of hiring two of the biggest, most experienced guns in the Georgia criminal defense bar: attorneys Bruce Harvey and Don Samuel. Just as Tex could spring for a top-of-the-line King Ranch SUV, he could also pay the fees of this pair of expensive lawyers and their supporting staffs.

The second arrow in Tex's legal quiver was the presumption of innocence. No matter how bad things look on the face of it, no matter how dead certain a cop, a steely eyed prosecutor, or a clamoring mob are of a red-handed suspect's guilt, every defendant in America is entitled to the presumption at their trial that they did not commit the crime with which they are charged—unless and until they are proven legally guilty after a fair trial or they make a valid confession to the crime. Standard law texts describe this presumption in ringing terms.

> The American legal system is based on the presumption of innocence. A defendant may not be compelled to testify against himself or herself, and the prosecution is required as a matter of the due process of law to establish every element of a crime beyond a reasonable doubt to establish a defendant's guilt.[3]

The presumption of innocence does not appear in the Constitution. But the U.S. Supreme Court established its place in American criminal law in an 1895 bank fraud case, *Coffin v. United States*.[4] In that case, the Court reversed a bank officer's criminal conviction in part because the trial judge had refused to give the jury an instruction on the presumption. "The principle that there is a presumption of innocence in favor of the accused is the undoubted law, axiomatic and elementary, and its enforcement lies at the foundation of the administration of our criminal law."[5] Most standard jury instructions in criminal trials today inform the jury of the defendant's right to a presumption of innocence.[6]

The presumption of innocence is often misstated in lay writing and sometimes in legal discourse. Although many observers argue that the presumption should attach to a person as soon as they encounter the criminal justice system, and some mistakenly believe that it does, it does not in fact arise in law until the criminal trial commences. The prevailing legal doctrine was expressed by the Supreme Court in the case of *Bell v. Wolfish*, "The presumption of innocence is a doctrine that allocates the burden of proof in criminal trials. . . . But it has no application to a determination of the rights of a pretrial detainee during confinement before his trial has even begun."[7]

As Wharton School Professor William S. Laufer has explained, "the perception of an accused's innocence, whether factual or legal, is overcome by standards of proof associated with search and seizure of evidence, arrest, indictment, detention, and plea bargaining."[8] In other words, police and prosecutors act on the presumption that a suspect is probably guilty, rather than innocent, once they have decided that the evidence meets the legal thresholds necessary to legally arrest the suspect, charge them with a crime, detain them, and search their premises. If everyone were actually presumed innocent at the outset of the criminal justice process, no one would ever be arrested and charged. On the other hand, conclusions about these supposedly neutral legal thresholds may be, and often are, influenced by racial and ethnic stereotypes—the lens of racial sorting.

There is a difference between *legal* guilt or innocence and *factual* guilt or innocence. Thus, the right to a presumption of innocence during a criminal trial does not bar, even in theory, the conclusions that we are all free to draw about all manner of things that we see and hear in our daily lives, including practical judgments about the factual guilt of a person arrested for or suspected of committing a crime. Based on the facts as we know them, or think we know them, or casually suppose them to be about an alleged crime, we are all perfectly entitled legally and constitutionally to decide for ourselves that the butler did it (unless we happen to be serving on a jury, in which case we are morally and legally bound to keep an open mind).

Invocation of this legal rule of evidence is a common resort of public figures. Politicians and other cultural stars often claim the right to a presumption of innocence when they are enmeshed in scandal, caught out in a circumstance that is not a crime but certainly an embarrassment. They are entitled to no such thing as a matter of law or constitutional protection. As law professor and former federal prosecutor Kim Wehle wrote, the presumption of innocence is "an overused and badly misunderstood phrase that gets tossed around whenever politicians are accused of wrongdoing. . . . Politicians who come under fire for abusing their office do not get a legal presumption of innocence. People only get the presumption of innocence if they are indicted and facing trial for crimes. The presumption of innocence is for criminal defendants, not presidents."[9]

Thus, for example, it may or may not be the fair thing to do to reserve judgment on President Donald Trump, who has been accused of emitting tens of thousands of lies about important matters, adversely affecting national security and imperiling millions of American lives, during his term of office.[10] But giving him the benefit of the doubt about whether he lied is a social meme, not a requirement of law or the Constitution. It would be if he were charged with a criminal offense and on trial. For another example, Thomas Jipping, deputy director of the Edwin Meese III Center for Legal and Judicial Studies and a Senior Legal Fellow at the Heritage Foundation, should have known better when he argued, "The presumption of innocence may be one of the casualties of the campaign against Supreme Court nominee Brett Kavanaugh," during the latter's contentious nomination hearing.[11] Indeed, the nominee may have felt like he was on trial. But he was no more entitled to the presumption of innocence than is any other political figure dancing on the red-hot griddle of public opinion. Whether the public gave Kavanaugh the benefit of the doubt had nothing to do with the viability of the presumption in criminal trials.

Tex's social, economic, and political station amped up his due process rights. No one slapped handcuffs on him, or even questioned him, the night he shot Diane in the back. He wasn't booked or locked up in an odorous holding cell, nor did he suffer the indignity of a publicly released booking photo, the social media equivalent of the infamous "perp walk."[12] For three months Tex was free to stroll around Atlanta and rest up at his ranch while the police pondered his case. Except for whatever psychological or moral burden he may have felt about having shot his wife to death, Tex could go on about his life.

Tex also enjoyed the benefit of a heads up from someone in authority when the police finally made the decision to charge him. No cops showed up at his condominium or ranch to take him into custody. On the contrary, when he learned that warrants would be issued for his arrest, he arranged to turn himself in at the Fulton County Jail on the evening of Wednesday, December 21, 2016. The next day, Thursday, was Tex's seventy-fourth birthday. He spent that day in custody, appearing before a magistrate judge for a preliminary hearing. On Friday Tex left the jail about 3:00 p.m. He was required to post a two hundred thousand dollar bond, surrender his passport, wear an ankle monitor, stay away from Diane's former employer, and not carry firearms.[13] In all, it was about as painless a process as it gets for a person charged with manslaughter.

Things would go downhill for Tex from there.

By mid-April 2017 the Fulton County district attorney's office was well along its way to indicting Tex for more serious crimes. One of the prosecutor's last steps was executing several search warrants, including a search of Tex's condominium. Investigators found a Glock semiautomatic pistol and ammunition stuffed in his sock drawer. A hearing was held on the charge that Tex had violated one of the conditions of his parole. During that hearing, a neighbor recounted an incident from several years past. Her tale illuminated Tex's penchant for gunplay. The neighbor told the court that one day she mentioned to Tex that she had seen a buzzard on her balcony. A few days later, she happened to be a guest in the McIver's apartment when the buzzard appeared on Tex's balcony. The balcony's sliding glass door was open. Tex got a handgun and fired at the bird through the screen door. The bird escaped unharmed. The judge was persuaded. Tex's probation was revoked, and he was sent back to jail.[14]

A few days later a grand jury returned an indictment charging him with seven counts, including felony murder.

SHORT CIRCUIT

Many persons of color, minority ethnicity, and low income accused of crimes, even crimes less serious than those with which Tex was charged, never get to the top of the shining hill of due process in the first place. They have nowhere to tumble down from. For them, lofty presumptions of innocence, a solicitous right to counsel, and prosecutorial burdens of proof are mere table scraps from the banquet of due process protection that Tex enjoyed. These unfortunates start at the bottom of the criminal process and stay at the bottom. "The reality is that most of these due process protections are enjoyed by only a tiny minority of criminal defendants," scholar William R. Kelly and federal judge Robert Pitman wrote in their book *Confronting Underground Justice*.[15]

In the words of Georgetown University Law Professor Paul Butler, the United States has "two systems of justice, separate and unequal." Butler was commenting on an incident in Minneapolis in which a Latino journalist for CNN and his crew were arrested by police while broadcasting live from a demonstration, whereas a white colleague in a nearby location was treated courteously by the police. To law professor Butler, the incident illustrated how race and ethnicity define what he described as "'opposite' systems of justice—one for white people and another for racial minorities, especially African Americans, Latinx and Native American people."[16]

Others see class and elitism as a major factor. Criticizing favoritism in the legal process shown by the Trump administration to the president's confidante Roger Stone, author Radley Balko criticized America's "tiered system of justice" and argued that "when someone gets a break from the laws that apply to everyone else because that person has unique access to power, it's a net loss for justice."[17] Representative Adam B. Schiff voiced the same concern after Trump commuted Stone's sentence, which was based on seven felony convictions. "With this commutation, Trump makes clear that there are two systems of justice in America: one for his criminal friends, and one for everyone else."[18] As outrageous as Trump's abuse of his pardoning power may seem to critics, these cases amount to no more than an indiscernible fraction among the tens of thousands of criminal cases in which people whose name nobody knows suffer on the "opposite" side of the criminal justice system.

Whether the driving force is race or class or both, for all of its noble pronouncements, the American system of criminal law operates very much like the "inside/outside" system that historian Sven Beckert described in *Empire of Cotton*. One of the mechanisms of the American inside/outside system of law that short circuits due process and equal protection rights for the vast majority of persons of any race or ethnicity charged with crimes is that they never go to trial. The criminal trial is the point at which such important protections as the presumption of innocence and the prosecutor's duty to prove all of the elements of a crime beyond a reasonable doubt kick in—not to mention the Constitution's intended protection against arbitrary justice by ensuring trial by a jury. Instead of going to trial, however, most defendants enter into a deal, a "plea bargain," with their prosecutor. They waive their procedural rights and admit guilt to *something* in order to avoid the risk of a harsher sentence. Judges endorse the process because it helps them "move the docket"—keep the criminal law assembly line humming along. A defendant who rejects the prosecutor's offer and insists on going to trial runs the risk of angering the judge who might then impose a stiffer penalty than the one offered in the plea bargain. At least 95 percent of criminal convictions are obtained through plea bargains, according to Kelly and Pitman.

This is Beckert's system of "inside/outside" law with a vengeance—a tiny stratum of "inside" defendants actually enjoy the rights enshrined in American criminal law theory. Those outside of this privileged few get pushed onto the grim Crime Control Model conveyor belt. The "tremendous power and discretion" that the system of plea bargaining gives prosecutors makes them "judge and jury as well as prosecutor since they determine who is innocent or guilty and also determine more often than not what the punishment will be." [19]

This wasn't how Herbert Packer thought that things would turn out in America. He was optimistic about the future of American criminal procedure when he wrote about his two models in 1966. Packer thought he saw a trend toward the Due Process Model, and the obstacle course that it erected. The pursuit of racial justice, he thought, would impel the course of the law in that direction.

Perhaps the most powerful propellant of the trend toward the Due Process Model has been provided by the Negro's struggle for his civil rights and the response to that struggle by law enforcement in the Southern states—as well, it needs to be said, by law enforcement in some Northern cities. . . . Our heightened national consciousness about the problems of urban poverty likewise contributes to and sustains the trend in the direction of the Due Process Model. [20]

But the very factors that Packer thought would move the dial toward enhanced due process have had the opposite effect, according to many critical observers. "[T]his latest round of African American advances set the gears of white opposition in motion," scholar Carol Anderson wrote of the white power structure's reaction to black success in courts and Congress in her book *White Rage*.[21] The decisions of the Warren Court and the passage of major federal civil rights legislation in 1964 and 1965 were seen as existential threats by the established order of white power. "The coincidence of these circumstances and threats provided much of the motivation for launching a sea change in criminal justice policy, the birth of what has come to be called 'tough on crime' or 'crime control,'" argue Pitman and Kelly.[22] Scholars Geoffrey Stone and David Strauss point out a broader reactionary trend in their book, *Democracy and Equality: The Enduring Constitutional Vision of the Warren Court*. Republican presidents have appointed about two-thirds of the sitting justices in the fifty years since Earl Warren's retirement, preferring "nominees who would actively move the law in an aggressively conservative direction on such issues as gun control, affirmative action, campaign finance, and so on."[23]

The politics of race and the glitter of corporate money have supercharged this reactionary trend. For fifteen years or more, "law and order" was the copyrighted hallmark of Republican politics, a centerpiece of the presidential administrations of Richard Nixon, Ronald Reagan, and George H. W. Bush. The latter's 1988 presidential campaign attacked Democratic candidate Michael Dukakis for having supported good conduct furloughs for convicted prisoners. But this ostensible law and order campaign featured the deliberately cynical subtext of racial fear. The Bush campaign used attack ads and promoted news media articles featuring William Horton, a black convicted felon released on furlough who went on to commit a number of heinous crimes. Renamed "Willie" by Bush's campaign manager—an act evocative of the slave masters' arbitrary power over slaves' names—the images of William Horton sounded the dog whistle of subtle but powerful racial allusion that became a lead player in the Republican political orchestra. Overlooked in most accounts is the role that Al Gore played during his contest with Dukakis for the Democratic presidential nomination. Gore first raised the issue of good conduct furloughs in an April 1988 debate with Dukakis (although without racial subtext). Gore's law and order thrust failed to help him. But Republicans picked up on the issue's racial potential, using grimly enhanced images of "Willie" Horton.[24] In Carol Anderson's words, "Crime and blackness soon became synonymous in a carefully constructed way that played to the barely subliminal fears of darkened, frightening images flashing across the television screen."[25]

Democrats learned that they could play the same tune on the same whistle. "The politics of crime control took an unusual turn in the 1992 presidential campaign when the [Bill] Clinton camp and the national Democratic Party decided it was time for liberals to be tough on crime and to take some of the political leverage for themselves."[26] The result was the Violent Crime Control and Law Enforcement Act of 1994, a controversial tough-on-crime omnibus bill. Senator Joe Biden "reveled in the politics of the 1994 law, bragging after it passed that 'the liberal wing of the Democratic Party' was now for '60 new death penalties,' '70 enhanced penalties,' '100,000 cops,' and '125,000 new state prison cells.'"[27] Money became "a key player" in this system as prisons and detention centers were increasingly "privatized," run by large corporations.[28] The more prisoners, the more money these private interests make. It is no wonder that these private sector players "spend considerable sums of money on lobbying efforts to promote these policies."[29]

Although Democrats backed away from their law and order politics, Donald Trump embraced the theme with vigor in his 2016 campaign, and in June 2020 announced in a Rose Garden speech that he was "your president of law and order."[30]

NEW KIDS ON THE LEGAL SCHOLARSHIP BLOCK

This 180-degree turn away from Packer's optimistic forecast has attracted substantial criticism from the proponents of critical race theory, "an intellectual movement that analyzes how the law maintains dominance and privilege of white society and how the law perpetuates the subordinate status of African Americans."[31] The movement emerged in the 1970s, as a number of lawyers, activists, and legal scholars realized that "the heady advances of the civil rights era of the 1960s had stalled . . . and were being rolled back."[32] The movement today is broader than the critical legal studies nucleus from which it sprang. It informs analytical thought in other disciplines such as education and sociology.

According to two of its leading proponents, critical race theory differs from traditional civil rights activism, "which stresses incrementalism and step-by-step progress" within the established system of law. Instead it "questions the very foundations of the liberal order, including equality theory, legal reasoning, Enlightenment rationalism, and neutral principles of constitutional law."[33] In short, most of the Western intellectual canon—at least as it applies to law, ethics, and social issues—is rejected by critical race theorists. They argue that in spite of its high-minded constructs, that canon has not only failed to deliver justice fairly and equally to people of color, but justified the violent suppression of their justice rights.

Traditional legal reasoning assumes that there is only one "correct" answer to a legal problem. The application of ruling precedent and logic to a given set of facts—legal reasoning—will produce that one right answer. Critical race theory proposes that there can be many such answers, depending on how the decider interprets the significance of various facts and the soundness of ostensible precedent. Thus, a white decider may see a set of facts and principles in a way profoundly different from how a person of color or another ethnicity might see the same set. The movement has often excluded and sometimes disparaged white academics on the grounds that they are at best insensitive and unable to grasp or articulate the realities of minority experience, or at worst active agents sustaining a racist intellectual order.[34] "White males tempted to participate in the conversation were condemned in advance as interlopers, even imperialists."[35]

The movement's teaching and academic texts make frequent and prominent use of exemplary storytelling, sometimes anecdotal and sometimes wholly fictional. The use of such stories is unlike the traditional study of adjudicated law cases from which universal legal principles are divined and law students are taught to "think like a lawyer." Another technique is investigating and constructing detailed background stories about the principals involved in landmark cases to show the influence of racial thinking in how the issues were articulated and decided. "One premise of legal storytellers is that members of this country's dominant racial group cannot easily grasp what it is like to be nonwhite."[36] The stories used in critical legal studies are intended to fill gaps in experience and perspective that never make it into the law books.

Dorothy E. Roberts is one of these intellectual critics. She holds appointments at the University of Pennsylvania in the Law School and in the departments of Africana Studies and Sociology. She writes and lectures on gender, race, and class in legal issues. Roberts wrote about the criminal justice system in 1993—almost thirty years *after* Packer's expression of hope and twenty-seven years *before* the turmoil of the spring of 2020. The subordinate position of persons of color in the American criminal justice system, Roberts argued, is neither the result of benign neglect nor an accident. It is a system of intention:

> Not only is race used to identify criminals, it is embedded in the very foundation of our criminal law. Race helps to determine who the criminals are, what conduct constitutes a crime, and which crimes society treats most seriously. . . . The American criminal justice system has historically served as a means of controlling blacks. This control is accomplished through very concrete means. Local police departments patrol black neighborhoods as if they were occupied territories. The idea of local control of police in most communities seems to most Americans to be as farfetched as the proverbial fox minding the hen house. Police serve not to protect black citizens, but to protect white citizens from black criminals. It is not surprising that many black Americans view the police with fear, anger, and distrust.[37]

Just one year earlier, the *New York Times* described these academic proponents of critical race theory as "legal scholarship's newest kids on the block" who were working "to correct the problem of the law's [white] voice."[38] The emerging intellectual force included Latino, Native American, and Asian scholars as well as black professors. Since then, critical race theory has become a powerful and growing presence in contemporary analysis of race and law, in turn influencing lay activism and the political dialogue on public policy.

Not surprisingly, critical race theory has sparked resistance.[39] Among its critics are some prominent scholars of color and minority ethnicity.[40] Opponents of critical race theory object to its use of storytelling, its skepticism about traditional presumptions of objectivity and merit, and the proposition that voices of people of color and minority ethnicity are more valid than white voices on the subjects of race and racism.[41] According to the theory's own proponents, its "adversaries are perhaps most concerned with what they perceive to be critical race theorists' nonchalance about objective truth. For the critical race theorist, objective truth, like merit, does not exist in social science and politics."[42]

Richard A. Posner, chief judge of the U.S. Court of Appeals for the Seventh Circuit and a lecturer at the University of Chicago Law School, is one of the harshest critics. "Every intellectual movement has a lunatic fringe," he wrote in a book review for the *New Republic* magazine in 1997. "Radical legal egalitarianism is distinguished by having a rational fringe and a lunatic core. The latter is constituted by the critical race theorists and the other legal academics who have swallowed postmodernism hook, line, and sinker."[43] Posner charged that the movement "turns its back on the Western tradition of rational inquiry, foreswearing analysis for narrative. . . . By repudiating reasoned argumentation, the storytellers reinforce stereotypes about the intellectual capacities of nonwhites."[44]

In an extensive critique of critical race theory in 1989, law professor Daniel Subotnik warned that

> [d]iscouraging white legal scholars from entering the national conversation about race . . . has generated a kind of cynicism in white audiences which, in turn, has had precisely the reverse effect of that ostensibly desired by [critical race theory advocates]. It drives the American public to the right and ensures that anything [critical race theory] offers is reflexively rejected.[45]

The late Harvard Law Professor Derrick Bell is often credited as the "movement's intellectual father figure," dating back to articles he wrote in the 1960s and 1970s.[46] As early as 1969 Bell wrote, "For the poor, the police do not protect, but contain; they do not assist, but rather harass, and their presence in the ghetto is not to keep peace but to maintain control."[47] He later authored a legal textbook, *Race, Racism, and American Law*, which through six editions continues to be a major source for the study of the problems that its title suggests. In 1992, Bell told the *New York Times* that blacks were worse off and more subjugated in America than at any time since slavery. The only difference, he said, was that in 1992 there was "a more effective, more sophisticated means of domination."[48]

Among Bell's core beliefs was what he called "the interest convergence dilemma," which held that whites would only support efforts to improve the lives of people of color when it was in their own interest.[49] He called a set of two corollary rules "The Derrick Bell Pre-Memorial Principle of Racial Loss and Gain." Rule One, he wrote, dictated that "Society is always willing to sacrifice the rights of Black people in order to protect important economic or political interests of Whites." Rule Two held that "law and society recognize the rights of African Americans and other people of color only when, and only for as long as, such recognition serves some economic or political interests of greater importance to Whites."[50]

A 1992 profile of Bell described him as a "devoutly angry man." Among the many at whom he was angry, according to the article, were his former black professorial colleagues at Harvard University. He was angry at a younger black colleague, Professor Randall Kennedy, a prolific author on issues of race, culture, and criminal law.[51] Bell was also angry at Henry Louis Gates Jr., a prominent black Harvard professor who had written a long article for the *New York Times* about the danger of black anti-Semitism. Gates had written that "[w]hile anti-Semitism is generally on the wane in this country, it has been on the rise among black Americans. . . . The trend has been deeply disquieting for many black intellectuals."[52] According to the *Times* profile, Bell was critical of Gates and said that blacks "should be very careful about criticizing each other, because whites love it so much when they do."[53]

Seventeen years later, Professor Gates would find himself ensnared in a confrontation with police that became a notorious example of what many saw as racially biased law enforcement. The incident thrust Gates and President Barack Obama onto the stage of high-profile political drama that was at least as instructive as any illustrative story conjured up by a critical race theory academic.

FOR THE GOOD AND THE GREAT—OR JUST "SOME CRIMINAL"

The original version of Harvard's alma mater song described how "the good and the great, in their beautiful prime, thro' thy precincts have musingly trod."[54] By any measure, Professor Henry Louis Gates Jr. is one of Harvard's best and greatest. The director of the Hutchins Center for African and African American Research at Harvard, Gates is an "Emmy Award-winning filmmaker, literary scholar, journalist, cultural critic, and institution builder" who has authored or co-authored twenty-one books and created fifteen documentary films. In 1981, Gates was a member of the first class to be awarded "genius grants" by the MacArthur Foundation.[55]

None of Gates's stellar achievements were apparent to Sgt. James Crowley of the Cambridge Police Department, a white man, when he confronted Gates in the professor's own home at 17 Ware Street on the afternoon of July 16, 2009. Nor would it likely have mattered much to a police officer who appeared to be most interested in forcing Gates to bend his knee to authority.[56] Within six minutes of responding to a vague and unfounded report of a possible burglary in progress at Gates' residence, Crowley had confronted the academic in his own home, then enticed him outside and arrested him on a charge of disorderly conduct—which he could not have done inside the professor's own home. Crowley's cleverly engineered "cover charge" was dismissed when cooler heads prevailed.

Proponents of both sides of this incident have promoted lengthy versions of what happened, parsing each of the 360 seconds it took Crowley to arrest Gates. But the crucial facts are actually few, and they are undisputed.[57]

Gates had just returned to his home in Cambridge after a long flight from China, where he had been working on a new documentary project. He and his driver found that the front door to Gates' house was damaged and jammed. The house was a residence provided to Gates by Harvard University. Gates entered through the back door, turned off the alarm, and the two men leaned against the front door to force it open. While they were thus gaining entrance to the professor's home, a passerby saw the two men's efforts. This first passerby in turn told a second passerby that what she had just seen might possibly have been an illegal entry, although she wasn't sure—it could have been simply a resident having trouble entering his own home. The second passerby called the Cambridge Police Department and described the ambiguous situation. The police dispatcher raised the question of race for the first time in the process, asking the caller whether the men were white, Hispanic, or black. The caller replied that she was not sure about the two men's race, but thought that one might be Hispanic. The dispatcher sent out a radio call, to which Sgt. Crowley responded.

By the time Crowley arrived on the scene, Gates was inside his home and calling the appropriate Harvard office to report the problem with the front door lock. Although both of the two passersby deny that they had said anything about black men, Crowley's report shows that he had decided that the suspicious subjects were black men by the time he went up onto the front porch. What he saw inside the home was indeed a middle-aged black man. (The driver had since left.)

Crowley asked the black man to step outside.

Gates refused to come out, accused the officer of being racist, and said, perhaps repeatedly, "This is what happens to black men in America." Crowley entered the house and asked Gates for identification. The professor produced both his Harvard identification card and his driver's license, which confirmed his address as the very house in which the two men were standing. At this point it should have been clear from the documents that Gates was indeed in his own home. But Crowley inexplicably continued to act is if he doubted Gates' explanation and the plain evidence of Gates' identification documents. He refused to leave, although Gates asked him to. After he had shown Crowley his identification and observed the officer's continuing doubt, Gates asked, "Why are you doing this? Is it because I'm a black man and you're a white officer? I don't understand why you don't believe this is my house."[58]

Crowley told the police dispatcher to keep sending backup police officers and to notify the Harvard police. By this time both men had become "heated." Gates asked for Crowley's name and badge number. Crowley told Gates he would give his credentials to him if the professor stepped outside. As the sergeant knew, the moment Gates stepped outside, he was in a public place, and rightfully or wrongly, Crowley could claim that the professor's heated words were creating a public "tumult" under the Massachusetts statute. Gates was arrested, taken to jail, and booked. His mug shot was transmitted around the world by news media the moment the story of his arrest broke.

Within days, prosecutors dropped the charge, which not only was unfounded but was obviously a "cover charge," an arrest tactic that policemen often use when a subject refuses to accord them the respect (i.e., deference) to which they incorrectly think their badge entitles them.

"What it made me realize was how vulnerable all black men are, how vulnerable all people of color are, and all poor people, to capricious forces like a rogue policeman, and this man clearly was a rogue police-man," Gates later said of the incident.[59]

An official review of the incident by a panel commissioned by the city of Cambridge went to tedious length to establish that both men contrib-uted to the tension. The report belabored the obvious fact that "the inci-dent was sparked by misunderstandings and failed communications be-tween the two men." A sixty-four-page monument to anodyne verbosity, the report went further and blamed *both* men for not backing down. "Once Professor Gates showed Sergeant Crowley his identification and Crowley explained why he was at Gates' home," the report intoned, "the potential threat was diminished, and the behavior of both men should have begun to change. But instead of de-escalating, both men continued to escalate the encounter."[60]

Only one of the two men, however, had a duty under law to de-escalate once the "potential threat was diminished," and it was not Profes-sor Gates. That man was Sergeant Crowley.

The law is clear that police have a duty to bear verbal abuse from citizens—assuming that Gates' language was abusive, as opposed to merely accurately descriptive. As Georgetown Law Professor Christy Lo-pez explained, "The First Amendment generally prohibits law enforce-ment officials from arresting people for how they talk to (or yell at) the police. Even speech that is loud, disrespectful, profane, and insulting is protected in most circumstances." This includes so-called fighting words that might not ordinarily be protected speech but are "construed more narrowly when the words are directed at police officers." More is simply expected of police officers than ordinary civilians. In the words of the Supreme Court, "a properly trained officer may reasonably be expected to 'exercise a higher degree of restraint' than the average citizen, and thus be less likely to respond belligerently to 'fighting words.'"[61]

Unfortunately, many law enforcement officers either don't know or don't care about their duty to stay calm and carry on. "There is abundant evidence that police overuse disorderly conduct and similar statutes to arrest people who 'disrespect' them or express disagreement with their actions."[62] The colloquial terms for the putative grounds for such arrests is "contempt of cop," a play on the actual legal offense of contempt of court. The difference is that "contempt of cop arrests are by definition abusive: they are arrests made with no valid legal reason."[63] Some officers, like Sgt. Crowley, are clever enough to realize that although they cannot make a valid arrest for being yelled at, they can make what is known as a "cover arrest . . . meant to help justify or explain an officer's use of force or other exercise of authority where there may have been no legitimate justification for that exercise of authority."[64]

Once Crowley had seen Gates's identification, which conclusively established the professor was where he had a right to be, in his own home, he should have disengaged. As Cambridge lawyer Lowry Heussler observed in her acidic review of Crowley's conduct in the case:

> Read Crowley's report and stop on page two when he admits seeing Gates' Harvard photo ID. I don't care what Gates had said to him up until then, Crowley was obligated to leave. He had identified Gates. Any further investigation of Gates' right to be present in the house could have been done elsewhere.[65]

Clearly, Sgt. Crowley did not intend to gracefully let go of this insolent middle-aged black man. On the contrary, Crowley was actively escalating the police show of force by calling for more officers from two jurisdictions. "Crowley is upset and he's mad at Gates. He's been accused of racism. Nobody likes that, but if a cop can't take an insult without retaliating, he's in the wrong job. When a person is given a gun and a badge, we better make sure he's got a firm grasp on his temper."[66]

Crowley had just enough of a grasp on his temper to understand that if he lured Gates outside of his home into a public space, and fudged his report a bit, he could make a cover arrest for disorderly conduct.

> By telling Gates to come outside, Crowley establishes that he has lost all semblance of professionalism. It has now become personal and he wants to create a violation of [the disorderly conduct statute]. He gets Gates out onto the porch because a crowd has gathered providing onlookers who could experience alarm. Note his careful recitation (tumultuous behavior outside the residence in view of the public).[67]

But

> if the facts are as Crowley asserted in his arrest report, the arrest was unlawful. Nothing in Sergeant Crowley's report, or any other evidence, suggests that Professor Gates's "tumultuous" behavior went

beyond words, and there is no evidence that these words, however loud, rude, or obnoxious were so inflammatory as to inflict injury or tend to incite an immediate breach of the peace. Professor Gates's behavior, as described by Sergeant Crowley, falls squarely in the realm of speech protected by the First Amendment. [68]

A week after the incident, President Barack Obama held a press conference on his health care reform initiative. The last questioner asked him about the arrest of Professor Gates. Obama's answer set off a frenzy of criticism from defenders of the police, tinged with charges of racial favoritism.

> I don't know, not having been there and not seeing all the facts, what role race played in [Gates case]. But I think it's fair to say, number one, any of us would be pretty angry; number two, that the Cambridge police acted stupidly in arresting somebody when there was already proof that they were in their own home; and, number three, what I think we know separate and apart from this incident is that there's a long history in this country of African-Americans and Latinos being stopped by law enforcement disproportionately. That's just a fact. [69]

In an effort to defuse tensions, the president invited Gates and Crowley to a meeting at the White House. After talking privately, the two men adjourned to the White House lawn, where they shared beverages and small talk with President Obama and Vice President Joe Biden. The media dubbed the meeting "the beer summit." Gates has later stated that he has since decided that Crowley is not a racist. [70]

Trump's first attorney general, Jeff Sessions, recounted a disturbing and peculiarly distorted version of the beer summit during an interview for a lengthy *New York Times Magazine* profile, published in July 2020 while he was trying to win back his old Senate seat, after having been dumped and disgraced by Trump:

> The mantra was: "Back to the men and women in blue," Sessions told me. "The police had been demoralized. There was all the Obama— there's a riot, and he has a beer at the White House with some criminal, to listen to him. Wasn't having a beer with the police officers. So we said, 'We're on your side. We've got your back, you got our thanks.'" [71]

Thus was the renowned and accomplished Harvard scholar Henry Louis Gates Jr. reduced to being just "some criminal" by the attorney general of the United States.

Incredibly, almost eleven years later to the day, and on the other side of the country, another black academic's right to be in her home was rudely challenged by a Santa Clara University security officer. The confrontation with Danielle Fuentes Morgan, an assistant professor of English, was sparked by a visit by her brother, Carlos Fuentes. Police challenged the brother's right to be in the neighborhood, demanded that Morgan vouch for him, and insisted that she produce identification to prove that she was entitled to be in the home. "No one ever wakes up in the morning thinking that these things will happen," Morgan said. But, she added, "being Black in America means there is an expectation that you have to show your papers."[72]

One can only sadly wonder how law enforcement officers see the less distinguished people of color with whom they daily interact.

AT THE MARGINS

Misconduct by armed law enforcement officers has been repeatedly shown to have every potential to escalate to fatal levels. But what about the conduct of supposedly law-abiding citizens at the margins of the criminal justice system who—like Tex shooting at a carload of teenagers—decide to enforce the law on their own terms?

8

NO N WORDS ANYWHERE

It is clear from Tex McIver's reckless behavior—from firing at a car full of teenagers in 1990, to shooting recklessly at a bird in a heavily populated area, to finally whipping out his revolver and killing his wife in 2016—that he had a distorted view of himself as an honorable vigilante, a bizarre sort of private law enforcement officer, a throwback to the good old days of slave patrols and Southern honor.

Acting as a lone-ranging citizen, Tex was ready to shoot not only when he was in actual mortal danger, but when he was annoyed or irritated by behavior that he unilaterally regarded as unacceptable. Tex had his own peculiarly violent way of making America great. Given the combination of his Blue Lives Matter and we-don't-call-911 signs, the tens of guns he owned, the gun-slinger's paraphernalia littered around his ranch, and his friendship with the local sheriff, it is also likely that Tex imagined that such brash behavior would win the beaming approval of those officially charged with enforcing the law.

Experience has shown that Tex is not alone in holding this self-righteous view of himself as a privileged enforcer of law and order. And, in fact, organizations like the neighborhood watch that cost Trayvon Martin his life in Florida, and legal institutions like the "citizen's arrest" have perpetuated many of the race-based premises of the American system of slave control. "Although slave patrols officially ceased to operate at the close of the Civil War, their functions were assumed by other Southern institutions . . . their lawless violent aspects were taken up by vigilante groups like the Ku Klux Klan."[1]

The distorted lens of racial perception plays a prominent role in many cases in which such enforcers presume to take action. News media regularly report instances when white private citizens butt in and call the cops on legal and perfectly normal behavior by black persons. These are but the visible cases among many more that occur without public notice. A few notable incidents include the case of a white woman in Manhattan who called police after a black man out bird watching in Central Park asked her to leash her dog, as park rules required. "I'm going to tell them there's an African American man threatening my life," the white woman told him, pulling out her cellphone and dialing 911.[2] A professor at Ball State University in Indiana called the police after a black student refused to change his classroom seat. The student was charging his computer and preferred to stay where he was.[3] A bank in Detroit called the police on a black man who was trying to deposit checks he had received in settlement of a discrimination lawsuit he had brought against a former employer. The authenticity of the checks could easily have been verified, but bank officials instead acted on their suspicions of attempted wrongdoing by a black man.[4] The president of a white homeowners' association in a gated community in Oklahoma blocked a black deliveryman's truck and called the police. The customer who had taken the delivery eventually came out and "defused" the situation.[5]

At a more overtly dangerous level, it is becoming increasingly common for heavily armed private Americans to confront other Americans who displease them, not only for allegedly breaking the law, but for expressing contrary political or cultural views, as in peaceful demonstrations, and even for daring to act as elected legislators.[6]

The police are the main, but not the only, means of criminal law enforcement in the United States. There is a spectrum of auxiliary private actors and actions in the gray areas of criminal procedure. These are aimed, at least in principle, at helping to prevent crime and apprehend lawbreakers. (Wild cards like Tex McIver have no legitimate place within that range of actors, but nonetheless pop up with distressing frequency.) The spectrum ranges from the merchant who restrains a shoplifter or resists a holdup with lethal force; to the private citizen who decides to intervene in what they perceive to be an ongoing crime; to patrols of private groups, such as neighborhood watches and unofficial border militia; to armed private security guards licensed by state and local authorities. Although the law might endorse the actions of these auxiliary actors in some specific circumstances, much of the legal territory is uncharted or vague. With the rise of formal police agencies, legislators and judges have devoted themselves to writing laws and rendering judgments that empower or regulate police and their actions. Private actors have been left to navigate murky doctrines from ancient common law, getting involved at their own risk. The tensions of race and racial perceptions are unrestrained along most of this spectrum.

CITIZEN'S ARRESTS

The practice of ordinary citizens taking it upon themselves to arrest other ordinary citizens is a particularly dangerous point on the violent margins of race and the American criminal justice system.[7] The citizen's arrest is made outside of an extensive body of law that constrains sworn law enforcement officers—the prior restraint of procedure, such as arrest warrants, and the bounds of doctrine, such as reasonable suspicion and probable cause. The vigilante lurks in the shadow of the citizen's arrest. The lens through which racial differences are viewed is for all practical purposes unrestrained and uncorrected in these private confrontations.

"In theory, [the citizen's arrest] makes sense," University of South Carolina Law Professor Seth W. Stoughton wrote. "Public safety is everyone's responsibility, after all. In practice, however, citizen's arrest doctrines have set the stage for tragic, unnecessary and avoidable confrontations and deaths." Private arrest authority, Stoughton continued, "is too often badly misused by those who believe their higher social status gives them authority over someone they perceive as having lower status. Frequently, this falls along racial lines."[8]

"It can get messy. . . . A citizen who is being arrested is much less inclined to be cooperative if it's not somebody with a blue uniform on," Ronald L. Carlson, a law professor at the University of Georgia, told the *New York Times*.[9] The resistance of the person being arrested escalates the confrontation and invites fatal results.

Different from arrest by sworn law enforcement officers, the idea of the citizen's arrest in Anglo-American law goes back to the Statute of Winchester, enacted in 1285 under King Edward I of England. The statute established more regular criminal procedures in England than existed under the earlier common law because, "robberies, murders, and arsons be more often used than they have been heretofore."[10] Felons often went free under the old arrest procedures because local citizens were reluctant to indict miscreants for various reasons, including favoring their neighbors over strangers who were victims of these neighbors' crimes. Henceforth, the statute declared, citizens would be punished for failing to go after criminals. They were required to raise a "hue and cry," to arouse neighbors to chase and apprehend felons, and had a duty to join the chase.

Before the establishment of regular police forces in the American colonies, citizen's arrests and the hue and cry were common. Today, most states and the District of Columbia either have citizen's arrest laws on the books or allow them to be made under common law doctrine.[11] In many states, including Georgia, a private person is allowed to make a citizen's arrest only when a felony has been committed in their presence.[12] In general, a citizen may use deadly force only when the criminal actually committed a "dangerous felony," including murder, manslaughter, mayhem, kidnapping, arson, burglary of a dwelling, robbery, forcible sodomy, and forcible rape.[13] A private person who uses deadly force acts at their peril—if it turns out that no dangerous felony was committed, the arresting citizen is liable to criminal prosecution and payment of damages in civil law.[14]

Georgia's citizen's arrest law was enacted in 1863 specifically to help masters control their slave population.

> Georgian units in the Confederate army were primarily stationed in Virginia. The Union army was preparing to invade the state from Tennessee. Enslaved Africans were fleeing plantations to join Union forces. . . . With its criminal justice system in a state of collapse, the 1863 code revision empowered white Georgians to replace law enforcement and slave patrols to keep the enslaved Black population under control.[15]

In more recent times, the concept of the citizen's arrest in Georgia has gone from being featured approvingly in a profile of "one man's little stand against crime" in Atlanta's newspaper in 1989, to calls for its repeal (and the repeal of similar laws or abolishment of common law doctrine in other states) in 2020.[16] A cook who intervened and prevented a carjacking at the Midtown Promenade shopping center in 1989 was praised as a "good Samaritan" and won an Atlanta police meritorious service award.[17] But in subsequent years several other attempted citizen's arrests resulted in criminal charges against the would-be law enforcers. In 2000 a man chased down four teenagers he suspected of having earlier broken into his home. He forced them into his Jeep at gunpoint and took them back to his house. He was subsequently charged with the felony of false imprisonment.[18] Two housemates were convicted of misdemeanor battery after they grabbed at gunpoint two boys they claimed were attempting to break into their home. The men tied the boys up, drenched them with a water hose, slapped them, and threatened worse. A jury declined to convict the men of the more serious charge of kidnapping.[19]

When such encounters involve black or brown "suspects" seen through the racial lens of white enforcers, anecdotal experience shows that the chances of a deadly outcome are great.

"EVERY DAY ON THE NEWS"

At about 6:00 p.m. on the evening of May 7, 2019, a twenty-one-year-old white woman named Hannah Payne was sitting in her black Jeep Cherokee near an intersection of two major roadways just south of Atlanta's airport. Payne had a Georgia Weapons Carry License, popularly known as a concealed carry permit.[20] A handgun was in a holster strapped to her side.[21] Hannah's mother Margaret Payne later explained why her daughter was packing a handgun that day.

"Just everyday protection, you know, the society we live in," she explained with unconscious irony. "You hear about it every day on the news. Innocent people getting shot, innocent people are getting broken into. She travels around Atlanta with her job. It's just personal protection and everybody has the right to do that."[22]

As Hannah waited in traffic, she saw a red 2002 Dodge Dakota pickup truck run a red light and strike a tractor-trailer truck. The driver of the pickup was Kenneth Herring, a sixty-two-year-old black man. No one was hurt. The accident caused no serious damage.

A Georgia state corrections officer also witnessed the accident and spoke to Herring, according to the testimony of Detective Keon Hayward. Payne called the 911 emergency line to report the accident. Herring got out of his truck and remained at the accident scene for about twenty minutes. During this period he appeared to be disoriented. He walked around his truck several times and repeatedly asked, "What happened? Who hit me? What's going on?"

There was no evidence that Herring was intoxicated or under the influence of drugs. Based on his experience working in a prison infirmary, the corrections officer thought that Herring was having a "medical emergency," specifically that he was experiencing "diabetic shock," a lay term for hypoglycemia, a condition in which one's blood sugar is lower than normal. Among the symptoms of hypoglycemia are "Confusion, abnormal behavior, or both, such as the inability to complete routine tasks."[23] Studies have shown that "driving performance is affected adversely by moderate hypoglycemia, causing problems such as inappropriate speeding or braking, ignoring road signs and traffic lights and not keeping to traffic lanes."[24] Concerned about Herring's medical condition and his agitation, the corrections officer suggested that Herring sit back down in his pickup truck. Herring got into his truck. He then unexpectedly started driving away from the scene.

Payne was on the phone with the 911 dispatcher, who instructed her to stay at the scene and specifically told her not to follow Herring. Police were on the way, the dispatcher said, and it would be safer for Hannah if she remained at the scene. But Payne insisted on chasing after Herring, staying on the line with the dispatcher, who repeatedly told her to break off the chase.

Payne eventually caught up with Herring, roughly one mile away. At about 6:20 p.m. she blocked his truck with her jeep. Rush hour traffic was heavy, and Herring could neither back up nor go around Payne's Jeep. Payne would later claim that Herring bumped into her Jeep with his truck. But police said that at no point during the entire incident did the two vehicles come into contact. According to four witnesses, Payne got out of her Jeep and walked back to Herring's truck. At some point, she drew her gun from its holster. Because she was still on the line with the dispatcher, what Hannah Payne said to Kenneth Herring was recorded, as well as being heard by some of the witnesses.

"Get out of the car, get out of the fucking car!" Payne is reported to have shouted at Herring. "Get out of the fucking car." Some witnesses claimed that Payne also said, "I'm going to shoot you."

Witnesses saw her striking Herring through his open window, hitting him with her left hand while holding the handgun in her right hand. Herring did not appear to be fighting back, witnesses said. He was rather holding his arms up, trying to deflect Payne's blows. At some point, Payne's gun went off. The bullet struck Herring mid-body, inflicting a fatal wound. A witness saw Payne go back to her Jeep and change her clothes. Hannah told the dispatcher that Herring had shot himself with her gun. Law enforcement authorities believe that, on the contrary, it was she who shot Herring.

Whatever the truth of those fateful seconds when the gun went off and killed him, Kenneth Herring became one of the "innocent people getting shot" that Margaret Payne cited to justify her daughter's driving around Atlanta in her Jeep Cherokee with a handgun strapped to her side. But Hannah Payne's lawyer urged the court at a preliminary hearing to see the bright side of things. Hannah was an "All-American girl" who played in her high school band, he argued. "She's a young individual that got on the phone with 911 and thought she was helping out," he added. "At her age, she learned a very valuable lesson."[25] The nature and extent of any "lesson" that she learned is not clear.

Hannah Payne was subsequently indicted on five felony counts, including felony murder, malice murder, aggravated assault, false imprisonment, and possession of a firearm during a felony. Her trial has been postponed several times, and the case is pending at this writing. Hannah's defense lawyer called the fatal shooting an act of self-defense in the course of a citizen's arrest gone bad. Clayton County's district attorney, Tracy Graham Lawson, acidly dismissed Payne's claim of self-defense. "You cannot claim self-defense and use deadly force unless you're not the initial aggressor—she is [the aggressor]," Lawson said. Moreover, she pointed out, Georgia law would allow a "citizen's arrest" only if the citizen witnesses a felony. But the vehicle accident was merely a misdemeanor traffic offense. "I guess she thinks she's the police or wants to be a police officer . . . she's blocked him in and he . . . [is unarmed], and then she shoots him."[26]

The notion of an armed white woman chasing down and then shooting to death an unarmed black man old enough to be her father over a fender-bender shocked many. Questions of race and profiling by Hannah were naturally raised. Herring's widow, Christine Herring, compared his death to the fatal shooting of teenager Trayvon Martin in Florida.

In Atlanta a "robocall" from a white supremacist group popped up in support of Hannah Payne. It was laced with racial hatred. "Negroes aren't American," the message spewed. "They aren't really fully human. It's time to send them all to Africa. She's been cast as the criminal when in fact it was the Negro."[27]

Payne's parents and friends—many of whom were people of color, including her boyfriend—rejected the robocall's support and adamantly insisted that race could not have entered into Hannah's actions.

"She's the sweetest, most caring [person]," her mother said. "Hannah does not see color. She sees right, she sees wrong. That's who she is."[28]

But research demonstrates that even people who would object to being labeled as "racist" or "discriminating" may harbor *unconscious* racism that affects their actions in a variety of ways in society generally and specifically in the criminal justice system. According to Dr. David Williams, professor of African and African American Studies at Harvard University, "the research shows that when people hold a negative stereotype about a group and meet someone from that group, they often treat that person differently and honestly don't even realize it."[29]

Much of the research to which Dr. Williams referred is based on Implicit Association Tests (IAT). In these laboratory, computerized tests, subjects are first briefly shown an "attitude object" (for example, a white or black person) and then required to select as quickly as possible a "dimension" choice, either evaluative (such as "good" or "bad") or attributive (such as "guilty" or "not guilty"). The time between the two steps is recorded and analyzed. The time dimension helps measure the person's subconscious perceptions. The less time there is for deliberate reflection and correction of the subject's initial connection between the attitude objects and dimension choices, the more likely it is that the subjects' unconscious attitudes will be demonstrated.[30]

There are many different IAT procedures, testing areas other than race, such as gender perceptions. The authors of a 2010 paper in the *Ohio State Journal of Criminal Law* reported that the results of IATs on race consistently show that white Americans express a strong white preference on the IAT. An early study of death penalty defense lawyers came up with the surprising result that these special defense attorneys, whom one would naturally think would be free of bias, "harbored strong implicit bias against African Americans." Another study of judges conducted at a judicial conference found that the participants "displayed an implicit preference for White over Black. That is, participants were faster to group together photos of White faces with Good words compared to Black faces with Good words."[31]

If judges, death penalty defense lawyers, and ordinary people have unwitting racial biases, it's possible that an angry, adrenalin-pumped, and armed Hannah Payne was indeed acting on unconscious racial bias when she confronted Kenneth Herring—whether she knew it or not. And if people who truly believe that they have no racial bias and would be offended to be labeled as racist can nevertheless act on unconscious perceptions of race and racial attributes, what might be expected of someone with overtly expressed racial biases?

That question was answered by another fatal white-on-black shooting in the course of an attempted citizen's arrest in Georgia. The alleged murder was one of several killings of black men that ignited a revolutionary confrontation in the spring of 2020.

WHITE RICE, BLACK LABOR, RED BLOOD

In his argument for abolishing citizen's arrests for private persons, law professor Ira P. Robbins explained that "it is exceedingly difficult for private individuals to understand the doctrine's subtleties and to effectuate arrests lawfully, safely, and without fear of reprisal. Implementation is ripe for abuse."[32] But even without arrest power, he pointed out, citizens can still play a useful role in law enforcement. "In the age of smartphones and other hi-tech devices, private citizens can easily gather photographic and video evidence of a crime without subjecting themselves or the suspect to the risks associated with a citizen's arrest."[33]

In the spring of 2020, there was a cascade of just such citizen-gathered video evidence of multiple cases of crimes—criminal violence by sworn law enforcement officers against persons of color. The videos set off a paroxysm of protests, primarily under the Black Lives Matter banner, against police brutality. Videos taken on cellphones by witnesses and subjects of police actions, or retrieved from surveillance cameras, repeatedly disproved claims of law enforcement officers and their supervisors about violent conduct, ranging from the use of chemical sprays to beatings and fatal chokeholds and shootings.[34] Activists argue that these cases are not unusual or random incidents, but the tip of an iceberg of structural and historical race-based violence in the American law enforcement system.

The killing of Ahmaud Arbery in Satilla Shores, a suburb of Brunswick, Georgia, by three private citizens attempting a citizen's arrest was prominent among these incidents. The story of Arbery's murder included a tragic irony—the video was recorded by one of the three vigilantes. The damning evidence in that video led to the arrest and indictment of all three white participants for the crime of murder. Seeing the images of Ahmaud Arbery's final moments was compared by many to watching a lynching.

Facts dragged out of the reluctant officials who first dealt with the case exposed ugly, systemic factors linked to a long history of racial bias and unchecked police violence. These facts implicated the local police in condoning—perhaps even encouraging—armed violence by private citizens, exposed the complicity of local prosecutors in helping police cover up the vigilantes' criminal conduct by shutting down the case, and revealed several prosecutors' violations of Georgia conflict of interest laws. It showed a "good old boy" network with tendrils that wound all the way back to Atlanta and wrapped around voter suppression and Tex McIver.

The port city of Brunswick lies on Georgia's southeastern coast, just about midway between Savannah and Jacksonville, Florida. Brunswick won praise during the civil rights revolution of the 1960s as a "model Southern city," a less prominent version of Atlanta, "the city too busy to hate." In both cases, local leaders were said to have taken a cooperative path to the attempted integration of the races that convulsed other cities all over America. And in both cases, another generation has raised questions about the depth and durability of whatever change might be credited to the leaders of that era.[35]

Brunswick is the county seat of Glynn County and is its only municipality. Created in 1777, Glynn County is one of Georgia's original eight counties. Like much of Georgia, it was carved out of land taken from Creek Indians. The city was named in honor of England's King George III, who was of the royal House of Brunswick.[36] The U.S. Census Bureau most recently estimated that about eighty-five thousand people live in Glynn County, of whom 69 percent are white and 27 percent black.[37] The county is home to the Federal Law Enforcement Training Centers, where officers from 105 U.S. government agencies are sent to train. It is located northwest of Brunswick.[38]

Satilla Shores is a tiny community just south of the city. There are but five short streets in Satilla Shores. A mostly white suburb, it curls along a bend in the Little Satilla River, part of a network of waterways and marshes in the Georgia Lowcountry.

A bit further to the south, the larger Satilla River runs to the coast. The Satilla River was one of four along which white slave owners operated large and profitable rice plantations from the earliest days of slavery in Georgia. There was, the *New Georgia Encyclopedia* observes, "a very close connection—indeed, a near identity—between black labor and white rice in Georgia."[39] About a half-hour's drive north up Interstate 95 is one of Glynn County's tourist attractions, the Hofwyl-Broadfield Plantation State Historic Site. According to the Georgia Department of Natural Resources, "This beautiful plantation represents the history and culture of Georgia's rice coast. . . . The plantation owners were part of the genteel low-country society that developed during the antebellum period."[40]

The benefits of Southern gentility did not extend to the black slaves upon whose labor that pleasant society was built. An average of forty-eight slaves worked on the typical rice plantation. That work required them to do long days' work bent over with hoes; use primitive, labor-intensive threshing and reaping methods; and constantly work exposed to unhealthy marsh country elements.[41] "The rice too is whitening . . . but there is no living near it with the putrid water that must lie on it, and the labour required for it is only fit for slaves, and I think the hardest work I have seen them engaged in," a Scottish "lady of quality" wrote in her late-eighteenth-century journal documenting her travels in the Caribbean and American South.[42] "For much of the day, slaves worked in knee-deep water. This . . . environment fostered illnesses, such as dysentery and malaria, that ravaged slaves' health and shortened their lives," scholar Watson W. Jennison wrote in his book about the history of slavery in Georgia. "The work regime for slaves on rice plantations in Georgia was strenuous, periodically exhausting, and year-around."[43]

Emancipation did not much improve the lives of former slaves in Georgia rice country. The collapse of rice plantations after the slaves were freed was "profoundly painful and dislocating to Lowcountry blacks, both economically and socially."[44]

Satilla Shores was described by the *New York Times* as "a mixed bag of blue- and white-collar retirees, young working-class families, lifelong residents and transplants from northern states."[45] The community is almost exclusively white. U.S. Highway 17 was an historic racial dividing line, a barrier between white Satilla Shores on one side and the black community known as Fancy Bluff on the other. Although a handful of people of color have in recent years moved into Satilla Shores, it can hardly be described as welcoming. Confederate flags fly from the homes of some of the white householders. A resident of mixed Puerto Rican and Dominican descent told the *New York Times* that when he waves to his neighbors from his yard, "A lot of people don't even wave back to us."[46]

Law enforcement is handled by the Glynn County Police Department. The county is one of only about a dozen counties (out of 159) in Georgia in which a county police department—rather than a county sheriff's office—provides primary law enforcement in unincorporated areas and under agreements with some municipalities. Such county police departments are seen as more responsive to the local politicians who appoint them. The Glynn county sheriff is responsible for running the jails and providing courtroom security.

Georgia's judiciary has a complex structure. Each of the state's 159 counties—second only to Texas in number—has a Superior Court in which felonies are tried. The counties are divided into forty-nine judicial circuits. The judicial circuits include varying numbers of counties, some only one county. The Brunswick Judicial Circuit includes Glynn and four other counties. Criminal prosecutions in each judicial circuit are overseen by a district attorney, an elected office with a four-year term. As is the case virtually everywhere in the American criminal justice system, Georgia's district attorneys have wide discretion in deciding whether and which crimes to prosecute, and wield powerful influence in their recommendations for sentencing.[47] Jackie Johnson, a graduate of the University of Georgia law school and a career prosecutor, has been district attorney of the Brunswick Judicial Circuit since 2010.[48]

Both the Glynn County Police Department and District Attorney Johnson were under fire for perceived problems even before the Arbery murder became widely known. But the fallout from that shooting intensified pressure to abolish the county police department and to fire Johnson.[49]

In February 2020, less than a week after Ahmaud Arbery was shot to death—and while the facts of his homicide were still being covered up—Glynn County Police Chief John Powell and three active or former police officers were indicted on charges stemming from an internal investigation into misconduct by police officers working on a drug task force. That investigation originally looked into allegations that one of the officers was having sexual relations with an informant, using drugs himself, and supplying them to informants. The resulting indictment charged the defendants with a range of crimes including violation of oath, attempt to commit a felony, influencing a witness, perjury, and making false statements to the Georgia Bureau of Investigation (GBI).[50]

The drug task force investigation exposed a culture of covering up corruption at the highest levels in the Glynn County Police Department. Immoral misconduct is one thing. Shooting an unarmed civilian to death is another. And the fatal shooting of a young white woman by two white Glynn county police officers in 2010 still festers a decade later as an example of unchecked police brutality. Prosecutor Johnson also has been under fire for her alleged help in shielding the officers involved from accountability for their actions.

The shooting occurred after the slow speed police chase of thirty-five-year-old Caroline Small, a mother of two. The unarmed woman's putative offense was reckless driving. So, in essence, this was a lengthy, slow motion traffic stop. The chase ended when Small's Buick Century spun out and was hemmed in on all sides by two police cars, a ditch, and a utility pole. A thorough investigation of the case by the *Atlanta Journal-Constitution* in 2015, based on reports and photographs of the incident as well as independent interviews, established conclusively that there was no place left for Small to go. More specifically, the space between the police cars hemming her in was too small for her car to have gotten out of the box she was in, even though she did feebly try. But two police officers—Sergeant Robert C. Sasser and Officer Michael T. Simpson—nevertheless claimed that they felt threatened by her apparent attempt to move the car. The newspaper's report described in detail what happened to Caroline Small:

> Officer Sasser's dash cam video shows Small backing up into the utility pole, then pulling forward and bumping into his county vehicle. At roughly the same time, Georgia State Patrol Trooper Jonathan Malone is seen running behind Small's vehicle in an effort to extract her from the driver's side, but he retreats when he sees Glynn County officers with their guns pointed at the Buick.
>
> "Let me get out there and get her out," Malone calls out to the other officers, according to the GBI audio transcripts.
>
> "Hold on, hold on," one unknown officer responds.
>
> "If she moves the car, I'm going to shoot her," Simpson says.

Moments later gunfire erupts and Small is hit by police bullets.

After the shooting, Sasser and Simpson are heard on video discussing the shoot.

"Where did you hit her?" Simpson asks, according to a GBI transcript.

"I hit her right in the face," Sasser says.

"I watched the bridge of her nose. . . . I pulled the trigger and I watched it hit her at the same time I think I fired," Simpson says.[51]

The brutality of the shooting and the two shooters' callous comments shocked other law enforcement officers. "This is the worst one I've ever investigated," a retired GBI agent who supervised the 2010 criminal investigation into the officers' actions told the newspaper. "I don't think it's a good shoot. I don't think it's justified."[52]

A grand jury declined to indict the officers. A federal judge threw out a civil lawsuit, ruling that although the shooting was "unnecessary," it did not violate Small's constitutional rights. That lawsuit was one of at least seventeen brought against the department over the last decade.[53]

The newspaper's report on its own investigation into the shooting concluded that

> Glynn County police officers interfered with the GBI's investigation from the start, seeking to protect the officers, the department tampered with the crime scene and created misleading evidence that was shown to the grand jury, and the local district attorney [Johnson] shared the state's evidence with the officers nearly two months before the grand jury convened and cut an unusual deal with them just before it met.[54]

In June 2018 one of the two officers involved, Sasser, shot and killed his estranged wife and her boyfriend, then committed suicide. Simpson, the other officer, had earlier died of cancer.[55] Some activists argued that had Sasser been properly investigated and disciplined for the 2010 shooting of Caroline Small, the ultimate trail of violence he left would have been avoided. The *Atlanta Journal-Constitution* detailed the alleged missteps of the Brunswick prosecutor's office in a 2020 investigatory story about a senior assistant district attorney who the paper charged "has a dark legacy of problem cases over the years—cases in which judges later found he cheated to win."[56]

Accountability, or its lack, have long-term consequences.

BLACK HUE, WHITE CRY

When Ahmaud Arbery was shot to death on February 23, 2020, the investigation of his death fell into the hands of the tainted Glynn County Police Department and the tarnished district attorney of the Brunswick Judicial District.[57] The investigation would be marked by an elaborate series of moves by police and several prosecutors intended to hush up the shooting and exonerate the three vigilantes involved.

On Sunday, February 23, 2020, Ahmaud Arbery dressed in his jogging outfit and headed out for a run. Eight years earlier, he had been a star linebacker on the Brunswick High School football team, dreaming of a career in the National Football League. But his five feet, ten inches stature was too small for the pros. After his high school graduation, Arbery wandered in and out of several educational and employment opportunities, but he seemed never to find a consistent stride. He also had a few brushes with the law. Defenders of his killers would later magnify these scrapes as evidence of Arbery's contributory badness, as if two or three misdemeanors justified a vigilante death penalty. Most recently, Ahmaud had been working at his father's lawn care business and, according to his family and friends, devoting himself to his fitness. A former employer and mentor saw Arbery a few days before he was shot to death. "He said he was getting into shape, and was in a good place," the friend was reported as saying. "I told him he was looking good, real good."[58]

At about 1:00 p.m., Arbery crossed U.S. Highway 17 and entered the Satilla Shores neighborhood. At least some of the white residents of the community were concerned about what they perceived to be a recent increase in crime in the neighborhood. Among them were Gregory McMichael, aged sixty-four, his son Travis McMichael, aged thirty-four, and William "Roddie" Bryan, aged fifty.

GBI investigators would later find evidence that among these three men, at least Travis McMichael had a record of using racial slurs. GBI Special Agent Richard Dial testified in a preliminary hearing that the investigation found multiple posts using the N word by Travis on social media. The posts were discovered on Travis's cellphone and on social media sites—both before and after Arbery's death.[59] As an example, Dial stated that in January 2020 someone sent Travis a picture or video on Instagram. "He made some comment that it would only be better if they had 'blown the f—ing n—er's head off,'" Dial said. He also stated that when Travis was in the U.S. Coast Guard, "he made the statement that he loved his job because he's out on a boat and there aren't any n-words anywhere."[60]

Some observers reported that the residents of Satilla Shores were "on edge" because of a recent rash of crime. "We've been having a lot of burglaries and break-ins around here lately," Travis McMichael told a 911 operator earlier in the month, when he called in to report a suspicious person in the neighborhood. In fact, however, police had not filed any burglary reports for some months, although between August 2019 and February 2020 there had been "87 calls from Satilla Shore reporting various activity, including suspicious behavior, trespassing and thefts."[61] In fact, Glynn County Police told CNN, the only record of a recent burglary in Satilla Shores was on January 1, 2020, when Travis McMichael reported to police that a Smith & Wesson 9mm pistol had been stolen from his unlocked truck.[62]

Two factors that research demonstrates affect perceptions about crime may have contributed to an exaggerated view of Satilla Shore's supposed crime wave. One factor is that "[although] crime is commonly perceived in geographic terms, it is also perceived in social terms. That is, there appear to be widely accepted images of dangerous persons, with the result that some persons in the population are feared more than others."[63] It is no surprise that the persons feared most are young males and in particular young males of color. The findings "suggest that blacks (or, most probably, young black males) are frequently typified as criminals or potential criminals and, as a consequence, are feared more than others."[64]

Tex McIver demonstrated his acceptance of "widely accepted images of dangerous persons" of color when he asked for his revolver the night he killed his wife. Ahmaud Arbery regularly jogging through a predominantly white neighborhood may have likewise triggered inflated perceptions of criminal danger, especially in the mind of someone like Travis McMichael, who thinks and acts in racist terms.

In addition to the youth and race factor, polling data over a long period of time shows that "Americans' perceptions of crime are often at odds with the data." Respondents to polls are "usually more likely to say crime is up than down, regardless of what official statistics show."[65] Presidents Richard Nixon, George H. W. Bush, Donald Trump, and other politicians have notoriously exploited these distorted perceptions of crime for political gain, a means of inciting white racial fears under the false flag of "law and order."[66]

One important thing is clear. Whether or not Satilla Shores was experiencing an increase in petty crimes like "suspicious behavior" and "trespassing," there is no evidence of a violent crime wave, or for that matter any violent crime—no assaults, no homicides, no rapes—in the neighborhood during the period residents were supposedly concerned about increasing crime. What Satilla Shore's vigilantes seemed to be most concerned about was a series of harmless trespasses into a house that had been under construction for some time. Incursions by a number of people of varying ages onto the property triggered the posse in the McMichaels, some of their neighbors, and the Glynn County Police Department.

Ahmaud Arbery was one of the triggers.

The construction site in question was not far from the McMichaels' residence and only a block away from where Arbery was shot. The property's owner, Larry English, did not live in Satilla Shores and had installed a motion-activated security camera. The camera picked up people going into the site and sent a text and video to English when that happened. When English received alerts, he often called the police, who went to check on the property. No one was ever caught. Nothing was ever taken from the site. It hadn't been vandalized.[67]

Nevertheless, the repeated trespasses were burrs under the saddles of the McMichaels and the county police department. Gregory McMichael had retired in 2019 as an investigator from the Brunswick district attorney's office. Prior to that, he had been an officer in the Glynn County Police Department. He apparently, and quite naturally, kept up his law enforcement ties. In December 2019, Glynn County police officer Robert Rash texted property owner English to tell him that Gregory McMichael lived nearby and was willing to help with the trespass problem.

"Greg is retired Law Enforcement and also a Retired Investigator from the DA's office," Rash texted English, adding McMichael's phone number. "He said please call him day or night when you get action on your camera."[68] English ignored the offer and says he later forgot it. He never called McMichael, nor did he have any other contact with him.

Officer Rash's text came to light only months later, when the layers of evident police misconduct began to be peeled back under public scrutiny. The unusual text raised questions about the propriety of Officer Rash's offer. In essence, it informally deputized Gregory McMichael. Moreover,

the text raised an apparent conflict of interest when county police were
called to investigate the McMichaels and their role in Arbery's homicide.

Law enforcement officials scathed the Glynn County police action.
One of those who raised such questions was Louis M. Dekmar, chief of
police of the city of LaGrange, Georgia. Dekmar served terms as president of the Georgia Association of Chiefs of Police and of the International Association of Chiefs of Police. "I'm not aware of any accepted
policy for referring someone that requires a police response to delegate
that response to a former law enforcement officer who happens to live in
the neighborhood," Dekmar told the *Atlanta Journal-Constitution* newspaper. "If it's not a real conflict, it's certainly a significant perception of
one."[69] Charlie Bailey, a former senior assistant district attorney in Fulton
County, ripped the "highly irregular" police offer. "I've never heard, in
my time as a prosecutor, of police enlisting a civilian to do something that
the police are sworn to do," he said. "You're not supposed to have civilians acting as police."[70]

Another critic was S. Lee Merritt, a lawyer for the Arbery family. "We
believe this communication deputized a group of untrained men in the
Satilla Shores community to hunt down suspected trespassers, causing the
events of February 23, 2020," he said.[71] "If anybody was going to stop
this from happening it was law enforcement. Instead, they encouraged
it."[72]

When Ahmaud Arbery jogged by the construction on the last day of
his life, he took a short break and went inside the property. From the
evidence of the surveillance video it is clear that he took nothing. It is
also possible that he may have gone onto the site to get water from a tap.
At most, he had committed nothing more serious than a misdemeanor
trespass. GBI Investigator Dial testified that for Arbery to be charged
with the felony of burglary, it would have to be shown that he entered
"with the intention of committing a felony or a theft. Neither fact could I
establish in my investigation."[73]

When Ahmaud left, he was seen by a resident. A hue and cry by
cellphone was raised. The report that county police filed immediately
after the incident described the first moments of the three vigilantes'
mobilization:

> McMichael stated there have been several Break-ins in the neighbor-
> hood and further the suspect was caught on surveillance video. McMi-

chael states that he was in his front yard and saw the suspect from the
break-ins "hauling ass" down Satilla Drive . . . McMichael stated he
then ran inside his house and called to Travis (McMichael) and said
"Travis the guy is running down the street lets go." McMichael stated
he went to his bedroom and grabbed his .357 Magnum and Travis
grabbed his shotgun because they "didn't know if the male was armed
or not."[74]

The McMichaels jumped into their pickup truck. Travis was driving
and Gregory was standing in the truck bed. The .357 Magnum revolver
that Gregory brandished had been issued to him when he was a Glynn
County police officer.[75]

"They decided he was somewhere he shouldn't be and they decided to
catch him," agent Dial testified. As noted previously, there had been no
reported "break-ins" in Satilla Shores, only a handful of misdemeanor
offenses. The McMichaels on that day and at that moment had not witnessed a felony, the threshold for justifying a citizen's arrest under Georgia law.

What was left was Ahmaud Arbery, a black man, simply being "somewhere he shouldn't be," a circumstance that has not been *legal* justification for armed interference with a black man since the days of slave
patrols and Jim Crow terror against "vagrants." W.E.B. Du Bois described that hateful circumstance in his 1903 book, *The Souls of Black
Folk*:

> A black stranger in Baker County, Georgia, for instance, is liable to be
> stopped anywhere on the public highway and made to state his busi-
> ness to the satisfaction of any white interrogator. If he fails to give a
> suitable answer, or seems too independent or "sassy," he may be ar-
> rested or summarily driven away.[76]

Seeing Arbery's pursuit by his white interrogators, Roddie Bryan got
into his truck and joined in. At some point he began recording the chase,
apparently with a dash camera. Prosecutors have stated that they have
access to a video made by Bryan that is longer than the one the public has
seen. Special Agent Dial testified that Bryan repeatedly blocked Arbery,
preventing him from leaving the neighborhood.[77] Originally, Arbery was
running in front of and away from the McMichael's pickup truck. Bryan
was behind the truck. But when Arbery doubled back and ran past the

truck in the other direction, he came between Bryan and the McMichaels. Bryan attempted to box Arbery in. His truck struck Arbery hard enough to leave a dent and cotton fibers from the young man's clothing stuck to his car.[78]

Arbery doubled back again, running away from Bryan and toward the McMichael's truck. It is at this point, about four minutes into the hunt, that the video recorded by Bryan documents what happened. A *New York Times* minute-by-minute reconstruction of the events—based on Bryan's tape, a home surveillance video, and the record of phone calls—documents Ahmaud Arbery's final seconds of life:

> Arbery doesn't know where to run. He veers right, then left and then darts around the right side of the [McMichael's] vehicle. Arbery comes around the front of the truck. We see his white T-shirt through the windshield and here is Travis now leaning toward him. This is the instant the first shot is fired. Arbery is hit in the chest, his right lung, ribs, and sternum are injured. The two men wrestle over the gun. Gregory shouts: "Travis!" Arbery punches Travis. In the back of the truck, Gregory drops the cellphone. A second blast goes off out of frame. But we see the shotgun smoke here. Arbery is heavily bleeding. He throws another punch. Travis fires a final shot, which hits Arbery in his left upper chest.[79]

The coroner ruled that Arbery died at 1:46 p.m.

Ahmaud Arbery was "chased, hunted down and ultimately executed," Jesse Evans, the case's ultimate lead prosecutor, charged in a hearing.[80] And according to Roddie Bryan, racial animus was at the heart of Arbery's death. He told investigators that after Travis McMichael shot Arbery to death, he stood over the young man's body and shouted, "F—ing n—!"[81]

A GLYNN COUNTY HOEDOWN

Two and a half months—seventy-four days—were to pass before the McMichaels were arrested and another two weeks after that before Bryan was arrested. In the meantime the facts of Ahmaud Arbery's death were suppressed, and a fantastic story was invented to explain his death, all amounting to a rolling cover-up that involved several prosecutors and the police.

The Glynn County hoedown began the moment Glynn County police officer Jake Brandeberry wrote up his report of the incident.

> McMichael stated they saw the unidentified male and shouted "stop, stop, we want to talk to you." McMichael stated they pulled up beside the male and shouted stop again at which time Travis exited the truck with the shotgun. McMichael stated the unidentified male began to violently attack Travis and the two men then started fighting over the shotgun at which point Travis fired a shot and then a second later there was a second shot. Michael stated the male fell face down on the pavement with his hand under his body. McMichael stated he rolled the man over to see if the male had a weapon. [82]

This was the birth of a notion, a contrived explanation shifting the entire blame for Ahmaud Arbery's death to himself. Virtuous citizens—not incidentally armed with a shotgun and a .357 Magnum police-issued revolver—chased down and cornered an unarmed black man who (quite improbably) then violently attacked Travis, the man wielding the shotgun, an extraordinarily dangerous weapon at close range. Self-defense mandated that Travis shoot to protect himself from the unarmed but (stereotypically) violent black man. The audacity of this bottom-of-the-deck card deal boggles the impartial mind. And yet, improbable as this scenario seems, it was accepted without apparent question by the minions of the Glynn County Police Department. They sent the McMichaels and Bryan on their way.

Later that day, a police investigator called Arbery's mother, Wanda Cooper Jones, and told her that her son had been involved in a burglary and was confronted by the homeowner. The two fought over the homeowner's gun, multiple shots were fired, and Ahmaud was killed. [83] A commentator later captured the racial context that cried out from Arbery's bloodied body:

> It's a useful mental exercise to imagine two black men, one armed with a .357 magnum, the other with a warm shotgun, having this conversation with a white police officer over the dead body of an unarmed white man. The elder black man explains that, unfortunately, the white man died from a gunshot wound. But, he notes, the white

man had been seen on a surveillance video, and there had recently been some break-ins in the neighborhood. [84]

The facts of the case were kept from the Arbery family and the general public for over two months. It was if Ahmaud Arbery's violent death never occurred. Meanwhile, a carousel of prosecutors cycled through the case, each handing it off within what Ahmaud's mother later called "the good ole boy network."[85]

Jackie Johnson, the Brunswick Judicial Circuit district attorney—who was criticized for her handling of the aftermath of the Christine Small homicide—reportedly decided on the day of Arbery's death that her office had a conflict of interest because Gregory McMichael had been an investigator in the office. She asked George E. Barnhill, district attorney for Waycross Judicial Circuit, to take over the case, even though, as it later developed, he too had an apparent conflict of interest. In the face of its known conflict, her office nevertheless discussed the shooting with Glynn County Police by phone several times that day. Moreover, Johnson waited three days until she notified Georgia State Attorney General Chris Carr's office of the conflict and suggested Prosecutor Barnhill—after he had already made his decision not to prosecute. This was the first of several missteps, including violations of Georgia procedural law, that prompted state and federal investigations of the two prosecutors' actions in the Arbery case. [86]

According to independent critics, Johnson should have notified Carr's office immediately, without enlisting Barnhill to take over the case. "Once you have a conflict, the prosecutor's office is done—no indictments, no accusations, no bonds and no finding a substitute prosecutor," according to a PowerPoint presentation of training offered by Carr's office and by the Prosecuting Attorneys' Council of Georgia. Recommending a replacement was not uncommon, a spokesperson for Attorney General Carr's office said. "What would be uncommon is if a prosecutor who has a conflict makes the unilateral decision to bring in another prosecutor on his or her own or asks or allows another prosecutor to take actions that would be inappropriate given their own conflict," she said. [87]

Barnhill, district attorney for Georgia's Waycross Judicial Circuit, also recused himself after Arbery's mother found out that Barnhill's son, an assistant prosecutor, used to work with Gregory McMichael in the Brunswick District Attorney's Office. [88] Barnhill's son had not only worked with McMichael for several years, but had been directly involved in one of Ahmaud Arbery's scrapes with the law.

But Barnhill was dug in. After his recusal, he wrote a tendentious, three-page letter to the Glynn County chief of police, going over the case and justifying his prior conclusion that the evidence did not support prosecution.

"We do not see grounds for an arrest of any of the three parties," Barnhill wrote. "It appears Travis McMichael, Greg McMichael, and Bryan William [sic] were following, in 'hot pursuit,' a burglary suspect with solid first hand probable cause, in their neighborhood, and asking/telling him to stop. It appears their intent was to stop and hold this criminal suspect until law enforcement arrived. Under Georgia Law this is perfectly legal." The prosecutor also recycled the theory that Travis McMichael was acting in self-defense, after Ahmaud supposedly grabbed Travis's shotgun. "A brief skirmish ensues in which it appears Arbery strikes McMichael and appears to grab the shotgun and pull it from McMichael. . . . Just as importantly, while we know McMichael had his finger on the trigger, we do not know who caused the firings."[89]

Barnhill's "gratuitous and detailed opinion" won him a stinging rebuke from the National District Attorneys Association, which noted that his involvement with the case should have ended as soon as he recused himself.

> These actions can have an intended or unintended ability to influence potential grand jurors or trial jurors, while also making the new special prosecutor's job to objectively seek the truth significantly more difficult. No prosecutor should inject his or her opinion into a pending case to the point where she or he becomes a potential witness and risks compromising the just outcome of a case.[90]

The organization's president, Duffie Stone, told the *Atlanta Journal-Constitution* that Barnhill's letter crossed a clear line that prosecutors everywhere know is wrong. "It's not how you do it," said Stone. "It's assumed that when you conflict yourself out of a case you have to stop at that point. You can't seek to influence it. This is highly unusual."[91]

It's not as if Barnhill was a stranger to vigorous prosecutions. His office spent years hounding a black official on trumped-up charges of "voter fraud." The case dates to 2012, when Olivia Pearson showed a first-time voter how to operate a voting machine. There was no evidence that Pearson attempted to influence the voter's ballot. The incident was referred to the Georgia State Election Board—on which Tex McIver then served. The board decided that state law "might have" been violated. Barnhill's office took the bit in its teeth and secured Pearson's indictment on charges of voter fraud. It doggedly pursued her through two trials, the first of which ended in a hung jury when a lone black juror held out against conviction. Six years after the original event, it took another jury only twenty minutes to find Pearson not guilty. The case was widely seen as a blatant attempt at suppressing the black vote.[92]

Everything changed in the Ahmaud Arbery case on May 5, 2020, when Roddie Bryan's dash cam video was leaked to social media and "went viral." The entire world could at last see with its own eyes the hunt and kill operation. The incident was one of the first to inspire large demonstrations in the angry spring of 2020. The GBI took over the investigation the next day. Two days later, on May 7, the McMichaels were arrested and charged with murder and aggravated assault. Two weeks later, Bryan was also charged.

The case finally landed in the office of the Cobb County district attorney, Joyette M. Holmes. On June 24, 2020, the three men each were indicted on nine counts: malice murder, four counts of felony murder, two counts of aggravated assault, false imprisonment, and criminal attempt to commit false imprisonment.[93]

As in many similar cases, defenders of the killers have attempted to smear the victim with hints of some kind of contributory badness, implying that Ahmaud Arbery may have got what was coming to him. Russell Moore, president of the Southern Baptist Convention's public-policy arm, the Ethics & Religious Liberty Commission, shredded that line of argument in a thundering online essay:

> [T]he arguments, already bandied about on social media, that "Arbery wasn't a choirboy" are revolting. We have heard such before with Trayvon Martin and in almost every case since. For all I know, Arbery was a choirboy. But even if he were the complete opposite (let's suppose just for the sake of argument), that is no grounds to be chased down and shot by private citizens. There is no, under any Christian vision of justice, situation in which the mob murder of a person can be morally right.

STRANGE JUSTICE

In the end, Gregory and Travis McMichael and Roddie Bryan were the beneficiaries of what they had brutally denied Ahmaud Arbery—due process under law, a regular procedure of professional investigation, presentation of the facts to a grand jury, indictment, the chance for a jury trial, and an appeals process.

Like the tens of dozens of other black men shot dead on suspicions raised by the twice-ground lens of race, Ahmaud Arbery got an untimely death and a funeral.

CONCLUSION

A great deal more could be written about the death of Diane McIver and the legal, moral, and psychological trials of Tex McIver. A jury of Tex's peers convicted him of deliberately murdering his wife, and he is at this writing spending the remainder of his life in a Georgia prison. How and why the jury was persuaded is in itself an engaging tale of legal combat waged by titans of the law on both sides of the case.

But enough.

The point of this book has not been the telling of the true crime saga of Diane McIver's murder. It has been rather been to show in a brief but hopefully illuminating way how the past of America's slavery, and the slave master's fear of those held in bondage, has been the prologue of the intense national agony we are enduring today. The lens of race fashioned over centuries warps much of our vision today with violent results. Tex's fearful brandishing of his gun is but one example with a fatal end.

Can we change? There is room for both pessimism and optimism at this pivotal moment in our history.

Pessimism can be justified by the nation's continuing inability to find a common civil language with which to examine our past and its effects, and to set about correcting our errors and expunging our evils to make America the noble country its founding documents declare it to be. Optimism is inspired by the growing recognition—particularly but not exclusively among young people, persons of color, and members of ethnicities other than white northern European—that America's ideals are indeed a light unto the world, and that we can and must reform ourselves to live up to those ideals. That is not an easy task, nor is it one to be accomplished quickly. Generational change is a powerful force for change. But fear, hate, political expediency, and most of all the battle lines of a polarized nation stand in the way.

Events that occurred after this manuscript was completed underscored the ambiguous nature of change in the United States. Kamala Harris's political revival catapulted her into the highest national office ever held by a woman—vice president of the United States. But two weeks before her inauguration, a violent attack upon the nation's capital vividly illustrated the depth and power of the country's political and cultural divisions.

America's fate before the bar of history is yet to be determined. The jury is still out.

NOTES

1. THE LENS OF RACIAL PERCEPTION

1. Matt Wray, *Not Quite White: White Trash and the Boundaries of Whiteness* (Durham, NC: Duke University Press, 2006), 140.

2. See, for example, R. J. Rummel's survey of what he concludes were the 169,198,000 victims of "democide" (genocide and government mass murder) in the twentieth century alone. Most of these murders can be linked to the brutal treatment of social categories of "others" out of favor with those wielding absolute power through the state. R. J. Rummel, *Death by Government* (New Brunswick, NJ: Transaction Publishers, 1994).

3. Wray, *Not Quite White*, 141.

4. William Julius Wilson, *More than Just Race: Being Black and Poor in the Inner City* (New York: W.W. Norton & Company, 2009), 15.

5. Ariela J. Gross, *What Blood Won't Tell: A History of Race on Trial in America* (Cambridge, MA: Harvard University Press, 2008), 306.

6. Ronald J. Allen, et al., *Comprehensive Criminal Procedure*, third edition (New York: Wolters Kluwer Law & Business, 2011), 6.

7. See John Yoo, "Executive Power Run Amok," *New York Times*, February 6, 2017, https://www.nytimes.com/2017/02/06/opinion/executive-power-run-amok.html?

8. Anatole France, *Wikiquote*, https://en.wikiquote.org/wiki/Anatole _France.

9. For a complete overview of the Jim Crow period, its artifacts, and their effects, see Henry Louis Gates, *Stony the Road: Reconstruction, White Supremacy, and the Rise of Jim Crow* (New York: Penguin Press, 2019); David Pilgrim, *Watermelons, Nooses, and Straight Razors: Stories from the Jim Crow Museum*

(Oakland, CA: PM Press, 2018); David Pilgrim, *Understanding Jim Crow: Using Racial Memorabilia to Teach Tolerance and Promote Social Justice* (Oakland, CA: PM Press, 2015).

10. For an overview, see "Der Stürmer," Holocaust Education & Archive Research Team, http://www.holocaustresearchproject.org/holoprelude/dersturmer.html.

11. For an overview of how the North benefited from slavery, see Anne Farrow, Joel Lang, and Jenifer Frank, *Complicity: How the North Promoted, Prolonged, and Profited from Slavery* (New York: Ballantine Books, 2005).

12. Watson M. Jennison, *Cultivating Race: The Expansion of Slavery in Georgia, 1750–1860* (Lexington: The University Press of Kentucky, 2012), 5.

2. ALABAMA

1. The events in this chapter are a literary recreation based on factual material derived from the author's interview with Diane McIver's close friend, Dani Jo Carter, and descriptions of Diane's childhood by her cousin, reported in "5 Things to Know about Diane McIver," *Atlanta Journal-Constitution*, April 23, 2018, https://www.ajc.com/news/local/things-know-about-diane-mciver/tfktDC2Xtwvm1rAIG4IiAL/.

3. MIDNIGHT MATTERS

1. Waller Wynne, "Culture of a Contemporary Rural Community," *Rural Life Studies*, January 1943, U.S. Department of Agriculture, Bureau of Agricultural Economics, 4 (available at Google Books).

2. Ira Berlin, *Many Thousands Gone: The First Two Centuries of Slavery in North America* (Cambridge: Belknap Press, 1998), 1.

3. Stuart Banner, *How the Indians Lost Their Land: Land and Power on the Frontier* (Cambridge, MA: Harvard University Press, 2005), 87.

4. "Putnam County," New Georgia Encyclopedia, https://www.georgia encyclopedia.org/articles/counties-cities-neighborhoods/putnam-county.

5. Wynne, "Culture of a Contemporary Rural Community," 13.

6. "Showing off Lake Oconee," *Atlanta Journal Constitution*, January 30, 2001 (downloaded from *Atlanta Journal Constitution* archives).

7. Introduction to Joel Chandler Harris, *Uncle Remus: His Songs and Sayings* (New York: Penguin Classics, electronic edition, 2001).

8. Henry Louis Gates, *Stony the Road: Reconstruction, White Supremacy, and the Rise of Jim Crow* (New York: Penguin Press, 2019), 96.

9. Details of the McIvers' possessions are based on "Everything Tex and Diane McIver Owned Is Being Sold. Everything," *Atlanta Journal-Constitution*, Jennifer Brett, August 1, 2018, https://www.ajc.com/entertainment/everything-tex-and-diane-mciver-owned-being-sold-everything/B2orOkkTVJxLQRD7W7tSmJ/; "McIver Ranch Sold for $1 Million at Auction Saturday," Union-Recorder (Milledgevill, GA), August 8, 2018, https://www.unionrecorder.com/news/mciver-ranch-sold-for-million-at-auction-satur-day/article_aee6e99e-9b1b-11e8-980c-f37104457d5c.html; "Buckhead Compa-ny Co-hosting Auction for McIvers' Eatonton Ranch Property," *Northside Neighbor*, July 31, 2018, https://www.mdjonline.com/neighbor_newspapers/northside_sandy_springs/news/buckhead-company-co-hosting-auction-for-mci-vers-eatonton-ranch-property/article_c0acfc40-9503-11e8-952a-7bcdc4e4eed9.html; Joe Kovac Jr., "Convicted Killer Tex McIver's Ranch—and Everything In It—On Auction Block," *The Telegraph* (Macon, GA), July 31, 2018, https://www.macon.com/news/local/article215823435.html; Richard Elli-ot, "Tex and Diane McIver's 85-Acre Ranch Set to Hit Auction Block," *WSB-TV*, August 1, 2018, https://www.wsbtv.com/news/local/everything-tex-and-diane-mciver-owned-to-be-sold/803692241/; Media release, "6.77-Carat Di-amond Ring Brings $31,000 and a Large Figural Hall Bench Attributed to Horn-er Realizes $28,320 at Ahlers & Ogletree, January 14th-16th," March 6, 2017, https://www.aandoauctions.com/january-2017-signature-estates-auction-post-auction-report/.

10. Tom Wolfe, *A Man in Full* (New York: The Dial Press, 2005), 5.

11. Concise definitions of these terms can be found in Matthew Lippman, *Law and Society*, second edition (Thousand Oaks, CA: Sage Publications, Inc., 2018), 4: "*Values* are the core beliefs about what is moral and immoral. . . . *Norms* are the 'action aspect' of values and tell us how to act in a situation. . . . *Folkways* are the customs that guide our daily interactions and behavior. . . . *Mores* are deeply and intensely held norms about what is right and wrong." These elements of culture, taken together, are powerful influences on the shaping of law and its administration.

12. William Alexander Percy, *Lanterns on the Levee: Recollections of a Planter's Son* (Baton Rouge: Louisiana State University Press, 1941); John O. Hodges, *Delta Fragments: The Recollections of a Sharecropper's Son* (Knox-ville: The University of Tennessee Press, 2013).

13. Lillian Smith, *Killers of the Dream* (New York: W.W. Norton & Compa-ny, 1994).

14. W. J. Cash, *The Mind of the South* (New York: Vintage Books Reprint, 1991); Tracy Thompson, *The New Mind of the South* (New York: Free Press, 2013).

15. Annie Gowen and Tyler Bridges, "From Piyush to Bobby: How Does Jindal Feel about His Family's Past?" *Washington Post*, June 23, 2015, https://www.washingtonpost.com/politics/from-piyush-to-bobby-how-does-jindal-feel-about-his-familys-past/2015/06/22/7d45a3da-18ec-11e5-ab92-c75ae6ab94b5_story.html.

16. "Nikki Haley," Biography.com, https://www.biography.com/political-figure/nikki-haley.

17. Johanes Rosello, "Nuestra Comunidad: Latina Politician Makes Georgia History," *Atlanta Journal Constitution*, January 20, 2017, https://www.ajc.com/news/local/nuestra-comunidad-latina-politician-makes-georgia-history/WT8WKZYuJ9cxX14fClpvpM/.

18. Neal Becton, "Atlanta's 'Chambodia,' a 'Burb With a Global Flavor," *Washington Post*, April 18, 1999, https://www.washingtonpost.com/archive/lifestyle/travel/1999/04/18/atlantas-chambodia-a-burb-with-a-global-flavor/aef19940-19d1-462f-b9bd-8ca000e63562/.

19. Dan Child, "Georgia Civil War Commission," *New Georgia Encyclopedia*, April 12, 2020, https://www.georgiaencyclopedia.org/articles/arts-culture/georgia-civil-war-commission.

20. "Civil War 'Trails' Proposed," *Atlanta Journal-Constitution*, September 27, 2000 (downloaded from *Atlanta Journal-Constitution* archives); "State Hopes Tourists will Follow Sherman's March to Sea," *Atlanta Journal-Constitution*, November 21, 1999 (downloaded from *Atlanta Journal-Constitution* archives).

21. See, for example, Edward Rothstein, "Not Forgotten," *New York Times*, March 16, 2011, https://www.nytimes.com/2011/03/17/arts/design/in-the-south-civil-war-has-not-been-forgotten.html.

22. James Oliver Horton and Lois E. Horton, eds., *Slavery and Public History: The Tough Stuff of American Memory* (Chapel Hill: The University of North Carolina Press, 2006), 44.

23. Rothstein, "Not Forgotten."

24. Stanley M. Elkins, *Slavery: A Problem in American Institutional and Intellectual Life* (New York: Grosset & Dunlap, 1963), 1.

25. Unless otherwise noted, quotes of Benton in this section are from Chris Joyner, "Ga. Lawmaker: KKK Made 'People Straighten Up,'" *Atlanta Journal-Constitution*, January 28, 2016, https://www.ajc.com/blog/investigations/lawmaker-kkk-made-people-straighten/QUYypM8evZYmlZojQ9ZdmO/.

26. Maya T. Prabhu, "Georgia Lawmaker Attacks John Lewis' Legacy, Loses Chairmanship," *Atlanta Journal-Constitution*, August 14, 2020, https://

www.ajc.com/politics/georgia-lawmaker-attacks-john-lewis-legacy-loses-chairmanship/NFDH2LKPE5HHXHFJP3STO62CUA/.

27. Joshua A. Lynn, *Preserving the White Man's Republic: Jacksonian Democracy, Race, and the Transformation of American Conservatism* (Charlottesville: University of Virginia Press, 2019), 10.

28. Kevin M. Kruse, *White Flight: Atlanta and the Making of Modem Conservatism* (Princeton: Princeton University Press, 2005), 237. The descriptions of Diane McIver's adult personality and character here and throughout the book are based primarily on the author's interviews with several of her close friends and co-workers, supplemented by other sources as noted.

29. Margaret Mitchell, *Gone With the Wind* (New York: Scribner, 2011), 159.

30. Kruse, *White Flight*, 237.

31. Wolfe, *A Man in Full*, 97.

32. Najja Parker, "Atlanta Rapper Young Thug Selling Buckhead Mansion for $3M," *Atlanta Journal-Constitution*, February 12, 2019, https://www.ajc.com/news/world/atlanta-rapper-young-thug-selling-buckhead-mansion-for/upLa0QMY5CtObwA0Md3WTM/.

33. Steve Fennessy, "Tex and Diane McIver Had It All. Now She's Dead, and He's Going on Trial for His Life," *Atlanta Magazine*, October 11, 2017, https://www.atlantamagazine.com/great-reads/tex-mciver/.

34. For a summary biography of Tex McIver, see Lisa Hester, "Fisher & Phillips Partner Tex McIver Receives Highest Award from National Fraternity," *Midtown GA Patch*, October 24, 2012, https://patch.com/georgia/midtown/amp/12032978/fisher-phillips-par.

35. "Obit of McIver Jr., Claud L. 'Mac' - Oklahoma County, Oklahoma," The USGenWeb Project, October 23, 2005, http://files.usgwarchives.net/ok/oklahoma/obits/mno/m2160026.txt.

36. Jerry Grillo, "The Immigration Dilemma," *Georgia Trend Magazine*, December 1, 2010, https://www.georgiatrend.com/2010/12/01/the-immigration-dilemma/.

37. "Atlanta Attorney Says Gun in His Lap Went Off, Striking His Wife," *Atlanta Journal-Constitution*, March 23, 2018, https://www.ajc.com/news/local/atlanta-attorney-says-gun-his-lap-went-off-striking-his-wife/1pA2ZtJkQI94 xnIr9J0zcL/.

38. Ross Douthat, "Confessions of a Columnist," *New York Times*, January 2, 2016, https://www.nytimes.com/2016/01/03/opinion/sunday/confessions-of-a-columnist.html.

39. Alexander Burns and Maggie Haberman, "Trailing Hillary Clinton, Donald Trump Turns to Political Gymnastics," *New York Times*, September 5, 2016, https://www.nytimes.com/2016/09/01/us/politics/trump-campaign.html.

40. Alan Rappeport, "New National Poll Shows Donald Trump and Hillary Clinton Essentially Tied," *New York Times*, September 6, 2016, https://www.nytimes.com/2016/09/07/us/politics/poll-donald-trump-hillary-clinton.html.

41. "With Clinton Leading Trump in Georgia, Reed Wants Campaign to Push," *Atlanta Journal-Constitution*, August 9, 2016 (downloaded from *Atlanta Journal-Constitution* archives).

42. "Ga. GOP Officials Uncomfortable with, but Committed to, Trump," *Atlanta Journal-Constitution*, August 21, 2016 (downloaded from *Atlanta Journal-Constitution* archives).

43. Roger Cohen, "President Donald Trump," *New York Times*, November 9, 2016, https://www.nytimes.com/2016/11/10/opinion/president-donald-trump.html.

44. Esquire Editors, "American Rage: The Esquire/NBC News Survey," January 3, 2016, https://www.esquire.com/news-politics/a40693/american-rage-nbc-survey/.

45. "Here's Donald Trump's Presidential Announcement Speech," *time.com*, June 16, 2015, https://time.com/3923128/donald-trump-announcement-speech/.

46. "Here's Donald Trump's Presidential Announcement Speech."

47. Sarah Posner and David Neiwert, "Meet the Horde of Neo-Nazis, Klansmen, and Other Extremist Leaders Endorsing Donald Trump," *Mother Jones*, September 21, 2016, https://www.motherjones.com/politics/2016/09/trump-supporters-neo-nazis-white-nationalists-kkk-militias-racism-hate/.

48. The Editorial Board, "Donald Trump's Alt-Right Brain," *New York Times*, September 5, 2016, https://www.nytimes.com/2016/09/06/opinion/donald-trumps-alt-right-brain.html.

49. Glenn Thrush and Maggie Haberman, "Trump Gives White Supremacists an Unequivocal Boost," *New York Times*, August 15, 2017, https://www.nytimes.com/2017/08/15/us/politics/trump-charlottesville-white-nationalists.html.

50. The Editorial Board, "Donald Trump's Alt-Right Brain."

51. "5 Things to Know about Diane McIver," *Atlanta Journal-Constitution*, April 23, 2018, https://www.ajc.com/news/local/things-know-about-diane-mciver/tfktDC2Xtwvm1rAIG4IiAL/.

52. Donald Trump has not fared well with his ghostwriters. Tony Schwartz, who wrote Trump's 1987 memoir, *The Art of the Deal*, later "denounced the book and called Trump a liar and a sociopath." Katy Guest, "Donald Trump, Beware—When the Ghostwriter Gives You Up," *The Guardian*, July 22, 2016, https://www.theguardian.com/books/2016/jul/22/donald-trump-beware-when-ghostwriter-gives-you-up. The ghostwriter of Trump's 2000 *The America We Deserve* said in 2015 that Trump has "no class" and announced in 2016 that he would not vote for Trump. Guest, "Donald Trump, Beware"; Jack Moore, "Don-

ald Trump's Former Ghostwriter Won't be Voting For Donald Trump," *GQ*, January 1, 2016, https://www.gq.com/story/donald-trump-ghostwriter-vote.

53. Fennessy, "Tex and Diane McIver Had It All."

54. See, for example, David W. Blight, "Trump Reveals the Truth About Voter Suppression," *New York Times*, April 11, 2020, https://www.nytimes.com/2020/04/11/opinion/sunday/republicans-voter-suppression.html; Eli Rosenberg, "'The Most Bizarre Thing I've Ever Been a Part Of': Trump Panel Found no Widespread Voter Fraud, Ex-member Says," *Washington Post*, August 3, 2018, https://www.washingtonpost.com/news/politics/wp/2018/08/03/the-most-bizarre-thing-ive-ever-been-a-part-of-trump-panel-found-no-voter-fraud-ex-member-says/.

55. See Jane Mayer, "The Voter-Fraud Myth," *New Yorker*, October 22, 2012, https://www.newyorker.com/magazine/2012/10/29/the-voter-fraud-myth; Theodore R. Johnson and Max Feldman, "The New Voter Suppression," Brennan Center for Justice, January 17, 2020, https://www.brennancenter.org/our-work/research-reports/new-voter-suppression; Justin Levitt, "The Truth About Voter Fraud," Brennan Center for Justice, November 9, 2007, https://www.brennancenter.org/our-work/research-reports/truth-about-voter-fraud.

56. Brentin Mock, "Like It or Not, Voter ID Is Not Working," Citylab.com, March 3, 2016, https://www.citylab.com/equity/2016/03/voter-id-is-not-working-photo-laws/471957/.

57. Ford Motor Company brochure, "2013 Expedition+EL," 2012.

58. "The King Ranch Legacy," https://king-ranch.com/.

59. Fennessy, "Tex and Diane McIver Had It All."

60. "New Details, More Questions in Exec's Death," *Atlanta Journal-Constitution*, October 1, 2016 (downloaded from *Atlanta Journal-Constitution* archives).

61. "New Details, More Questions in Exec's Death."

62. "Former McIver Spokesman Tells of Race Comments; Bill Crane Says He Refused to Change the Story about Fatal Night," *Atlanta Journal-Constitution*, April 10, 2018 (downloaded from *Atlanta Journal-Constitution* archives).

63. "Former McIver Spokesman Tells of Race Comments."

4. VICTIMS

1. Andrea Castillo, "How Two Black Women in L.A. Helped Build Black Lives Matter from Hashtag to Global Movement," *Los Angeles Times*, June 21, 2020, https://www.latimes.com/california/story/2020-06-21/black-lives-matter-los-angeles-patrisse-cullors-melina-abdullah.

2. Stephanie Elam and Jason Kravarik, "Black Lives Matter's surprising target: Los Angeles County's First Black District Attorney," *CNN*, July 15, 2020, https://www.cnn.com/2020/07/10/us/jackie-lacey-la-da-black-lives-matter/index.html.

3. Sam Levin, "'I Will Shoot You': Husband of LA District Attorney Pulls Gun on Black Lives Matter Activists," *The Guardian*, March 2, 2020, https://www.theguardian.com/us-news/2020/mar/02/jackie-lacey-husband-gun-black-lives-matter-la.

4. Misdemeanor Complaint, *California v. Lacey*, Superior Court of California, County of Los Angeles, filed August 3, 2020; Tim Elfrink, "Husband of Los Angeles District Attorney Charged with Pointing a Gun at BLM Protesters," *Washington Post*, August 5, 2020, https://www.washingtonpost.com/nation/2020/08/05/jackie-lacey-blm-protesters-gun/.

5. Sam Levin, "Husband of LA District Attorney Charged after Pointing Gun at Black Lives Matter Protesters," *The Guardian*, August 4, 2020, https://www.theguardian.com/us-news/2020/aug/04/husband-los-angeles-district-attorney-charged-with-pointing-a-gun-at-black-lives-matter-protesters.

6. Lori Craig, "District Attorney Jackie Lacey: Born to be an Advocate," University of Southern California, *USC News*, October 28, 2014, https://news.usc.edu/70188/district-attorney-jackie-lacey-born-to-be-an-advocate/.

7. Peter Beinart, "Progressives Have Short Memories," *The Atlantic*, December 4, 2019, https://www.theatlantic.com/ideas/archive/2019/12/kamala-harris-was-impossible-bind/602971/.

8. Tim Arango, "Two Prosecutors Were Shaped by 1980s Los Angeles. Now They Have Opposing Views on Criminal Justice," *New York Times*, October 3, 2019, https://www.nytimes.com/2019/10/03/us/los-angeles-district-attorney-george-gascon.html.

9. Link to tweet available in Jeremy B. White, "Schiff Renounces Jackie Lacey as Los Angeles DA Bleeds Reelection Support," *Politico*, June 20, 2020, https://www.politico.com/states/california/story/2020/06/20/schiff-renounces-jackie-lacey-as-los-angeles-da-bleeds-reelection-support-1293900.

10. Sentinel News Service, "Atty. Gen. Kamala Harris backs Jackie Lacey," *Los Angeles Sentinel*, August 16, 2012, https://lasentinel.net/atty-gen-kamala-harris-backs-jackie-lacey.html.

11. Larry Altman, "Sen. Kamala Harris Endorses Gascon in Tight LA County DA Race," *Los Angeles Daily News*, February 18, 2020, https://www.dailynews.com/2020/02/18/sen-harris-endorses-gascon-in-tight-la-da-race/.

12. Chuck McCutcheon and David Mark, "Politics Ain't Beanbag," *Christian Science Monitor*, November 14, 2014, https://www.csmonitor.com/USA/Politics/Politics-Voices/2014/1114/Politics-ain-t-beanbag.

13. For an overview of America's ongoing culture war, see "American Tsunami—The Causes and Consequences of Polarization," in "Introduction," Tom Diaz, *Tragedy in Aurora—The Culture of Mass Shootings in America* (Lanham, MD: Rowman & Littlefield, 2019), 16–26.

14. Quoted with citations in Tom Diaz, *The Last Gun—How Changes in the Gun Industry Are Killing Americans and What It Will Take to Stop It* (New York: The New Press, 2013), 192.

15. For an overview of the early Balkan Wars, see Richard C. Hall, "Balkan Wars 1912–1913," in *International Encyclopedia of the First World War*, edited by Ute Daniel, et al., issued by Freie Universität Berlin, October 8, 2014, https://encyclopedia.1914-1918-online.net/article/balkan_wars_1912-1913.

16. An example of variable demographics and polling is the shift in priorities among young people from gun control to racial justice described in Giovanni Russonello, "What Happened to the Young Voters Focused on Guns?" *New York Times*, August 3, 2020, https://www.nytimes.com/2020/08/03/us/politics/gun-control-voters.html.

17. Andrew Glass, "Reagan Declares 'War on Drugs,' October 14, 1982," *Politico*, October 14, 2010, https://www.politico.com/story/2010/10/reagan-declares-war-on-drugs-october-14-1982-043552.

18. Lawrence Bobo, James R. Kluegel, and Ryan A. Smith, "Laissez-Faire Racism: The Crystallization of a Kinder, Gentler, Antiblack Ideology," in Steven A. Tuch and Jack K. Martin, eds., *Racial Attitudes in the 1990s: Continuity and Change* (Westport, CT: Praeger Publishers, 1997), 16.

19. Bobo, Kluegel, and Smith, "Laissez-Faire Racism," 41.

20. Wilson, *More than Just Race*, 16.

21. Associated Press, "'What Do You Have to Lose?' Donald Trump Appeals for Black Vote," *The Guardian,* August 19, 2016, https://www.theguardian.com/us-news/2016/aug/20/what-do-you-have-to-lose-donald-trump-appeals-for-black-vote.

22. Donald J. Trump with Dave Shiflett, *The America We Deserve* (Los Angeles: Renaissance Books, 2000), 91. Excerpts here are from Scribd.com, https://www.scribd.com/book/182526899/The-America-We-Deserve. Shiflett, the book's actual writer, later denounced Trump. Jack Moore, "Donald Trump's Former Ghostwriter Won't Be Voting For Donald Trump," *GQ*, January 1, 2016, https://www.gq.com/story/donald-trump-ghostwriter-vote.

23. Trump, *The America We Deserve*, 93.

24. Trump, *The America We Deserve*, 93.

25. Trump, *The America We Deserve*, 101.

26. Jeff Sessions, "Being Soft on Sentencing Means More Violent Crime. It's Time to Get Tough Again," *Washington Post*, June 16, 2017, https://www.washingtonpost.com/opinions/jeff-sessions-being-soft-on-sentencing-

means-more-violent-crime-its-time-to-get-tough-again/2017/06/16/618ef1fe-4a19-11e7-9669-250d0b15f83b_story.html.

27. German Lopez, "Jeff Sessions Turned Trump's 'Tough on Crime' Dreams into Reality," *Vox*, November 7, 2018, https://www.vox.com/policy-and-politics/2018/11/7/18073074/jeff-sessions-resigns-war-on-drugs-crime.

28. Cornel West, "Foreword," in Michelle Alexander, *The New Jim Crow: Mass Incarceration in the Age of Colorblindness* (New York: The New Press, 2012).

29. Alexander, *The New Jim Crow*, 6. For comprehensive statistical overviews of state, local, and federal imprisonment in the United States, see Wendy Sawyer and Peter Wagner, "Mass Incarceration: The Whole Pie 2020," Prison Policy Initiative, March 24, 2020, https://www.prisonpolicy.org/reports/pie2020.html; and "Fact Sheet: Trends in U.S. Corrections," The Sentencing Project, June 2019, available at https://www.sentencingproject.org/.

30. Alexander, *The New Jim Crow*, 6.

31. Alexander, *The New Jim Crow*, 2.

32. Alexander, *The New Jim Crow*, 185.

33. Alexander, *The New Jim Crow*,186.

34. Alexander, *The New Jim Crow*, 186.

35. Kamala D. Harris, *Smart on Crime: A Career Prosecutor's Plan to Make Us Safer* (San Francisco: Chronicle Books, 2009), 14.

36. Josie Duffy Rice, "Cyrus Vance and the Myth of the Progressive Prosecutor," *New York Times*, October 16, 2017, https://www.nytimes.com/2017/10/16/opinion/cy-vance-progressive-prosecutor.html?.

37. NBC 4 News, "Incumbent Jackie Lacey Conceded Defeat in the Race to Become LA County's Top Prosecutor," November 6, 2020, https://www.nbclosangeles.com/news/politics/decision-2020/jackie-lacey-george-gascon-los-angeles-county-district-attorney-decision-2020/2453809/.

38. See, for example, Jose A. Del Real, Kayla Ruble, and Vickie Elmer, "For Black Activists, Biden's Selection of Harris as Running Mate Brings Pride but also Compromise," *Washington Post*, August 14, 2020, https://www.washingtonpost.com/politics/for-black-liberals-bidens-selection-of-harris-as-running-mate-brings-pride-but-also-compromise/2020/08/14/ecb87c82-dd87-11ea-b205-ff838e15a9a6_story.html.

39. Reuters, "Black Activists Praise Biden's Pick of Harris, but Warn Challenges Remain," *New York Times*, August 12, 2020, https://www.nytimes.com/reuters/2020/08/12/us/politics/12reuters-usa-election-biden-race.html?; German Lopez, "The Controversial 1994 Crime Law that Joe Biden Helped Write, Explained," *VOX*, June 20, 2019, https://www.vox.com/policy-and-politics/2019/6/20/18677998/joe-biden-1994-crime-bill-law-mass-incarceration.

40. Tim Arango, "Two Prosecutors Were Shaped by 1980s Los Angeles."

41. Lori Craig, "District Attorney Jackie Lacey: Born to be an Advocate."

42. Harris, *Smart on Crime*, 81.

43. Shirley Hawkins, "Jackie Lacey Makes History," *Los Angeles Sentinel*, November 7, 2012, https://lasentinel.net/jackie-lacey-makes-history.html.

44. Wilson, *More than Just Race*, 20.

45. Wilson, *More than Just Race*, 21.

46. "Henry Louis Gates Jr. on What Really Happened at Obama's 'Beer Summit,'" *New York Times Magazine*, January 31, 2020, https:// www.nytimes.com/interactive/2020/02/03/magazine/henry-louis-gates-jr-inter-view.html.

47. Hawkins, "Jackie Lacey Makes History."

48. This description of Trayvon Martin's homicide is adapted with additional sourcing from Diaz, *The Last Gun*, 134–37.

49. Lizette Alvarez and Cara Buckley, "Zimmerman Is Acquitted in Killing of Trayvon Martin," *New York Times*, July 14, 2013, https://www.nytimes.com/ 2013/07/15/us/george-zimmerman-verdict-trayvon-martin.html?.

50. Channing Joseph and Ravi Somaiya, "Demonstrations Across the Country Commemorate Trayvon Martin," *New York Times*, July 20, 2013, https:// www.nytimes.com/2013/07/21/us/demonstrations-across-the-country-com-memorate-trayvon-martin.html?.

51. "Transcript: Obama Speaks of Verdict Through the Prism of African-American Experience," *New York Times*, July 19, 2013, https://www.nytimes .com/2013/07/20/us/politics/transcript-obama-speaks-of-verdict-through-the -prism-of-african-american-experience.html?.

52. This description of the organization of the Black Lives Matter movement is based primarily on "Herstory: Black Lives Matter Los Angeles," https:// www.blmla.org/herstory; and Jamil Smith, "The Power of Black Lives Matter," *Rolling Stone*, June 16, 2020, https://www.rollingstone.com/culture/culture-fea-tures/black-lives-matter-jamil-smith-1014442/.

53. Smith, "The Power of Black Lives Matter."

54. Smith, "The Power of Black Lives Matter."

55. Castillo, "How Two Black Women in L.A. Helped Build Black Lives."

56. Smith, "The Power of Black Lives Matter."

57. Michael Edison Hayden, "George Zimmerman Explains His Rationale for Auctioning Pistol That Killed Trayvon Martin," ABC News, May 24, 2016, https://abcnews.go.com/US/george-zimmerman-explains-rationale-auctioning-pistol-killed-trayvon/story?id=39330161.

58. James W. Loewen, *Sundown Towns: A Hidden Dimension of American Racism* (New York: The New Press, 2018), xii.

59. Loewen, *Sundown Towns*, 194.

60. Loewen, *Sundown Towns*, 195.

61. U.S. Department of Justice, Civil Rights Division, "Investigation of the Ferguson Police Department," Washington, DC, March 4, 2015, 6.

62. U.S. Census Bureau, "Quick Facts: Ferguson city, Missouri," https://www.census.gov/quickfacts/fergusoncitymissouri.

63. Civil Rights Division, "Investigation of the Ferguson Police Department," 7.

64. Loewen, *Sundown Towns*, x.

65. For a short overview, see Wesley Lowery, "Black Lives Matter: Birth of a Movement," *The Guardian*, January 17, 2017, https://www.theguardian.com/us-news/2017/jan/17/black-lives-matter-birth-of-a-movement.

66. Michelle Ye Hee Lee, Fact Checker, "'Hands Up, Don't Shoot' Did Not Happen in Ferguson," March 19, 2015, *Washington Post*, https://www.washingtonpost.com/news/fact-checker/wp/2015/03/19/hands-up-dont-shoot-did-not-happen-in-ferguson/.

67. See, for example, Jack Dunphy, "The Stubborn Facts in Ferguson," *National Review*, October 27, 2014, https://www.nationalreview.com/2014/10/stubborn-facts-ferguson-jack-dunphy/.

68. Jonathan Capehart, "'Hands Up, Don't Shoot' was Built on a Lie," *Washington Post*, March 16, 2015, https://www.washingtonpost.com/blogs/post-partisan/wp/2015/03/16/lesson-learned-from-the-shooting-of-michael-brown/.

69. Michelle Ye Hee Lee, Fact Checker, "'Hands Up, Don't Shoot' Did Not Happen in Ferguson."

70. U.S. Department of Justice, "Memorandum: Department of Justice Report Regarding the Criminal Investigation into the Shooting Death of Michael Brown by Ferguson, Missouri Police Officer Darren Wilson," March 4, 2015, 6.

71. U.S. Department of Justice, "Memorandum: Department of Justice Report Regarding the Criminal Investigation," 80.

72. U.S. Department of Justice, "Memorandum: Department of Justice Report Regarding the Criminal Investigation," 7.

73. Rich Lowry, "The Ferguson Fraud," *National Review*, November 26, 2014, https://www.nationalreview.com/2014/11/ferguson-fraud-rich-lowry/.

74. Sandra Jordan, "Wesley Bell Elected STL County's First Black Prosecutor," *St. Louis American*, November 6, 2018, http://www.stlamerican.com/news/local_news/victory-night-for-wesley-bell-former-ferguson-councilman-makes-history/article_40e7f5ca-e24a-11e8-b793-83813ee3637c.html.

75. Jessica Wolfrom and Reis Thebault, "Prosecutor Will Not Charge the Police Officer Who Shot and Killed Michael Brown in Ferguson," *Washington Post*, July 30, 2020, https://www.washingtonpost.com/nation/2020/07/30/prosecutor-will-not-charge-police-officer-who-shot-killed-michael-brown-ferguson/; "Michael Brown Shooting: Officer Will not be Charged, Top Prosecutor Says,"

The Guardian, July 30, 2020, https://www.theguardian.com/us-news/2020/jul/30/michael-brown-ferguson-shooting-darren-wilson-not-charged.

76. "Editorial: New Investigation, Same Disappointing Result for Michael Brown's Family," *St. Louis Post-Dispatch*, August 1, 2020, https://www.stltoday.com/opinion/editorial/editorial-new-investigation-same-disappointing-result-for-michael-browns-family/article_5701d147-4932-5279-b693-35a8aec2ac1b.html.

77. Civil Rights Division, "Investigation of the Ferguson Police Department," 2.

78. Wesley Lowery, *"They Can't Kill Us All": The Story of the Struggle for Black Lives* (New York: Back Bay Books, 2016), 15.

79. Lowery, *"They Can't Kill Us All,"* 10.

80. Lowery, *"They Can't Kill Us All,"* 10.

81. Lowery, *"They Can't Kill Us All,"* 13.

82. Civil Rights Division, "Investigation of the Ferguson Police Department," 3.

83. Civil Rights Division, "Investigation of the Ferguson Police Department," 5.

5. HERITAGE

1. For summaries as of mid-2020, see "Editorial: A Very Abbreviated History of Police Officers Killing Black People," *Los Angeles Times*, June 4, 2020, https://www.latimes.com/opinion/story/2020-06-04/police-killings-black-victims; CNN Editorial Research, "Controversial Police Encounters Fast Facts," CNN, June 4, 2020, https://www.cnn.com/2015/04/05/us/controversial-police-encounters-fast-facts/index.html. Also see generally Lowery, *"They Can't Kill Us All"* for specific stories described in depth.

2. U.S. Bureau of the Census, "QuickFacts: United States," https://www.census.gov/quickfacts/fact/table/US/IPE120218.

3. "Fatal Force," *Washington Post*, https://www.washingtonpost.com/graphics/investigations/police-shootings-database/.

4. "Unarmed, Shot in Back: Police Never Charged," *Atlanta Journal-Constitution*, December 20, 2015. (Available in newspaper archives.)

5. Lowery, *"They Can't Kill Us All,"* 114.

6. "Ga. Racial Progress Uncertain: Relations Unchanged or Worse Since 1985, Poll Finds," *Atlanta Journal-Constitution*, January 12, 2015. (Available in newspaper archives.)

7. "AJC Poll Finds Stark Views on Police: Blacks, Whites Divided on Officers' Conduct," *Atlanta Journal-Constitution*, January 13, 2015. (Available in newspaper archives.)

8. Pew Research Center, "The Partisan Divide on Political Values Grows Even Wider," October 2017, 31–32, https://www.pewresearch.org/politics/2017/10/05/the-partisan-divide-on-political-values-grows-even-wider/.

9. "Black Lives Matter: An Activist's Evolution to Lead a Local Movement," *Atlanta Journal-Constitution*, August 7, 2016. (Available in newspaper archives.)

10. Black Lives Matter Atlanta, "About," https://www.blacklivesmatteratl .org/about.html.

11. "Black Lives Matter: An Activist's Evolution."

12. "Black Lives Matter has 'Changed the Conversation.'" *Atlanta Journal-Constitution,* January 1, 2016. (Available in newspaper archives.)

13. Mo Barnes, "Why There Is a Beef with Black Lives Matter Activists in Atlanta, Part 1," *Rolling Out Magazine*, March 23, 2018, https://rollingout.com/2018/03/23/why-there-is-a-beef-with-black-lives-matter-activists-in-atlanta-part-1/.

14. Barnes, "Why There Is a Beef with Black Lives Matter Activists."

15. Willoughby Mariano, "Black Lives Matter and Civil Rights Movements Confront Generation Gap," *Atlanta Journal-Constitution*, October 20, 2016, https://www.ajc.com/news/local-govt--politics/black-lives-matter-and-civil-rights-movements-confront-generation-gap/tnNrCB1gKKUOEgeIsEoNVO/.

16. "Black Lives," *Atlanta Journal-Constitution*, September 25, 2016. (Available in newspaper archives.)

17. "Black Lives."

18. Mariano, "Black Lives Matter and Civil Rights Movements Confront Generation Gap."

19. "Black Lives."

20. "Activism in Atlanta Reflects Our Changing World: New Movement Targets More than Racism, Has Wide Regional Impact," *Atlanta Journal-Constitution*, January 1, 2016.

21. "Millennial Activists Join Rallies for Civil Rights: A New Generation Provides Vitality to Social Movements," *Atlanta Journal-Constitution*, August 9, 2015. (Available in newspaper archives.)

22. Press Release, "PBS NewsHour/Marist Poll Demonstrates Both White and African American Residents Nationally Agree That Race Relations in the U.S. Have Deteriorated in Past Year," PBS, September 21, 2015, https://www.pbs.org/newshour/press-releases/pbs-newshourmarist-poll-demonstrates-white-african-american-residents-nationally-agree-race-relations-u-s-deteriorated-past-year.

23. Giovanni Russonello, "Race Relations Are at Lowest Point in Obama Presidency, Poll Finds," *New York Times*, July 13, 2016, https://www.nytimes.com/2016/07/14/us/most-americans-hold-grim-view-of-race-relations-poll-finds.html.

24. Russonello, "Race Relations Are at Lowest Point in Obama Presidency."

25. Lowery, *"They Can't Kill Us All,"* 15.

26. Nate Cohn and Kevin Quealy, "How Public Opinion Has Moved on Black Lives Matter," *New York Times*, June 10, 2020, https://www.nytimes.com/interactive/2020/06/10/upshot/black-lives-matter-attitudes.html.

27. Jeff Sharlet, "A Flag for Trump's America," *Harper's Magazine*, July 2018, https://harpers.org/archive/2018/07/a-flag-for-trumps-america/. See also Maurice Chammah and Cary Aspinwall, "The Short, Fraught History of the 'Thin Blue Line' American Flag," The Marshall Project, June 8, 2020, https://www.themarshallproject.org/2020/06/08/the-short-fraught-history-of-the-thin-blue-line-american-flag.

28. "Atlanta Protesters Call for Change, Peace; Thousands March in Rallies Organized by Civil Rights Groups," *Atlanta Journal-Constitution*, July 9, 2016. (Available in newspaper archives); John Ruch, "Black Lives Matter Protest March Held at Lenox Square Mall," *Reporter Newspapers*, July 9, 2016, https://www.reporternewspapers.net/2016/07/09/black-lives-matter-protest-march-held-lenox-square-mall/.

29. Manny Fernandez, Richard Pérez-Peña, and Jonah Engel Bromwich, "Five Dallas Officers Were Killed as Payback, Police Chief Says," *New York Times*, July 8, 2016, https://www.nytimes.com/2016/07/09/us/dallas-police-shooting.html.

30. Derryck Green, "Black Lives Matter has Failed Morally," *Atlanta Journal-Constitution*, July 24, 2016. (Available in newspaper archives.)

31. "Reed Praises 'Exhausted' Cops: Officers have Logged 6,000 Hours of Overtime; Activists Vow More Protests to Keep up Pressure," *Atlanta Journal-Constitution*, July 12, 2016. (Available in newspaper archives.)

32. John Ruch, "Black Lives Matter Protest March Held at Lenox Square Mall," *Reporter Newspapers*, July 9, 2016, https://www.reporternewspapers.net/2016/07/09/black-lives-matter-protest-march-held-lenox-square-mall/; Collin Kelley, "Arrests Made in Third Night of Protests in Downtown Atlanta," *Atlanta INtown Paper*, July 10, 2016, https://atlantaintownpaper.com/2016/07/arrests-made-in-third-night-of-protests-in-downtown-atlanta/; John Ruch, "Buckhead Black Lives Matter Protest Ends in Meeting with Mayor, Police Chief," *Reporter Newspapers*, July 12, 2016, https://www.reporternewspapers.net/2016/07/12/buckhead-black-lives-matter-protest-ends-meeting-mayor-police-chief/.

33. "Reed Praises 'Exhausted' Cops."

34. "NAACP: Atlanta Police 'Exemplary' during Protests," *Atlanta Journal-Constitution*, July 10, 2016. (Available in newspaper archives.)

35. Torpy at Large, "Protests Show the 'Atlanta Way,'" *Atlanta Journal-Constitution*, July 21, 2016. (Available in newspaper archives.)

36. Alan Judd, "Police Turn Georgia Capitol Protest into 'Battle Space,'" *Atlanta Journal-Constitution*, June 5, 2020, https://www.ajc.com/news/crime--law/for-police-protest-georgia-capitol-turned-into-combat/pmhfmZqW5X8l9zorWCW47M/?utm_source=Iterable&utm_medium=email&utm_campaign=campaign_1269944.

37. "Unarmed, Shot in Back: Police Never Charged," *Atlanta Journal-Constitution*, December 20, 2015. (Available in newspaper archives.)

38. Allen, et al., *Comprehensive Criminal Procedure*, 993.

39. "Unarmed, Shot in Back: Police Never Charged."

40. "New Grand Jury Rules for Ga. Officers Tested," *Atlanta Journal-Constitution*, October 7, 2017; "Five Georgia Officers Likely to Stand Trial in 2019 for Murder: 2015 Change to State Grand Jury Rules has 'Leveled the Playing Field,'" *The Atlanta Journal-Constitution*, December 16, 2018. (Available in newspaper archives.)

41. "Ex-cop's Case Sign of Big Shift in Georgia; Murder Charge Comes in Wake of Shooting," *Atlanta Journal-Constitution*, July 17, 2016. (Available in newspaper archives.)

42. "24-hour Protest Puts Focus on Shootings: Grand Jury Convening Today in Case of Officer Charged in Slaying," *Atlanta Journal-Constitution*, August 31, 2016. (Available in newspaper archives.)

43. "Ex-Atlanta Cop Indicted in Fatal Shooting," *Atlanta Journal-Constitution*, September 1, 2016. (Available in newspaper archives.)

44. "250 March Downtown in Wake of Police Shootings," *Atlanta Journal-Constitution*, September 24, 2016. (Available in newspaper archives.)

45. John Ruch, "Black Lives Matter Protesters Block Lenox Mall, Call for Boycott," *Reporter Newspapers*, September 25, 2016, https://www.reporternewspapers.net/2016/09/25/black-lives-matter-protesters-block-lenox-mall-call-boycott/.

46. Audrey Washington, "Black Lives Matter Protesters Demonstrate in Downtown, Buckhead," WSB-TV 2, September 25, 2016, https://www.wsbtv.com/news/local/atlanta/black-lives-matter-protesters-demonstrate-in-downtown-buckhead/449937532.

47. "Black Lives."

48. John P. Crank, *Understanding Police Culture*, second edition (Cincinnati, OH: Anderson Publishing Co., 2004), 2.

49. Crank, *Understanding Police Culture*, 3.

50. Crank, *Understanding Police Culture*, 3.

51. Crank, *Understanding Police Culture*, 97.

52. "Protesters, Reed Seek Common Ground Today on Easing Tensions with Police," *Atlanta Journal-Constitution*, July 18, 2016. (Available in newspaper archives.)

53. Crank, *Understanding Police Culture*, 257.

54. Crank, *Understanding Police Culture*, 258.

55. Crank, *Understanding Police Culture*, 264.

56. Crank, *Understanding Police Culture*, 266.

57. James Oliver Horton and Lois E. Horton, eds., *Slavery and Public History: The Tough Stuff of American Memory* (Chapel Hill: The University of North Carolina Press, 2006), 215.

58. Horton and Horton, *Slavery and Public History*, 37.

59. Horton and Horton, *Slavery and Public History*, 41.

60. Horton and Horton, *Slavery and Public History*, 41.

61. Horton and Horton, *Slavery and Public History*, 42.

62. Horton and Horton, *Slavery and Public History*, 44.

63. Horton and Horton, *Slavery and Public History*, 39.

64. Sven Beckert, *Empire of Cotton: A Global History* (New York: Alfred A. Knopf, 2014), 38.

65. Albert W. Alschuler, "Rediscovering Blackstone," *University of Pennsylvania Law Review*, November 1996, Vol. 145, No. 1, 2.

66. See, for example, *District of Columbia v. Heller*, 554 U.S. 570 (2008).

67. Quoted in Alschuler, "Rediscovering Blackstone," 28–29. The full text is available online at "Blackstone on the Absolute Rights of Individuals (1753)," Online Library of Liberty, https://oll.libertyfund.org/pages/blackstone-on-the-absolute-rights-of-individuals-1753.

68. Quoted in Hubert Williams and Patrick V. Murphy, U.S. Department of Justice, National Institute of Justice, "The Evolving Strategy of Police: A Minority View," January 1990, 7.

69. Williams and Murphy, "The Evolving Strategy of Police."

70. Williams and Murphy, "The Evolving Strategy of Police," 8.

71. Williams and Murphy, "The Evolving Strategy of Police," 8.

6. THE ASSEMBLY LINE

1. Matthew Lippman, *Law and Society*, second edition (Thousand Oaks, CA: Sage Publications, 2018), 44.

2. For an extended discussion, see Stanford University, Center for the Study of Language and Information, "Theories of Criminal Law," *Stanford Encyclopedia of Philosophy*, https://plato.stanford.edu/entries/criminal-law/.

3. Lippman, *Law and Society*, 23.

4. Allen, et al., *Comprehensive Criminal Procedure*, 6.

5. Geoffrey R. Stone and David A. Strauss, "The Legacy of the Warren Court," *American Heritage*, Winter 2020, Vol., 64, Issue 1, https://www.americanheritage.com/legacy-warren-court#.

6. Herbert L. Packer, "Two Models of the Criminal Process," *University of Pennsylvania Law Review*, November 1964, Vol. 113, No. 1; "Courts, the Police, and the Rest of Us," *Journal of Criminal Law and Criminology*, Vol. 57, No. 3, 1966; *The Limits of the Criminal Sanction* (Stanford, CA: Stanford University Press, 1968).

7. Packer, "Two Models of the Criminal Process," 9.

8. Packer, "Two Models of the Criminal Process," 10.

9. Packer, "Two Models of the Criminal Process," 16.

10. Packer, "Two Models of the Criminal Process," 13.

11. Allen, et al., *Comprehensive Criminal Procedure*, 6.

12. Report by the President's Commission on Law Enforcement and Administration of Justice, *The Challenge of Crime in a Free Society* (Washington: United States Government Printing Office, February 1967), 7.

13. Theodore F. T. Plucknett, *A Concise History of the Common Law* (Indianapolis: Liberty Fund 2010 reprint of fifth edition originally printed by Little, Brown and Co., 1956), 3.

14. Lawrence M. Friedman, *Crime and Punishment in American History* (New York: Basic Books, 1993), 20.

15. Friedman, *Crime and Punishment in American History*, 4.

16. Friedman, *Crime and Punishment in American History*, 4.

17. Friedman, *Crime and Punishment in American History*, 5.

18. A good measure of power is wealth. "The median white family had more than ten times the wealth of the median black family in 2016. . . . The widening racial wealth gap disadvantages black families, individuals, and communities and limits black citizens' economic power and prospects, and the effects are cyclical." Nick Noel, et al., "The Economic Impact of Closing the Racial Wealth Gap," McKinsey & Company, August 13, 2019, https://www.mckinsey.com/industries/public-sector/our-insights/the-economic-impact-of-closing-the-racial-wealth-gap#; "the racial wealth gap is not the result of individual missteps but is driven by systemic barriers such as structural racism, policies, programs, and institutional practices that facilitate wealth building for white families while inhibiting or stripping wealth from African American families." Kilolo Kijakazi, "50 Years after Martin Luther King's Death, Structural Racism Still Drives the Racial Wealth Gap," Blog of the Urban Institute, April 6, 2018, https://www.urban.org/urban-wire/50-years-after-martin-luther-kings-death-structural-racism-still-drives-racial-wealth-gap. Another measure is health. See, for exam-

ple, Maanvi Singh, "'Long Overdue': Lawmakers Declare Racism a Public Health Emergency," *The Guardian*, June 12, 2020, https:// www.theguardian.com/society/2020/jun/12/racism-public-health-black-brown-coronavirus.

19. Friedman, *Crime and Punishment in American History*, 5.

20. Allen, et al., *Comprehensive Criminal Procedure*, 4.

21. Allen, et al., *Comprehensive Criminal Procedure*, 569.

22. William J. Stuntz and Joseph L. Hoffman, *Defining Crimes*, second edition (New York: Wolters Kluwer Law & Business, 2014), 2.

23. For a general discussion of the classification of crimes, see Wayne R. LaFave, *Criminal Law*, fourth edition (St. Paul, MN: West Publishing Co., 2003), Section 1.6.

24. GA Code § 17-10-3 (2018).

25. Lawrence M. Friedman, *Crime Without Punishment: Aspects of the History of Homicide* (New York: Cambridge University Press, 2018), 1.

26. For general discussions of the law of homicide, see chapter 10, "Homicide," in Matthew Lippman, *Contemporary Criminal Law: Concepts, Cases and Controversies* (Thousand Oaks, CA: Sage Publications, Inc., 2019); chapter 14, "Murder," in LaFave, *Criminal Law*; Stuntz and Hoffman, *Defining Crimes* 609–11.

27. LaFave, *Criminal Law*, Section 15.1.

28. Lippman, *Contemporary Criminal Law*, 293; Plucknett, *A Concise History of the Common Law*, 445–46.

29. Stuntz and Hoffman, *Defining Crimes*, 609.

30. Ga. Code § 16-5-1 (a) (2018).

31. Ga. Code § 16-5-3 (a) (2018).

32. For a textbook discussion of direct and circumstantial evidence, see Jefferson L. Ingram, *Criminal Evidence*, eleventh edition (Waltham, MA: Elsevier Books, 2012), 98–104.

33. Clint Van Zandt, "The Real World vs. the CSI Syndrome," *The Abrams Report, NBC News*, http://www.nbcnews.com/id/8802371/ns/msnbc-the_abrams_report/#.XtZkssZ7lE4.

34. Friedman, *Crime Without Punishment*, 14.

35. Friedman, *Crime Without Punishment*, 15.

36. Friedman, *Crime Without Punishment*, 18.

37. For overviews of the Simpson and Anthony trials and evidence, see Christo Lassiter, "The O.J. Simpson Verdict: A Lesson in Black and White," 1 *MICH. J. RACE & L.* 69 (1996), https://repository.law.umich.edu/mjrl/vol1/iss1/3; Jennifer Dearborn, "The Case of Casey Anthony: Defending the American Jury System," *Rutgers Law Record*, August 11, 2011, https://lawrecord.com/2011/08/11/the-case-of-casey-anthony-defending-the-american-jury-system/.

38. John Berendt, *Midnight in the Garden of Good and Evil* (New York: Vintage Books, 1999).

39. Dep Kirkland, *Lawyer Games: After Midnight in the Garden of Good and Evil* (Indianapolis: Dog Ear Publishing, 2015).

40. From author's interview with Dani Jo Carter.

41. "Key Witness Gives Account of Night Ga. Lawyer Fatally Shot His Wife," CBS News, March 19, 2018, https://www.cbsnews.com/news/key-witness-gives-account-of-night-ga-lawyer-fatally-shot-his-wife/.

42. "The Kathryn Steinle Murder Trial: Why the Jury and Trump Saw Two Different Cases," *Los Angeles Times*, December 2, 2017, http://www.latimes.com/local/lanow/la-me-kate-steinle-analysis-20171202-story.html.

43. Matt Stevens, Thomas Fuller, and Caitlin Dickerson, "Trump Tweets 'Build the Wall' After Immigrant is Acquitted in Kathryn Steinle Case," *New York Times*, November 30, 2017, https://www.nytimes.com/2017/11/30/us/kate-steinle-murder-trial.html.

44. "Why Was Officer Peter Liang Convicted?" *The Atlantic*, March 3, 2016, https://www.theatlantic.com/national/archive/2016/03/peter-liang-police-shooting/471687/.

45. Jaeah Lee, "Why Was Peter Liang One of so Few Cops Convicted for Killing an Unarmed Man?" *Mother Jones*, April 8, 2016, https://www.motherjones.com/politics/2016/04/peter-liang-police-conviction-nypd/.

46. "Why Was Officer Peter Liang Convicted?"

47. Bill Torpy, "Tex McIver Is Unlikable and Dangerous. But a Murderer?" *Atlanta Journal-Constitution*, April 13, 2018, https://www.ajc.com/news/local/torpy-large-tex-mciver-unlikable-and-dangerous-but-murderer/bfxrXelfmcXpd5My7716pJ/.

48. James H. Welcome, "Carjacking Epidemic Plagues the City of Atlanta," *NewsmakersLive*, March 15, 2017, http://newsmakerslive.com/carjacking-epidemic-plagues-city-atlanta/; Christopher Coble, "Carjacking Spike in Atlanta: What Are the Charges and How Can You Avoid Being Carjacked?" *Findlaw Blog*, September 6, 2016, https://blogs.findlaw.com/blotter/2016/09/carjacking-spike-in-atlanta-what-are-the-charges-and-how-can-you-avoid-being-carjacked.html; U.S. Department of Justice, U.S. Attorney's Office, Northern District of Georgia, media release, "Five Sentenced in Violent Carjacking Spree Involving Seven Carjackings in Four Counties," November 19, 2015, https://www.justice.gov/usao-ndga/pr.

49. See, for example, "Carjacking Suspect Arrested after Chase," *Atlanta Journal-Constitution*, August 29, 2015; "Suspects in Midtown Carjacking Arrested," *Atlanta Journal-Constitution*, October 16, 2015; "Carjacking Victim Fought until the End," *Atlanta Journal-Constitution*, November 15, 2015 ; "4 Atlanta Teens Held in Cobb Carjacking, Slaying," *Atlanta Journal-Constitution*,

December 15, 2015; "Three Arrested in Attack at Clark Atlanta," *Atlanta Journal-Constitution*, May 7, 2016; "Woman Hits, Kills Pedestrian, Goes on Carjacking Spree," *Atlanta Journal-Constitution*, May 12, 2016; "Woman with Baby Reports Carjacking," *Atlanta Journal-Constitution*, June 20, 2016; "Boy, 8, Dies after Two Days on Life Support," *Atlanta Journal-Constitution*, July 1, 2016; "Man Arrested after Officer Shot at in Chase," *Atlanta Journal-Constitution*, July 6, 2016; "Man, 77, Shot in Carjacking Attempt," *Atlanta Journal-Constitution*, August 29, 2016 (articles available in *Atlanta Journal-Constitution* online archives).

50. "Carjacking Suspect Arrested after Chase."

51. "Woman with Baby Reports Carjacking."

52. Bill Torpy, "Tex McIver is Unlikable and Dangerous. But a Murderer?"

53. Allen, et al., *Comprehensive Criminal Procedure*, 6.

54. Shannon McCaffrey, "Detective in Tex McIver Murder Trial—'Accidents Happen,'" WSB-TV, April 22, 2019, https://www.wsbtv.com/news/local/atlanta/tex-mciver-murder-trial-day-14/724196376/; "Prosecutor: Gaps in Police Investigation of Tex McIver," *Atlanta Journal-Constitution*, March 31, 2018 (available in *Atlanta Journal-Constitution* archives); "The Cops vs. the DA," Breakdown, *Atlanta Journal-Constitution*, April 8, 2018, https://www.stitcher.com/podcast/the-atlanta-journalconstitution/ajc-breakdown/e/54020636.

55. "Reckless conduct" is defined thusly in Georgia law: "A person who causes bodily harm to or endangers the bodily safety of another person by consciously disregarding a substantial and unjustifiable risk that his act or omission will cause harm or endanger the safety of the other person and the disregard constitutes a gross deviation from the standard of care which a reasonable person would exercise in the situation is guilty of a misdemeanor," GA Code § 16-5-60 (b)(2018).

56. Fennessy, "Tex and Diane McIver Had It All."

57. "Joseph Henry Beasley, Biography," *The History Makers*, https://www.thehistorymakers.org/biography/joseph-henry-beasley-41.

58. "Black Activists Concerned about Handling of McIver; Some Worry that Atlanta Lawyer Getting Special Treatment," *Atlanta Journal-Constitution*, October 25, 2016 (available in *Atlanta Journal-Constitution* archives).

59. "Black Activists Concerned about Handling of McIver; Some Worry that Atlanta Lawyer Getting Special Treatment."

60. This description of the 1990 shooting, charges, and their disposition is based on "Tex McIver Faced Charges in 1990 Shooting of Teens' Car," *Atlanta Journal-Constitution*, October 18, 2016, https://www.myajc.com/news/local/tex-mciver-faced-charges-1990-shooting-teens-car/NgCSQDruQjiEL6gCVfsW7I/; "McIver Feared Crime, but Seemed to be the Menace," *Atlanta Journal-Constitution*, October 23, 2016 (available in *Atlanta Journal-Constitution* archives);

DeKalb County Public Services Department, Police Services Incident Report, February 28, 1990; DeKalb County Public Services Department, Police Services, Supplemental Report, April 5, 1990; DeKalb County Police, crime scene and property and evidence reports, February 28, 1990, undated witness statements, and arrest report, March 27, 1990; Dekalb Superior Court, Indictment, "The State versus Claud Lee McIver, III," May 19, 1990; DeKalb Superior Court, Order, November 29, 1990.

61. "McIver Feared Crime, But Seemed to be the Menace."

62. See American Bar Association, "Criminal Justice Standards for the Prosecution Function Fourth Edition (2017)," https://www.americanbar.org/groups/criminal_justice/standards/ProsecutionFunctionFourthEdition/; National District Attorneys Association, "National Prosecution Standards Third Edition," https://ndaa.org/resources/publications-videos/.

63. Richard E. Nisbett and Dov Cohen, *Culture of Honor: The Psychology of Violence in the South* (Boulder, CO: Westview Press, Inc., 1996), 4.

64. Nisbett and Cohen, *Culture of Honor*, 5.

65. Bertram Wyatt-Brown, *Southern Honor: Ethics and Behavior in the Old South* (New York: Oxford University Press, 2007), 3.

66. Wyatt-Brown, *Southern Honor*, 16.

67. Wyatt-Brown, *Southern Honor*, 371.

68. Edward L. Ayers, *Vengeance and Justice: Crime and Punishment in the 19th-Century American South* (New York: Oxford University Press, 1984), 18.

69. Wyatt-Brown, *Southern Honor*, 371.

70. Wyatt-Brown, *Southern Honor*, 53.

71. Nisbett and Cohen, *Culture of Honor*, 92.

72. Christian Boone, "Trial Watchers Consumed by McIver Saga and Power Couple's Life," *Atlanta Journal-Constitution*, April 5, 2018, https://www.ajc.com/news/crime--law/trial-watchers-consumed-mciver-saga-and-power-couple-life/4tg9LgIuE7ec4c2TNZ7qCJ/.

73. "Apology Issued after Atlanta Officer Draws Gun on 82-Year-Old Activist," *Atlanta Journal-Constitution*, September 27, 2019, https://www.ajc.com/news/breaking-news/apology-issued-after-atlanta-officer-draws-gun-year-old-activist/75RUCnMl2sSSukgxQtV01H/.

74. "Handling of Police Chief's Case Sparks Debate," *Atlanta Journal-Constitution*, March 23, 2015 (available in *Atlanta Journal-Constitution* archives).

75. "Handling of Police Chief's Case Sparks Debate."

76. David Markiewicz, "Former Peachtree City Chief Pleads Guilty in Shooting of Ex-wife," *Atlanta Journal-Constitution*, August 13, 2015, https://www.ajc.com/news/crime--law/former-peachtree-city-chief-pleads-guilty-shooting-wife/jJcxZvxhzWSyCwvQVrdsfM/.

77. Jenny Jarvie, "Georgia Sheriff Who Shot and Wounded Friend Was Acquitted in Previous Case," *Los Angeles Times*, May 14, 2015, https://www.latimes.com/nation/la-na-georgia-sheriff-20150514-story.html.

78. Tammy Joyner, "First Offender Act Leaves Clayton Sheriff Hill without Criminal Record," *Atlanta Journal-Constitution*, August 30, 2016, https://www.ajc.com/news/local-govt--politics/first-offender-act-leaves-clayton-sheriff-hill-without-criminal-record/zM0TijWDs1rJXWK5TiysOO/.

79. Complaint and Demand for Jury Trial, *Butler V. Staes*, U.S. District Court for the Central District of Illinois, filed January 21, 2020.

80. This account is based on Complaint and Demand for Jury Trial, *Butler V. Staes*; Alex Horton, "A Black Student Left His Team Bus to Stretch. Police Swarmed and Put a Gun to His Head, Lawsuit Says," *Washington Post*, February 15, 2020, https://www.washingtonpost.com/nation/2020/02/15/jaylan-butler-aclu-lawsuit/; Barb Ickes, "Quad-City Police: Swimmer in ACLU Lawsuit Resisted Arrest," *Quad-City Times* (Davenport, Iowa), April 18, 2020, https://qctimes.com/news/local/quad-city-police-swimmer-in-aclu-lawsuit-resisted-arrest/article_ca5339a7-33e4-585a-9aa8-55a420478b55.html.

81. Horton, "A Black Student Left His Team Bus to Stretch."

82. Complaint and Demand for Jury Trial, *Butler V. Staes*.

83. Complaint and Demand for Jury Trial, *Butler V. Staes*.

7. THROUGH A LENS DARKLY

1. Packer, *The Limits of the Criminal Sanction*, 149.

2. Allen, et al., *Comprehensive Criminal Procedure*, 5.

3. Lippman, *Contemporary Criminal Law*, 196.

4. *Coffin v. United States*, 156 U.S. 432 (1895).

5. 156 U.S. 453.

6. See, for example, "Pattern Criminal Federal Jury Instructions" adopted by the federal Seventh Circuit, Section 2.03, "Presumption of Innocence—Burden of Proof" ("The defendant is presumed to be innocent of [each of] the charge[s]"); New York state court instruction, "Presumption of Innocence" ("Throughout these proceedings, the defendant is presumed to be innocent").

7. *Bell v. Wolfish*, 441 U.S. 520 (1979), 533.

8. William S. Laufer, "The Rhetoric of Innocence," 70 *Wash. L. Rev.* 329 (1995), 357, https://digitalcommons.law.uw.edu/wlr/vol70/iss2/2.

9. Kim Wehle, "Why the Presumption of Innocence Doesn't Apply to Trump," *TheHill.com*, August 8, 2019, https://thehill.com/opinion/white-house/456757-why-the-presumption-of-innocence-doesnt-apply-to-trump.

10. Glenn Kessler, Salvador Rizzo, and Meg Kelly, "President Trump Made 16,241 False or Misleading Claims in His First Three Years," *Washington Post*, January 20, 2020, https://www.washingtonpost.com/politics/2020/01/20/president-trump-made-16241-false-or-misleading-claims-his-first-three-years/; Christian Paz, "All the President's Lies About the Coronavirus," *The Atlantic*, May 27, 2020, https://www.theatlantic.com/politics/archive/2020/05/trumps-lies-about-coronavirus/608647/; Michael Tomasky, "Why Does Trump Lie?" *New York Times*, June 11, 2020, https://www.nytimes.com/2020/06/11/opinion/trump-lies.html

11. Thomas Jipping, "Losing the Presumption of Innocence," The Heritage Foundation, September 28, 2018, https://www.heritage.org/courts/commentary/losing-the-presumption-innocence.

12. For a discussion of the perp walk, its history, and the issues it raises about the criminal justice process, see Clyde Haberman, "For Shame: A Brief History of the Perp Walk," *New York Times*, December 2, 2018, https://www.nytimes.com/2018/12/02/us/perp-walk.html.

13. Craig Schneider and Alexis Stevens, "Tex McIver Surrenders at Fulton Jail after Being Charged in Wife's Death," *Atlanta Journal-Constitution*, December 22, 2016, https://www.ajc.com/news/local/tex-mciver-surrenders-fulton-jail-after-being-charged-wife-death/ZAFjkWsjMupVrD8MHrm5SO/; "Bond Set for Prominent Atlanta Attorney Who Allegedly Fatally Shot His Wife," ABC News, December 22, 2016, https://abcnews.go.com/US/bond-set-prominent-atlanta-attorney-allegedly-fatally-shot/story?id=44344792; Laura Corley, "Atlanta Attorney Charged in Wife's Killing Is Free on Bond," *Telegraph* (Macon, GA), December 23, 2016, https://www.macon.com/news/local/crime/article122711619.html.

14. Adrianne Haney and Michael King, "Judge Decides to Revoke Bond for Tex McIver after Gun Found in His Condo," *11 Alive WXIA-TV*, April 26, 2017, https://www.11alive.com/article/news/crime/judge-decides-to-revoke-bond-for-tex-mciver-after-gun-found-in-his-condo/85-434303848; Fennessy, "Tex and Diane McIver Had It All."

15. William R. Kelly and Robert Pitman, *Confronting Underground Justice: Reinventing Plea Bargaining for Effective Criminal Justice Reform* (Lanham, MD: Rowman & Littlefield, 2018), 46.

16. Paul Butler, "Policing in the US is Not About Enforcing Law. It's About Enforcing White Supremacy," *The Guardian*, May 30, 2020, https://www.theguardian.com/commentisfree/2020/may/30/policing-in-the-us-is-not-about-enforcing-law-its-about-enforcing-white-supremacy.

17. Radley Balko, "The Roger Stone Case Highlights Our Pernicious System of Tiered Justice," *Washington Post*, February 13, 2020, https://

www.washingtonpost.com/opinions/2020/02/13/roger-stone-case-highlights-our-pernicious-system-tiered-justice/.

18. Peter Baker, Maggie Haberman, and Sharon LaFraniere, "Trump Commutes Sentence of Roger Stone in Case He Long Denounced," *New York Times*, July 10, 2020, https://www.nytimes.com/2020/07/10/us/politics/trump-roger-stone-clemency.html.

19. Kelly and Pitman, *Confronting Underground Justice*, 11.

20. Packer, "Courts, the Police, and the Rest of Us," *Journal of Criminal Law and Criminology*, 240.

21. Carol Anderson, *White Rage: The Unspoken Truth of Our Racial Divide* (New York: Bloomsbury, 2017), 99.

22. Kelly and Pitman, *Confronting Underground Justice*, 3. For a scholarly overview of the conservative trend, see Steven M. Teles, *The Rise of the Conservative Legal Movement: The Battle for Control of The Law* (Princeton, NJ: Princeton University Press, 2008).

23. Geoffrey R. Stone and David A. Strauss, *Democracy and Equality: The Enduring Constitutional Vision of the Warren Court* (New York: Oxford University Press, 2020), 161.

24. Sidney Blumenthal, "Willie Horton the Making of an Election Issue," *Washington Post*, October 28, 1988, https://www.washingtonpost.com/archive/lifestyle/1988/10/28/willie-horton-the-making-of-an-election-issue/4395a870-0f0e-4c5a-9eff-9ff1c009d59f/?; Erin Blakemore, "How the Willie Horton Ad Played on Racism and Fear," History.com, November 2, 2018, https://www.history.com/news/george-bush-willie-horton-racist-ad.

25. Anderson, *White Rage*, 104.

26. Kelly and Pitman, *Confronting Underground Justice*, 4.

27. German Lopez, "The Controversial 1994 Crime Law that Joe Biden Helped Write, Explained," *VOX*, June 20, 2019, https://www.vox.com/policy-and-politics/2019/6/20/18677998/joe-biden-1994-crime-bill-law-mass-incarceration.

28. For an overview of the private prison industry, see Kara Gotsch and Vinay Basti, "Capitalizing on Mass Incarceration: U.S. Growth in Private Prisons," The Sentencing Project, August 2018, https://www.sentencingproject.org/publications/capitalizing-on-mass-incarceration-u-s-growth-in-private-prisons/.

29. Kelly and Pitman, *Confronting Underground Justice*, 6.

30. Ed Kilgore, "Trump Is Reviving the Disgraceful Legacy of 'Law-and-Order' Politics," *New York Magazine*, June 3, 2020, https://nymag.com/intelligencer/2020/06/trump-law-and-order-politics-nixon-reagan.html.

31. Lippman, *Law and Society*, 442.

32. Richard Delgado and Jean Stefanic, *Critical Race Theory: An Introduction*, second edition (New York: New York University Press, 2012), 4.

33. Delgado and Stefanic, *Critical Race Theory*, 3.

34. See, for example, Michael Powell, "How a Famous Harvard Professor Became a Target Over His Tweets," *New York Times*, July 15, 2020, https://www.nytimes.com/2020/07/15/us/steven-pinker-harvard.html?.

35. Daniel Subotnik, "What's Wrong with Critical Race Theory: Reopening the Case for Middle Class Values," *Cornell Journal of Law and Public Policy*, 1998, Vol. 7: Issue 3, 681, 684, http://scholarship.law.cornell.edu/cjlpp/vol7/iss3/1.

36. Delgado and Stefanic, *Critical Race Theory*, 45.

37. Dorothy E. Roberts, "Crime, Race and Reproduction," Faculty Scholarship at Penn Law, 1993, 1945–46, https://scholarship.law.upenn.edu/faculty_scholarship/1383.

38. Stephanie B. Goldberg, "The Law, a New Theory Holds, Has a White Voice," *New York Times*, July 17, 1992, https://www.nytimes.com/1992/07/17/archives/the-law-a-new-theory-holds-has-a-white-voice.html?.

39. For one detailed criticism, see Subotnik, "What's Wrong with Critical Race Theory."

40. See, for example, Randall L. Kennedy, "Racial Critiques of Legal Academia," *Harvard Law Review*, June 1989, Vol. 102, No. 8, 1745–819. Available at JSTOR, http://www.jstor.com/stable/1341357.

41. See generally, chapter 6, "Critiques and Responses to Criticism" in Delgado and Stefanic, *Critical Race Theory*, 99–111.

42. Delgado and Stefanic, *Critical Race Theory*, 104.

43. Richard A. Posner, "The Skin Trade," *The New Republic*, October 13, 1997, 40.

44. Posner, "The Skin Trade," 42.

45. Subotnik, "What's Wrong with Critical Race Theory," 697.

46. Delgado and Stefanic, *Critical Race Theory*, 6.

47. Derrick A. Bell, Jr., "The Western Center on Law and Poverty," *Los Angeles Law Bulletin*, October 1968, quoted in Randall L. Kennedy, "Derrick Bell and Me" (March 8, 2019), Harvard Public Law Working Paper No. 19-13, https://ssrn.com/abstract=3350497 or http://dx.doi.org/10.2139/ssrn.3350497.

48. Linda Greenhouse, "The End of Racism, and Other Fables," *New York Times*, September 20, 1992, https://www.nytimes.com/1992/09/20/books/the-end-of-racism-and-other-fables.html?.

49. Fred A. Bernstein, "Derrick Bell, Law Professor and Rights Advocate, Dies at 80," *New York Times*, October 6, 2011, https://www.nytimes.com/2011/10/06/us/derrick-bell-pioneering-harvard-law-professor-dies-at-80.html.

50. Derrick Bell, "Affirmative Action: Another Instance of Racial Workings in the United States," *Journal of Negro Education*, Winter 2000, Volume 69, Issue 1/2, available atwww.questia.com. (Bell argues that affirmative action,

originally intended to help blacks, was transformed so as to primarily help white women.)

51. Kennedy summarized Bell's history and the relationship between the two scholars in Randall L. Kennedy, "Derrick Bell and Me."

52. Henry Louis Gates Jr., "Black Demagogues and Pseudo-Scholars," *New York Times*, July 20, 1992, https://www.nytimes.com/1992/07/20/opinion/black-demagogues-and-pseudo-scholars.html?.

53. Susan Chira, "At Lunch With: Derrick Bell; The Charms of a Devoutly Angry Man," *New York Times*, October 28, 1992, https://www.nytimes.com/1992/10/28/garden/at-lunch-with-derrick-bell-the-charms-of-a-devoutly-angry-man.html?.

54. HR69, Website of the Harvard-Radcliffe Class of 1969, http://hr69.org/harvardiana. The song's original lyrics have been changed to comport with demands for inclusion and excision of symbols associated with exclusion, slavery, and racism among other things. Thus, the "till the stock of the Puritans die" was deleted from the original lyrics. Matt Stevens and Anemona Hartocollis, "Harvard Seeks to Write 'Puritans' Out of Its Alma Mater," *New York Times*, April 7, 2017, https://www.nytimes.com/2017/04/07/us/harvard-alma-mater-contest.html. Along the same lines, Princeton University scrubbed the name Woodrow Wilson from its school of public and international affairs, on the ground that the late president's segregationist policies made him an "especially inappropriate namesake" for a public policy school. Lori Aratani, "Princeton Says It Will Remove Woodrow Wilson's Name From Its Public Policy School," *Washington Post*, June 28, 2020, https://www.washingtonpost.com/local/education/princeton-says-it-will-remove-woodrow-wilsons-name-from-campus-buildings/2020/06/27/26075bee-b898-11ea-aca5-ebb63d27e1ff_story.html. Georgia's public university system announced that it would examine whether the names of any buildings and colleges at its campuses should be changed. Ty Tagami, "Georgia University System to Review Names of Buildings and Colleges," *Atlanta Journal-Constitution*, June 17, 2020, https://www.ajc.com/news/state--regional-education/georgia-university-system-review-names-buildings-and-colleges/LzuItvOun7dFqoD9vxwSpK/. However, the president of Yale University rejected calls to "#CancelYale." Valerie Pavilonis, "'Cancel Yale'? Not Likely," *Yale Daily News*, June 28, 2020, https://yaledailynews.com/blog/2020/06/28/cancel-yale-not-likely/.

55. Biographical details from "Henry Louis Gates Jr., Harvard University," https://aaas.fas.harvard.edu/people/henry-louis-gates-jr.

56. For a book-length examination of the incident and its implications by a Harvard professor of law who was friend and legal counsel to Gates, see Charles Ogletree, *The Presumption of Guilt: The Arrest of Henry Louis Gates Jr. and Race, Class, and Crime in America* (New York: Palgrave Macmillan, 2010).

57. The description of the Gates arrest is based primarily on Ogletree, *The Presumption of Guilt*; "Missed Opportunities, Shared Responsibilities: Final Report of the Cambridge Review Committee," June 15, 2010; Abby Goodnough, "Harvard Professor Jailed; Officer Is Accused of Bias," *New York Times*, July 20, 2009, https://www.nytimes.com/2009/07/21/us/21gates.html; Krissah Thompson, "Harvard Scholar Henry Louis Gates Arrested," *Washington Post*, July 21, 2009, https://www.washingtonpost.com/wp-dyn/content/article/2009/07/20/AR2009072001358.html; Chris Arnold, "Sergeant Who Arrested Gates Tells His Story," NPR, July 24, 2009, https://www.npr.org/templates/story/story.php?storyId=106963782; Lowry Heussler, "Nightmare on Ware Street," in Ta-Nehisi Coates, "The Arrest of Henry Louis Gates," *The Atlantic*, August 12, 2010, https://www.theatlantic.com/national/archive/2010/08/the-arrest-of-henry-louis-gates/61365/; Donald E. Wilkes Jr., "The Arrest of Henry Louis Gates, Jr.," *Flagpole Magazine*, December 1, 2010, 8, h8ps://digitalcommons.law.uga.edu/fac_pm/82.

58. Thompson, "Harvard Scholar Henry Louis Gates Arrested."

59. Arnold, "Sergeant Who Arrested Gates."

60. "Missed Opportunities, Shared Responsibilities: Final Report of the Cambridge Review Committee," 3.

61. Christy E. Lopez, "Disorderly (mis)Conduct: The Problem with 'Contempt of Cop' Arrests," American Constitution Society, June 2010, https://www.acslaw.org/issue_brief/briefs-2007-2011/disorderly-misconduct-the-problem-with-contempt-of-cop-arrests/, 3. (Quoting *Lewis v. City of New Orleans*, 415 U.S. 130.)

62. Lopez, "Disorderly (mis)Conduct," 2.

63. Lopez, "Disorderly (mis)Conduct," 4.

64. Lopez, "Disorderly (mis)Conduct," 5.

65. Heussler, "Nightmare on Ware Street."

66. Heussler, "Nightmare on Ware Street."

67. Heussler, "Nightmare on Ware Street."

68. Lopez, "Disorderly (mis)Conduct," 2.

69. Michele Mcphee and Sara Just, "Obama: Police Acted 'Stupidly' in Gates Case," ABC News, July 22, 2009, https://abcnews.go.com/US/story?id=8148986&page=1.

70. "Henry Louis Gates Jr. on What Really Happened at Obama's 'Beer Summit,'" *New York Times Magazine*, January 31, 2020, https://www.nytimes.com/interactive/2020/02/03/magazine/henry-louis-gates-jr-interview.html.

71. Elaina Plott, "The Fall of Jeff Sessions, and What Came After," *New York Times Magazine*, July 14, 2020, https://www.nytimes.com/2020/06/30/magazine/jeff-sessions.html.

72. Teo Armus, "'I Wasn't Surprised. I Was Just Hurt': A Black Professor Says Campus Police Demanded Proof She Lives in Her Own House," *Washington Post*, August 24, 2020, https://www.washingtonpost.com/nation/2020/08/24/santa-clara-campus-police-professor/.

8. NO N WORDS ANYWHERE

1. Sally E. Haddon, *Slave Patrols: Law and Violence in Virginia and the Carolinas* (Cambridge: Harvard University Press, 2001), 4.

2. Teo Armus, "White Woman 'Terminated' from Job after Calling Police on Black Birdwatcher Who Asked Her to Leash Her Dog, Company Says," *Washington Post*, May 27, 2020, https://www.washingtonpost.com/nation/2020/05/26/amy-cooper-central-park/.

3. The Associated Press, "Student: Response to Professor Who Called Police not Enough," ABC News, January 24, 2020, https://abcnews.go.com/US/wireStory/student-response-professor-called-police-68517776.

4. Theresa Braine, "Detroit Man Settled Antidiscrimination Lawsuit with His Employer, then Bank Called Cops When He Went to Deposit the Checks," *New York Daily News*, January 23, 2020, https://www.nydailynews.com/news/national/ny-detroit-antidiscrimination-suit-bank-not-cash-check-20200124-osl3sx7knjc47camrl6vdpb354-story.html.

5. Mariel Padilla, "Black Deliveryman Says He Was Blocked and Interrogated by White Driver," *New York Times*, May 17, 2020, https://www.nytimes.com/2020/05/17/us/black-delivery-driver-okc-travis-miller.html?.

6. See, for example, David Frum, "The Chilling Effects of Openly Displayed Firearms," *The Atlantic*, August 16, 2017, https://www.theatlantic.com/politics/archive/2017/08/open-carry-laws-mean-charlottesville-could-have-been-graver/537087/; Mark Tran, "Men with Guns Swell Protest Crowds Outside Obama Meetings," *The Guardian*, August 17, 2009, https://www.theguardian.com/world/2009/aug/18/gun-protests-obama; David Welch, "Michigan Cancels Legislative Session to Avoid Armed Protesters," *Bloomberg News*, May 14, 2020, https://www.bloomberg.com/news/articles/2020-05-14/michigan-cancels-legislative-session-to-avoid-armed-protesters; Hannah Knowles, "A Tiny Ohio Town's Black Lives Matter Event was Overrun by Armed Counterprotesters," *Washington Post*, June 16, 2020, https://www.washingtonpost.com/nation/2020/06/16/bethel-ohio-black-lives-counterprotest/.

7. For a comprehensive scholarly discussion of the origins and problems in citizen's arrests, see Ira P. Robbins, "Vilifying the Vigilante: A Narrowed Scope of Citizen's Arrest," *Cornell Journal of Law and Public Policy*, 2016, Vol. 25, No. 3, Article 1, h7p://scholarship.law.cornell.edu/cjlpp/vol25/iss3/1.

8. Seth W. Stoughton, "Ahmaud Arbery's Killing Puts a Spotlight on the Blurred Blue Line of Citizen's Arrest Laws," *The Conversation*, May 29, 2020, https://theconversation.com/ahmaud-arberys-killing-puts-a-spotlight-on-the-blurred-blue-line-of-citizens-arrest-laws-139275.

9. Frances Robles, "The Citizen's Arrest Law Cited in Arbery's Killing Dates Back to the Civil War," *New York Times*, May 13, 2020, https://www.nytimes.com/article/ahmaud-arbery-citizen-arrest-law-georgia.html?.

10. Statute of Winchester, 13 Edward I, c. 1-6 (U.K.) (October 8, 1285), https://en.wikisource.org/w/index.php?title=Statute_of_Winchester&oldid=3719325.

11. Robles, "The Citizen's Arrest Law Cited"; Robbins, "Vilifying the Vigilante," 565.

12. LaFave, *Criminal Law*, Section 10.7(a), 558–59.

13. LaFave, *Criminal Law*, Sections 10.7, 558, and 10.7(d), 564.

14. LaFave, *Criminal Law*, Section 10.7(a), 562–63.

15. Alan J. Singer, "Citizen's Arrest: Racist at its Roots," *History News Network*, May 24, 2020, https://historynewsnetwork.org/article/175619.

16. Nicholas Reimann, "Georgia Lawmakers Look to Repeal 1863 Citizen's Arrest Law After Arbery Killing," *Forbes*, June 4, 2020, https://www.forbes.com/sites/nicholasreimann/2020/06/04/georgia-lawmakers-look-to-repeal-1863-citizens-arrest-law-after-arbery-killing/#7c1921d85e1d.; Robles, "The Citizen's Arrest Law Cited."

17. "One Man's 'Little Stand' Against Crime," *Atlanta Journal*, March 30, 1989 (available in *Atlanta Journal-Constitution* archives).

18. "Henry Man Charged after He 'Arrests' Teens," *Atlanta Journal Constitution*, July 4, 2000 (available in *Atlanta Journal-Constitution* archives).

19. "Citizen's Arrest Wins No Medals," *Atlanta Journal-Constitution*, December 15, 2005 (available in *Atlanta Journal-Constitution* archives).

20. See Georgia Code, O.C.G.A. 16-11-129 (2010), "License to Carry Weapon."

21. The events of the Hannah Payne incident are based on these sources: Clayton County Georgia Superior Court Records, Case No. 2019CR01737, filed June 20, 2019; Clayton County detective's testimony at preliminary hearing, Channel 11 News, https://www.youtube.com/watch?v=HTWPNDdT74c and https://www.youtube.com/watch?v=qScNpaKBGQo; Channel 11 News interview with Hannah Payne's parents, https://www.youtube.com/watch?time_continue=25&v=0JlOGlrjaDU&feature=emb_logo; Zachary Hansen, "Racist Robocall Defends Murder Suspect Who Intervened in Hit-and-Run," *Atlanta Journal-Constitution*, May 14, 2019, https://www.ajc.com/news/crime--law/racist-robocall-defends-murder-suspect-who-intervened-hit-and-run/gEh7ROIniIN7aKxnNAN86J/; Jonathan Raymond, "Shot Dead after a Hit and

Run: A Witness Accused of Murder; The Victim May Have Been in Diabetic Shock," *WXIA-TV*, May 28, 2019, https://www.11alive.com/article/news/crime/shot-dead-after-a-hit-and-run-a-witness-accused-of-murder-the-victim-may-have-been-in-diabetic-shock/85-21155108-40e9-4af1-b944-d1ede36356fb; Zachary Hansen, "Murder Suspect Who Intervened in Hit-and-Run Allegedly Ignored 911 Operator," *Atlanta Journal-Constitution*, May 28, 2019, https://www.ajc.com/news/crime--law/murder-suspect-who-intervened-hit-and-run-allegedly-ignored-911-operator/LD3CtlelcLkFciyRnEBWjJ/; Jonathan Raymond, "Woman who Allegedly Pursued and Killed Man after Hit-and-Run Can Be Released on Bond, Judge Rules," WXIA-TV, May 31, 2019, https://www.11alive.com/article/news/woman-who-allegedly-killed-man-after-hit-and-run-can-be-released-on-bond-judge-rules/85-b4710304-f2a0-4aea-b7bc-93a4d8fde637; Asia Simone Burns, "New Charges for Woman Accused of Intervening in Hit-and-Run, Fatally Shooting Driver," *Atlanta Journal-Constitution*, June 21, 2019, https://www.ajc.com/news/crime--law/new-charges-for-woman-accused-intervening-hit-and-run-fatally-shooting-driver/p6H9HhoKwWBYBgQ3F2JllO/; Tanasia Kenney, "Black Woman Judge to Decide Fate of Vigilante Who Shot, Killed Man Following Hit-and-Run Incident," *Atlanta Black Star*, December 23, 2019, https://atlantablackstar.com/2019/12/23/black-woman-judge-to-decide-fate-of-vigilante-who-shot-killed-man-following-hit-and-run-incident/; Robin Kemp, "Hannah Payne Murder Trial Delayed Again; Was Set for March 9," *Clayton Daily News* (Jonesboro, GA), February 27, 2020, https://www.news-daily.com/news/hannah-payne-murder-trial-delayed-again-was-set-for-march-9/article_6a12e888-5977-11ea-8828-93d05dd2f9bb.html.

22. Channel 11 News interview, https://www.youtube.com/watch?time_continue=25&v=0JlOGlrjaDU&feature=emb_logo.

23. "Hypoglycemia Overview," Mayo Clinic, https://www.mayoclinic.org/diseases-conditions/hypoglycemia/symptoms-causes/syc-20373685?p=1.

24. Alex J. Graveling and Brian M. Frier, "Driving and Diabetes: Problems, Licensing Restrictions and Recommendations for Safe Driving," *Clinical Diabetes and Endocrinology*, 2018, Vol. 1, No. 8, DOI 10.1186/s40842-015-0007-3.

25. Robin Kemp, "Hannah Payne Murder Trial on Hold Until February 2020," *Clayton News-Daily.com*, December 10, 2019, https://www.news-daily.com/news/hannah-payne-murder-trial-on-hold-until-february-2020/article_1ac5d394-1b88-11ea-a670-5b2171b23ea1.html; Frances Robles, "The Citizen's Arrest Law Cited in Arbery's Killing Dates Back to the Civil War."

26. Raymond, "Shot Dead after a Hit and Run."

27. Hansen, "Racist Robocall Defends Murder Suspect."

28. Channel 11 News interview.

29. Mikhail Lyubansky, "Studies of Unconscious Bias: Racism Not Always by Racists," *Psychology Today*, April 26, 2012, https://www.psychologytoday.com/us/blog/between-the-lines/201204/studies-unconscious-bias-racism-not-always-racists.

30. For scholarly descriptions and discussions of IAT testing and results, see, for example, Troy Duster, "Introduction to Unconscious Racism Debate," *Social Psychology Quarterly*, 2008, Vol. 71, No. 1, 6–11; Justin D. Levinson, Huajian Cai, and Danielle Young, "Guilt by Implicit Racial Bias: The Guilty/Not Guilty Implicit Association Test," *Ohio State Journal of Criminal Law*, 2009, Vol. 8, 187; Samuel R. Sommers and Michael I. Norton, "Race-Based Judgments, Race-Neutral Justifications: Experimental Examination of Peremptory Use and the Batson Challenge Procedure," *Law Hum Behav*, 2007, Vol. 31, 261–73.

31. Levinson, et al., "Guilt by Implicit Racial Bias."

32. Robbins, "Vilifying the Vigilante," 557.

33. Robbins, "Vilifying the Vigilante," 599.

34. Audra D. S. Burch and John Eligon, "Bystander Videos of George Floyd and Others Are Policing the Police," *New York Times*, May 29, 2020, https://www.nytimes.com/2020/05/26/us/george-floyd-minneapolis-police.html; Ryan J. Foley, "Video evidence increasingly disproves police narratives," *Denver Post*, June 9, 2020, https://www.denverpost.com/2020/06/09/video-evidence-increasingly-disproves-police-narratives/.

35. Orlando Montoya, "50 Years Later: The 'Quiet Conflict,'" *Georgia Public Broadcasting*, August 26, 2013, https://www.gpb.org/news/2013/08/26/50-years-later-the-quiet-conflict; Jenny Jarvie and Clare Busch, "In Brunswick, Georgia, Residents Reflect on the Shooting of Ahmaud Arbery," *Los Angeles Times*, May 8, 2020, https://www.latimes.com/world-nation/story/2020-05-08/in-brunswick-georgia-residents-reflect-on-the-shooting-of-ahmaud-arbery; Rick Rojas and John Eligon, "In Ahmaud Arbery's Hometown, Pain, Anger and Pride in a Shared Racial History," *New York Times*, May 10, 2020, https://www.nytimes.com/2020/05/10/us/ahmaud-arbery-shooting-brunswick-georgia.html.

36. "About Glynn," Glynn County, GA Official Website, https://www.glynncounty.org/1339/About-Glynn.

37. U.S. Census Bureau, "Quick Facts, Glynn County, Georgia," https://www.census.gov/quickfacts/fact/table/glynncountygeorgia,US/PST045219.

38. "Federal Law Enforcement Training Centers," *Wikipedia*, https://en.wikipedia.org/wiki/Federal_Law_Enforcement_Training_Centers.

39. Peter A. Coclanis, "Rice," *New Georgia Encyclopedia*, December 9, 2019, https://www.georgiaencyclopedia.org/articles/business-economy/rice.

40. Georgia Department of Natural Resources, "Hofwyl-Broadfield Plantation State Historic Site," https://gastateparks.org/HofwylBroadfieldPlantation.

201

The collapse of the rice industry following emancipation of black slaves was devastating for the region.

41. Ralph Betts Flanders, *Plantation Slavery in Georgia* (Chapel Hill: University of North Carolina Press, 1933, reprint by Literary Licensing, LLC), 42–43. Flanders is a useful source on many factual details of slavery in Georgia, but his commentary is of the flawed "lost cause" type and clearly influenced by his race-based perceptions.

42. Janet Schaw, *Journal of a Lady of Quality*, Evangeline Walker Andrews, editor (Lincoln, NE: University of Nebraska Press, 2005, accessed on Questia.com), 194. Schaw's writings are laced with manifest "white privilege." She has been characterized "by her immersion in and relish for the world of aristocratic privilege . . . consumed by the perquisites and appurtenances of such privilege." Keith A. Sandiford, *The Cultural Politics of Sugar: Caribbean Slavery and Narratives of Colonialism* (Cambridge, UK: Cambridge University Press, 2000, accessed through Questia.com), 91.

43. Watson M. Jennison, *Cultivating Race: The Expansion of Slavery in Georgia, 1750-1860* (Lexington: The University Press of Kentucky, 2012), 29.

44. Coclanis, "Rice."

45. Richard Fausset and Rick Rojas, "Where Ahmaud Arbery Ran, Neighbors Cast Wary Eyes," *New York Times*, May 22, 2020, https://www.nytimes.com/article/satilla-shores-ahmaud-arbery-killing.html.

46. Fausset and Rojas, "Where Ahmaud Arbery Ran."

47. For an overview of Georgia's system, see "Georgia Judicial System Structure," https://www.reformgeorgia.org/georgia-judicial-system-structure/.

48. Teresa Stepzinski, "Georgia Governor Appoints Brunswick District Attorney," *Florida Times-Union*, August 9, 2010, https://www.jacksonville.com/article/20100809/NEWS/801247031.

49. See, for example, Rick Rojas, Richard Fausset, and Serge F. Kovaleski, "Georgia Killing Puts Spotlight on a Police Force's Troubled History," *New York Times*, May 8, 2020, https://www.nytimes.com/2020/05/08/us/glynn-county-police-ahmaud-arbery.html; Taylor Cooper, "Jones Call on Governor to Remove DA Johnson, Police Abolition Bill Passes House Committee," *Brunswick News*, June 18, 2020, https://thebrunswicknews.com/news/local_news/jones-call-on-governor-to-remove-da-johnson-police-abolition-bill-passes-house-committee/article_7ef56dfa-9548-52dc-bc33-fd5c0701258d.html.

50. Jim Piggott, "Grand Jury Indicts Glynn County Police Chief, 3 Others," WJXT News4Jax, February 28, 2020, https://www.news4jax.com/news/georgia/2020/02/28/grand-jury-indicts-glynn-county-police-chief-3-others/; Kayla Davis, "Glynn County Police Chief, Three Officers Indicted, Accused of Multiple Oath Violations on Disbanded Drug Task Force," *First Coast News*, February 20, 2020, https://www.firstcoastnews.com/article/news/crime/glynn-county-

chief-of-police-three-officers-indicted-on-multiple-violations-of-oath-charges-related-to-disbanded-drug-task-force/77-c6a8ea57-5b78-4338-b95c-2d53c71028f8.

51. Brad Schrade, "Did Caroline Small Have to Die?" *Atlanta Journal-Constitution*, July 2, 2015, https://investigations.ajc.com/caroline-small-shooting/.

52. Schrade, "Did Caroline Small Have to Die?"

53. Larry Hobbs and Terry Dickson, "Suspended Glynn Police Officer Dead after Allegedly Killing Wife, Boyfriend," *Brunswick News*, June 29, 2018, https://thebrunswicknews.com/breaking/suspended-glynn-police-officer-dead-after-allegedly-killing-wife-boyfriend/article_0d995c95-3eae-5c5d-9e15-14d5da38720a.html.

54. Schrade, "Did Caroline Small Have to Die?"

55. Hobbs and Dickson, "Suspended Glynn Police Officer Dead."

56. Bill Rankin, Brad Schrade, and Joshua Sharpe, "Dark Legacy of Overturned Convictions Trails Longtime Prosecutor," *Atlanta Journal-Constitution*, July 24, 2020, https://www.ajc.com/news/dark-legacy-of-overturned-convictions-trails-longtime-prosecutor/4SDCY5SP3FGKPJ4GVUTM4OLAMM/.

57. This account of Ahmaud Artery's death is based upon the following sources, unless otherwise noted: Glynn County Police Department, "Public Release Incident Report for G20-11303," April 1, 2020; letter from George E. Barnhill, District Attorney, Waycross Judicial District to Captain Tom Jump, Glynn County Police Department, April 2, 2020; "Ahmaud Arbery's Final Minutes: What Videos and 911 Calls Show," undated transcript, *New York Times*, https://www.nytimes.com/article/satilla-shores-ahmaud-arbery-killing.html; Christian Boone and Bert Roughton Jr., "GBI to Launch State Investigation into Brunswick Area Shooting," *Atlanta Journal-Constitution*, May 5, 2020, https://www.ajc.com/news/local/bring-charges-against-brunswick-shooter/fz7taEww0Nqfedg8JgXm2K/; Russell Moore, "The Killing of Ahmaud Arbery and the Justice of God," May 6, 2020, https://www.russellmoore.com/2020/05/06/the-killing-of-ahmaud-arbery-and-the-justice-of-god/; Michael Brice-Saddler, Colby Itkowitz, and Cleve R. Wootson Jr., "Father and Son Charged in the Killing of Black Georgia Jogger, Ahmaud Arbery, after Footage Sparked Outrage," *Washington Post*, May 7, 2020, https://www.washingtonpost.com/politics/2020/05/07/killing-ahmaud-arbery-draws-condemnation-calls-prosecution/; Richard Fausset, "2 Suspects Charged with Murder in Ahmaud Arbery Shooting," *New York Times*, May 7, 2020, https://www.nytimes.com/2020/05/07/us/ahmaud-arbery-shooting-arrest.html; Christian Boone, "Father, Son Charged with Murder in Brunswick Area Shooting," *Atlanta Journal-Constitution*, May 8, 2020, https://www.ajc.com/news/local/father-son-charged-with-murder-brunswick-shooting/tWjmSXAeWlD2LKIN1dSmfK/; Dakin Andone, Angela Barajas, and Jason Morris, "A Suspect in the Killing of Ahmaud Arbery was Involved

in a Previous Investigation of Him, Recused Prosecutor Says," CNN, May 9, 2020, https://www.cnn.com/2020/05/08/us/ahmaud-arbery-mcmichael-arrests-friday/index.html; Joe Henke, "Travis McMichael Named in 2 Incidents Police Responded to in the Weeks before Ahmaud Arbery's Death," *11Alive (WXIA)*, May 13, 2020, https://www.11alive.com/article/news/crime/travis-mcmichael-named-in-2-police-reports-before-arbery-shooting/85-135bab7a-b5bb-40f6-bb1f-3294adb16cda; Brad Schrade, "Police Enlisted Suspect's Help Months before Arbery Shooting," *Atlanta Journal-Constitution*, May 15, 2020, https://www.ajc.com/news/crime--law/suspect-arbery-shooting-had-offered-help-police/gFMpkRpX0Zk5edjvXrE6sN/; Richard Fausset, "Suspect in Arbery Shooting Offered to Help Deal With Potential Trespasser," *New York Times*, May 16, 2020, https://www.nytimes.com/2020/05/16/us/ahmaud-arbery-gregory-mcmichael.html; Bert Roughton Jr. and Brad Schrade, "Records Show a Neighborhood on Edge before Arbery's Final Run," *Atlanta Journal-Constitution*, May 17, 2020, https://www.ajc.com/news/crime--law/records-show-neighborhood-edge-before-arbery-final-jog/P9shmCoRGj90XFWbKfApmJ/; Rick Rojas, "Investigators Say Man Who Filmed Arbery's Killing Was More Than a Witness," *New York Times*, May 22, 2020, https://www.nytimes.com/2020/05/22/us/ahmaud-arbery-william-roddie-bryan.html; Francis Wilkinson, "Ahmaud Arbery Was the Victim of Two Deadly Cultures," *Bloomberg.com*, June 2, 2020, https://www.bloomberg.com/opinion/articles/2020-06-02/ahmaud-arbery-was-killed-by-a-toxic-mix-of-racism-and-gun-culture; Christian Boone, "GBI: Arbery's Killer Uttered Racial Epithet after Firing Fatal Shots," *Atlanta Journal-Constitution*, June 4, 2020, https://www.ajc.com/news/crime--law/gbi-arbery-killer-uttered-racial-epithet-after-firing-fatal-shots/qVQrqQkOPrGxm4JRu5u3JN/; Cleve R. Wootson Jr., Annie Gowen, and Abigail Hauslohner, "Judge Advances Murder Trial for All Three White Men Charged in Death of Ahmaud Arbery," *Washington Post*, June 4, 2020, https://www.washingtonpost.com/nation/2020/06/04/fellow-shooter-called-georgia-jogger-f-ing-n-he-lay-dying-road-agent-testified/; Laura Italiano and Jorge Fitz-Gibbon, "Travis McMichael Allegedly Yelled Racial Slur at Ahmaud Arbery after Shooting," *New York Post*, June 4, 2020, https://nypost.com/2020/06/04/shooter-allegedly-yelled-racial-slur-at-ahmaud-arbery-during-attack/; Bill Hutchinson and Rachel Katz, "Ahmaud Arbery was Struck by Vehicle before He Was Shot Dead; Suspect Yelled Racial Slur: Investigator," ABC News, June 4, 2020, https://abcnews.go.com/US/suspects-struck-ahmaud-arbery-vehicle-shot-dead-yelled/story?id=71066667; Jorge Fitz-Gibbon, "Man who Filmed Ahmaud Arbery Shooting Admitted He Tried to Block Him In," *New York Post*, June 4, 2020, https://nypost.com/2020/06/04/man-who-filmed-ahmaud-arbery-shooting-admits-he-tried-to-block-him-in/; Katheryn Tucker, "Racial Slur Shocks Hearing in Ahmaud Arbery Murder Case," *Law.com Daily Report*, June 4, 2020, https://www.law.com/dailyrepor-

tonline/2020/06/04/racial-slur-shocks-hearing-in-ahmaud-arbery-murder-case/
?slreturn=20200526142925; Griff Witte and Michael Brice-Saddler, "Georgia
Grand Jury Indicts Three Men in Killing of Ahmaud Arbery," *Washington Post*,
June 24, 2020, https://www.washingtonpost.com/national/georgia-ahmaud-arb-
ery-indictment-murder/2020/06/24/e9aac6bc-b668-11ea-aca5-
ebb63d27e1ff_story.html.

58. Roughton and Schrade, "Records Show a Neighborhood on Edge."

59. Tucker, "Racial Slur Shocks Hearing."

60. Italiano and Fitz-Gibbon, "Travis McMichael Allegedly Yelled Racial
Slur."

61. Roughton and Schrade, "Records Show a Neighborhood on Edge."

62. Andone, et al., "A Suspect in the Killing of Ahmaud Arbery"; Wilkinson,
"Ahmaud Arbery Was the Victim." Burglary was defined in common law as the
breaking and entering of the dwelling house of another at night with the intent of
committing a felony. LaFave, *Criminal Law*, Section 21.1, 1017. The modern
offense has been broadly expanded in most states. The nighttime elements have
been dropped, and the locale extended, in some cases to include motor vehicles.

63. National Research Council, "Public Perceptions and Reactions to Violent
Offending and Victimization," 1994, *Understanding and Preventing Violence,
Volume 4: Consequences and Control* (Washington, DC: The National Acade-
mies Press), 18.

64. National Research Council, "Public Perceptions and Reactions," 19.

65. John Gramlich, "Voters' Perceptions of Crime Continue to Conflict with
Reality," Pew Research Center, November 16, 2016, https://
www.pewresearch.org/fact-tank/2016/11/16/voters-perceptions-of-crime-contin-
ue-to-conflict-with-reality/.

66. Terence McArdle, "The 'Law and Order' Campaign that Won Richard
Nixon the White House 50 Years Ago," *Washington Post*, November 5, 2018,
https://www.washingtonpost.com/history/2018/11/05/law-order-campaign-that-
won-richard-nixon-white-house-years-ago/; Rachel Withers, "George H.W.
Bush's "Willie Horton" Ad Will Always be the Reference Point for Dog-Whistle
Racism," *VOX*, December 1, 2018, https://www.vox.com/2018/12/1/18121221/
george-hw-bush-willie-horton-dog-whistle-politics; David Nakamura and Peter
Hermann, "After Announcing Modest Police Reforms, Trump Pivots Quickly to
a Law-and-Order Message in Appeal to His Base," *Washington Post*, June 26,
2020, https://www.washingtonpost.com/politics/after-announcing-modest-po-
lice-reforms-trump-pivots-quickly-to-a-law-and-order-message-in-appeal-to-his-
base/2020/06/26/622c6688-b7b6-11ea-a8da-693df3d7674a_story.html.

67. *New York Times* transcript, "Ahmaud Arbery's Final Minutes."

68. Schrade, "Police Enlisted Suspect's Help."

69. Schrade, "Police Enlisted Suspect's Help."

70. Fausset, "Suspect in Arbery Shooting Offered to Help."

71. Fausset, "Suspect in Arbery Shooting Offered to Help."

72. Schrade, "Police Enlisted Suspect's Help."

73. Fitz-Gibbon, "Man who Filmed Ahmaud Arbery Shooting."

74. Glynn County Police Department, "Public Release Incident Report."

75. Hutchinson and Katz, "Ahmaud Arbery was Struck by Vehicle."

76. W.E.B. Du Bois, *The Souls of Black Folk*, reproduced in *Three African-American Classics* (Mineola, NY: Dover Publications, Inc., 2007), 259.

77. Tucker, "Racial Slur Shocks Hearing."

78. Fitz-Gibbon, "Man who Filmed Ahmaud Arbery Shooting."

79. *New York Times* transcript, "Ahmaud Arbery's Final Minutes."

80. Boone, "GBI: Arbery's Killer Uttered Racial Epithet."

81. Boone, "GBI: Arbery's Killer Uttered Racial Epithet"; Tucker, "Racial Slur Shocks Hearing"; Italiano and Fitz-Gibbon, "Travis McMichael Allegedly Yelled Racial Slur."

82. Glynn County Police Department, "Public Release Incident Report."

83. Rojas, Fausset and Kovaleski, "Georgia Killing Puts Spotlight on a Police Force's Troubled History."

84. Christian Boone and Brad Schrade, "State Guidelines Ignored by Prosecutors in Arbery Death Probe," *Atlanta Journal-Constitution*, May 29, 2020, https://www.ajc.com/news/crime--law/state-guidelines-ignored-prosecutors-arbery-death-probe/tELbrJObvVhaVUQrqy9jHI/; Wilkinson, "Ahmaud Arbery Was the Victim."

85. Boone and Schrade, "State Guidelines Ignored by Prosecutors."

86. Boone and Schrade, "State Guidelines Ignored by Prosecutors"; Katheryn Tucker, "DAs Who Passed on Prosecution in Arbery Case Now Being Investigated," *Law.Com Daily Report*, May 15, 2020, https://www.law.com/dailyreportonline/2020/05/15/das-who-passed-on-prosecution-in-arbery-case-now-being-investigated/?slreturn=20200521133305.

87. Boone and Schrade, "State Guidelines Ignored by Prosecutors."

88. Brice-Saddler, Itkowitz, and Wootson, "Father and Son Charged in the Killing of Black Georgia Jogger"; Boone and Schrade, "State Guidelines Ignored by Prosecutors."

89. Letter from George E. Barnhill, April 2, 2020.

90. National District Attorneys Association, "NDAA Statement on District Attorney Recusal and Comments on Ahmaud Arbery Case," May 9, 2020, https://ndaa.org/ndaa-statement-on-district-attorney-recusal-and-comments-on-ahmaud-arbery-case/.

91. Boone and Schrade, "State Guidelines Ignored by Prosecutors."

92. Carrie Teegardin, "Jury Quickly Says 'Not Guilty' in Georgia Elections Case," *Atlanta Journal-Constitution*, March 15, 2018, https://www.ajc.com/blog/

investigations/jury-quickly-says-not-guilty-georgia-elections-case/uxbn-
ZO4AUxmBQfTmVGZjXK/; Samantha Michaels, "He Didn't File Charges in
the Arbery Case. But He Spent Years Accusing a Black Grandma of Voter
Fraud," *Mother Jones*, May 9, 2020, https://www.motherjones.com/crime-jus-
tice/2020/05/ahmaud-arbery-georgia-jogger-george-barnhill-olivia-pearson-vot-
er-fraud-charges/; Joel Anderson, "The District Attorney Who Saw 'No Grounds
for Arrest' in the Killing of Ahmaud Arbery Has a History," *Slate*, May 9, 2020,
https://slate.com/news-and-politics/2020/05/ahmaud-arbery-george-barnhill-
olivia-pearson.html.

93. Griff Witte and Michael Brice-Saddler, "Georgia Grand Jury Indicts
Three Men in Killing of Ahmaud Arbery," *Washington Post*, June 24, 2020,
https://www.washingtonpost.com/national/georgia-ahmaud-arbery-indictment-
murder/2020/06/24/e9aac6bc-b668-11ea-aca5-ebb63d27e1ff_story.html.

BIBLIOGRAPHY

Abramowitz, Alan I. *The Great Alignment: Race, Party Transformation, and the Rise of Donald Trump.* New Haven: Yale University Press, 2018.

Alexander, Michelle. *The New Jim Crow: Mass Incarceration in the Age of Colorblindness.* New York: The New Press, 2012.

Allen, Ronald J., et al., *Comprehensive Criminal Procedure*, third edition. New York: Wolters Kluwer Law & Business, 2011.

Ambrose, Andy. *Atlanta: An Illustrated History.* Athens, GA: Hill Street Press, 2003.

Anderson, Carol. *White Rage: The Unspoken Truth of Our Racial Divide.* New York: Bloomsbury, 2017.

Aronson, Marc, and Marina Budhos. *Sugar Changed the World: A Story of Magic, Spice, Slavery, Freedom, and Science.* New York: Houghton Mifflin Harcourt, 2010.

Ayers, Edward L. *Vengeance and Justice: Crime and Punishment in the 19th-Century American South.* New York: Oxford University Press, 1984.

Banner, Stuart. *How the Indians Lost Their Land: Land and Power on the Frontier.* Cambridge, MA: Harvard University Press, 2005.

Baptist, Edward E. *The Half Has Never Been Told: Slavery and the Making of American Capitalism.* New York: Basic Books, 2014.

Bazelon, Emily. *Charged: The New Movement to Transform American Prosecution and End Mass Incarceration.* New York: Random House, 2019.

Beckert, Sven. *Empire of Cotton: A Global History.* New York: Alfred A. Knopf, 2014.

Berendt, John. *Midnight in the Garden of Good and Evil.* New York: Vintage Books, 1994.

Berlin, Ira. *Many Thousands Gone: The First Two Centuries of Slavery in North America.* Cambridge, MA: Belknap Press, 1998.

Bernstein, William J. *A Splendid Exchange: How Trade Shaped the World.* New York: Grove Press, 2008.

Blackmon, Douglas A. *Slavery by Another Name: The Re-Enslavement of Black Americans from the Civil War to World War II.* New York: Anchor Books, 2009.

Bobo, Lawrence, James R. Kluegel, and Ryan A. Smith, "Laissez-Faire Racism: The Crystallization of a Kinder, Gentler, Antiblack Ideology," in Steven A. Tuch and Jack K. Martin, editors, *Racial Attitudes in the 1990s: Continuity and Change.* Westport, CT: Praeger Publishers, 1997.

Bolton, Charles C. *Poor Whites of the Antebellum South: Tenants and Laborers in Central North Carolina and Northeast Mississippi.* Durham, NC: Duke University Press, 1994.

Bridges, Herb, and Terryl C. Boodman. *Gone With the Wind: The Definitive Illustrated History of the Book, the Movie, and the Legend.* New York: Simon & Schuster, 1989.

Brown, John. *Slave Life in Georgia.* London: Forgotten Books, 2018 (reprint of 1855 original).

Caldwell, Erskine. *Tobacco Road*, in *The Caldwell Caravan*. New York: The World Publishing Company, 1946.

The Cambridge Ancient History, volume III, part 2. New York: Cambridge University Press, 1991.

Cash, W. J. *The Mind of the South*. New York: Vintage Books, 1991.

Cobb, James C. *Georgia Odyssey: A Short History of the State*, second edition. Athens: The University of Georgia Press, 2008.

Conway, Alan. *The Reconstruction of Georgia*. Minneapolis: University of Minnesota Press, 1966.

Cowan, Ruth Schwartz. *A Social History of American Technology*. New York: Oxford University Press, 1997.

Crane, Elaine Forman. *A Dependent People: Newport, Rhode Island in the Revolutionary Era*. New York: Fordham University Press, 1992.

Crank, John P. *Understanding Police Culture*, second edition. Cincinnati, OH: Anderson Publishing Co., 2004.

Crosby, Alfred W., Jr. *The Columbian Exchange: Biological and Cultural Consequences of 1492*. Westport, CT: Greenwood Press, 1972.

Curtin, Philip D. *The Rise and Fall of the Plantation Complex: Essays in Atlantic History*, second edition. New York: Cambridge University Press, 1998.

Davidson, Basil. *The African Slave Trade: Precolonial History, 1450-1850*. Boston: Little Brown, 1961.

Delgado, Richard, and Jean Stefanic. *Critical Race Theory: An Introduction*, second edition. New York: New York University Press, 2012.

Diaz, Tom. *The Last Gun—How Changes in the Gun Industry Are Killing Americans and What It Will Take to Stop It*. New York: The New Press, 2013.

Diaz, Tom. *Tragedy in Aurora—The Culture of Mass Shootings in America*. Lanham, MD: Rowman & Littlefield, 2019.

Dickey, James. *The Whole Motion: Collected Poems, 1945-1992*. Hanover, NH: University Press of New England, 1992.

Douglass, Frederick. *Narrative of the Life of Frederick Douglass*, in *Three African-American Classics*. Mineola, NY: Dover Publications, Inc., 2007.

Du Bois, W. E. B. *The Souls of Black Folk*, in *Three African-American Classics*. Mineola, NY: Dover Publications, Inc., 2007.

Duke, George, and Robert P. George. *The Cambridge Companion to Natural Law Jurisprudence*. New York: Cambridge University Press, 2017.

Elkins, Stanley M. *Slavery: A Problem in American Institutional and Intellectual Life*. New York: Grosset & Dunlap, 1963.

Engerman, Stanley L., editor. *Terms of Labor: Slavery, Serfdom, and Free Labor*. Stanford, CA: Stanford University Press, 1999.

Farrow, Anne, Joel Lang, and Jenifer Frank. *Complicity: How the North Promoted, Prolonged, and Profited from Slavery*. New York: Ballantine Books, 2005.

Finkleman, Paul, editor. *Slavery and the Law*. Madison, WI: Madison House Publishers, Inc., 1997.

Flanders, Ralph Betts. *Plantation Slavery in Georgia*. Chapel Hill: University of North Carolina Press, 1933 (reproduction).

Foner, Eric. *A Short History of Reconstruction: 1863-1877*. New York: Harper Perennial Modern Classics, 2015.

Friedman, Lawrence M. *American Law in the 20th Century*. New Haven, CT: Yale University Press, 2002.

Friedman, Lawrence M. *Crime and Punishment in American History*. New York: Basic Books, 1993.

Friedman, Lawrence M. *Crime Without Punishment: Aspects of the History of Homicide*. New York: Cambridge University Press, 2018.

Gates, Henry Louis, Jr. *Stony the Road: Reconstruction, White Supremacy, and the Rise of Jim Crow*. New York: Penguin Press, 2019.

Genovese, Eugene D. *From Rebellion to Revolution: Afro-American Slave Revolts in the Making of the Modern World*. Baton Rouge: Louisiana State University Press, 1979.

Genovese, Eugene D. *Roll, Jordan, Roll, the World the Slaves Made*. New York: Vintage Books, 1976.

Glancy, Jennifer A. *Slavery in Early Christianity*. New York: Oxford University Press, 2002. http://www.questia.com/read/103556599/slavery-in-early-christianity.

Goldenberg, David M. *The Curse of Ham: Race and Slavery in Early Judaism, Christianity, and Islam*. Princeton, NJ: Princeton University Press, 2005. http://www.questia.com/read/117793725/the-curse-of-ham-race-and-slavery-in-early-judaism.

Green, Constance McLaughlin. *Eli Whitney and the Birth of American Technology*. New York: Longman, 1956.

Gregory, James N. *The Southern Diaspora: How the Great Migration of Black and White Southerners Transformed America*. Chapel Hill: The University of North Carolina Press, 2005.

Gross, Ariela J. *What Blood Won't Tell: A History of Race on Trial in America*. Cambridge, MA: Harvard University Press, 2008.

Haddon, Sally E. *Slave Patrols: Law and Violence in Virginia and the Carolinas*. Cambridge, MA: Harvard University Press, 2001.

Harris, Kamala D. *Smart on Crime: A Career Prosecutor's Plan to Make Us Safer*. San Francisco: Chronicle Books, 2009.

Hietala, Thomas R. *Manifest Design: American Exceptionalism and Empire*, revised edition. Ithaca, NY: Cornell University Press, 2003.

Hinton, Elizabeth. *From the War on Poverty to the War on Crime: The Making of Mass Incarceration in America*. Cambridge: Harvard University Press, 2016.

Hobhouse, Henry. *Seeds of Change: Six Plants that Transformed Mankind*. New York: Shoemaker & Hoard, 2005.

Hochschild, Arlie Russell. *Strangers in Their Own Land: Anger and Mourning on the American Right*. New York: The New Press, 2016.

Hodges, John O. *Delta Fragments: The Recollections of a Sharecropper's Son*. Knoxville: The University of Tennessee Press, 2013.

Horton, James Oliver, and Lois E. Horton. *Slavery and the Making of America*. New York: Oxford University Press, 2005.

Horton, James Oliver, and Lois E. Horton, editors. *Slavery and Public History: The Tough Stuff of American Memory*. Chapel Hill: The University of North Carolina Press, 2006.

Hough, Richard M., and Kimberly D. McCorkle. *American Homicide*. Thousand Oaks, CA: SAGE Publications, Inc., 2017.

Hounshell, David A. *From the American System to Mass Production, 1800-1932*. Baltimore: The Johns Hopkins University Press, 1984.

Heuman, Gad, and Trevor Burnard, eds. *The Routledge History of Slavery*. New York: Rutledge, 2011.

Hunt, Peter. *Ancient Greek and Roman Slavery*. Hoboken, NJ: John Wiley & Sons, 2018.

Isenberg, Nancy. *White Trash: The 400-Year Untold History of Class in America*. New York: Viking, 2016.

Inglehart, Ronald. *The Silent Revolution: Changing Values and Political Styles among Western Publics*. Princeton: Princeton University Press, 1977.

Ingram, Jefferson L. *Criminal Evidence*, eleventh edition. Waltham, MA: Elsevier Books, 2012.

Jacobs, Harriet. *Incidents in the Life of a Slave Girl*. Mineola, NY: Dover Publications, Inc., 2001.

Jacobson, Matthew Frye. *Whiteness of a Different Color: European Immigrants and the Alchemy of Race*. Cambridge: Harvard University Press, 1998.

Jennison, Watson M. *Cultivating Race: The Expansion of Slavery in Georgia, 1750-1860*. Lexington: The University Press of Kentucky, 2012.

Johnson, Walter. *River of Dark Dreams: Slavery and Empire in the Cotton Kingdom*. Cambridge, MA: The Belknap Press, 2013.

Jones-Rogers, Stephanie E. *They Were Her Property: White Women as Slave Owners in the American South*. New Haven, CT: Yale University Press, 2019.

Kelley, Sean M. *The Voyage of the Slave Ship Hare: A Journey into Captivity from Sierra Leone to South Carolina*. Chapel Hill, NC: University of North Carolina Press, 2016.

Kelly, William R., and Robert Pitman. *Confronting Underground Justice: Reinventing Plea Bargaining for Effective Criminal Justice Reform*. Lanham, MD: Rowman & Littlefield, 2018.

Kennedy, Randall. *Race, Crime, and the Law*. New York: Vintage Books, 1997.

Kirkland, Dep. *Lawyer Games: After Midnight in the Garden of Good and Evil*. Indianapolis: Dog Ear Publishing, 2015.

Kruse, Kevin M. *White Flight: Atlanta and the Making of Modern Conservatism*. Princeton, NJ: Princeton University Press, 2005.

LaFave, Wayne R. *Criminal Law*, fourth edition. St. Paul, MN: West Publishing Co., 2003.

Liem, Marieke, and Frans Koenraadt. *Domestic Homicide: Patterns and Dynamics*. New York: Routledge, 2018.

Lippman, Matthew. *Law and Society*, second edition. Thousand Oaks, CA: SAGE Publications, 2018.

Lippman, Matthew. *Contemporary Criminal Law: Concepts, Cases and Controversies*. Thousand Oaks, CA: Sage Publications, Inc., 2019.

Loewen, James W. *Sundown Towns: A Hidden Dimension of American Racism*. New York: The New Press, 2018.

Lowery, Wesley. *"They Can't Kill Us All": The Story of the Struggle for Black Lives*. New York: Back Bay Books, 2016.

Lynn, Joshua A. *Preserving the White Man's Republic: Jacksonian Democracy, Race, and the Transformation of American Conservatism*. Charlottesville: University of Virginia Press, 2019.

McIlvenna, Noeleen. *The Short Life of Free Georgia: Class and Slavery in the Colonial South*. Chapel Hill, NC: University of North Carolina Press, 2015.

McPherson, James M. *Battle Cry of Freedom: The Civil War Era*. New York: Oxford University Press, 1988.

McPherson, James M. *Ordeal by Fire: The Civil War and Reconstruction*. New York: McGraw-Hill, 2001.

Mason, Lilliana. *Uncivil Agreement: How Politics Became our Identity*. Chicago: The University of Chicago Press, 2018.

Meltzer, Milton. *The Cotton Gin*. New York: Benchmark Books, 2004.

Meltzer, Milton. *Slavery, A World History*, updated edition. New York: De Capo Press, 1993.

Melusky, Joseph, and Keith A. Pesto. *The Death Penalty: A Reference Handbook*. Santa Barbara, CA: ABC-CLIO, 2017.

Merritt, Keri Leigh. *Masterless Men: Poor Whites and Slavery in the Antebellum South*. New York: Cambridge University Press, 2017.

Miller, Dan B. *Erskine Caldwell: The Journey from Tobacco Road*. New York: Alfred A. Knopf, 1995.

Mitchell, Margaret. *Gone With the Wind*. New York: Scribner, 2011.

Morgan, Kenneth. *Slavery and the British Empire: From Africa to America*. New York: Oxford University Press, 2007.

Morris, Thomas D. *Southern Slavery and the Law: 1619-1860*. Chapel Hill: University of North Carolina Press, 1999.

Muller, Ingo. *Hitler's Justice: The Courts of the Third Reich*. Cambridge, MA: Harvard University Press, 1991.

Nisbett, Richard E., and Dov Cohen. *Culture of Honor: The Psychology of Violence in the South*. Boulder, CO: Westview Press, 1996.

Northup, Solomon. *12 Years a Slave*. New York: GreyMalkin Media, 2014.

Oakes, James. *The Ruling Race: A History of American Slaveholders*. New York: W.W. Norton & Company, 1998.

Ogletree, Charles. *The Presumption of Guilt: The Arrest of Henry Louis Gates Jr. and Race, Class, and Crime in America*. New York: Palgrave Macmillan, 2010.

Packer, Herbert L. *The Limits of the Criminal Sanction*. Stanford, CA: Stanford University Press, 1968.

Parsons, Elaine Frantz. *Ku-Klux: The Birth of the Klan During Reconstruction*. Chapel Hill: The University of North Carolina Press, 2015.

Percy, William Alexander. *Lanterns on the Levee: Recollections of a Planter's Son*. Baton Rouge: Louisiana State University Press, 1941.

Pilgrim, David. *Watermelons, Nooses, and Straight Razors: Stories from the Jim Crow Museum*. Oakland, CA: PM Press, 2018.

Pilgrim, David. *Understanding Jim Crow: Using Racist Memorabilia to Teach Tolerance and Promote Social Justice*. Oakland, CA: PM Press, 2015.

Plucknett, Theodore F. T. *A Concise History of the Common Law*. Indianapolis: Liberty Fund 2010 reprint of fifth edition originally printed by Little, Brown and Co., 1956.

Putnam, Robert D. *Bowling Alone: The Collapse and Revival of American Community*. New York: Simon & Schuster Paperbacks, 2000.

Rawlings, William. *The Second Coming of the Invisible Empire: The Ku Klux Klan of the 1920s*. Macon, GA: Mercer University Press, 2016.

Rawlings, William. *The Strange Journey of the Confederate Constitution and Other Stories from Georgia's Historical Past*. Macon, GA: Mercer University Press, 2017.

Rediker, Marcus. *The Slave Ship: A Human History*. New York: Penguin Books, 2008.

Richardson, David, Suzanne Schwarz, and Anthony Tibbles, editors. *Liverpool and Transatlantic Slavery*. Liverpool: University of Liverpool Press, 2007.

Rummel, R. J. *Death by Government*. New Brunswick, NJ: Transaction Publishers, 1994.

Sandiford, Keith A. *The Cultural Politics of Sugar: Caribbean Slavery and Narratives of Colonialism*. Cambridge, UK: Cambridge University Press, 2000.

Schaw, Janet. *Journal of a Lady of Quality*. Evangeline Walker Andrews, editor. Lincoln, NE: University of Nebraska Press, 2005.

Sheridan, Richard B. *Sugar and Slavery: An Economic History of the British West Indies, 1623-1775*. Kingston, Jamaica: Canoe Press, 1974.

Smith, Lillian. *Killers of the Dream*. New York: W.W. Norton & Company, 1994.

Stampp, Kenneth M. *The Peculiar Institution: Slavery in the Ante-Bellum South*. New York: Vintage Books, 1989.

Stannard, David E. *American Holocaust: The Conquest of the New World*. New York: Oxford University Press, 1992.

Steinfeld, Robert J. *The Invention of Free Labor: The Employment Relation in English and American Law and Culture, 1350-1870*. Chapel Hill, NC: University of North Carolina Press, 1991.

Stinchcombe, Arthur L. *Sugar Island Slavery in the Age of Enlightenment: The Political Economy of the Caribbean World*. Princeton, NJ: Princeton University Press, 1995.

Stone, Geoffrey R., and David A. Strauss, *Democracy and Equality: The Enduring Constitutional Vision of the Warren Court*. New York: Oxford University Press, 2020.

Stuntz, William J., and Joseph L. Hoffman. *Defining Crimes*, second edition. New York: Wolters Kluwer Law & Business, 2014.

Tannenbaum, Frank. *Slave and Citizen: The Negro in the Americas*. New York: Alfred A. Knopf, 1947.

Tannenbaum, Frank. *Slave and Citizen: The Negro in the Americas*. New York: Alfred A. Knopf, 1947.

Teles, Steven M. *The Rise of the Conservative Legal Movement: The Battle for Control of The Law*. Princeton, NJ: Princeton University Press, 2008.

Thompson, Tracy. *The New Mind of the South*. New York: Free Press, 2013.

Time-Life Books editors. *Voices of the Civil War: Atlanta*. Alexandria, VA: Time-Life Books, 1996.

Trump, Donald J., with Dave Shiflett. *The America We Deserve*. Los Angeles: Renaissance Books, 2000.

Tushnet, Mark V. *Slave Law in the American South: State v. Mann in History and Literature*. Lawrence, KS: The University Press of Kansas, 2003.

Walker, Alice. *The Color Purple*. New York: Harcourt, Inc., 2003.

Washington, Booker T. *Up from Slavery*, in *Three African-American Classics*. Mineola, NY: Dover Publications, Inc., 2007.

Weaver, John C. *The Great Land Rush and the Making of the Modern World, 1650-1900*. Montreal: McGill-Queen's University Press, 2006.

Weightman, Gavin. *The Industrial Revolutionaries: The Making of the Modern World, 1776-1914*. New York: Grove Press, 2007.

Westermann, William L. *The Slave Systems of Greek and Roman Antiquity*. Philadelphia: American Philosophical Society, 1955. http://www.questia.com/read/3797806/the-slave-systems-of-greek-and-roman-antiquity.

Wiedemann, Thomas. *Greek and Roman Slavery*. London: Routledge, 1988. http://www.questia.com/read/109103591/greek-and-roman-slavery.

Wilson, William Julius. *More than Just Race: Being Black and Poor in the Inner City*. New York: W.W. Norton & Company, 2009.

Wolfe, Tom. *A Man in Full*. New York: The Dial Press, 2005.

Woodward, C. Vann. *The Strange Career of Jim Crow*. New York: Oxford University Press, 2002 (reprint of 1955 original release).

Wray, Matt. *Not Quite White: White Trash and the Boundaries of Whiteness*. Durham, NC: Duke University Press, 2006.

Wuthnow, Robert. *The Left Behind: Decline and Rage in Rural America*. Princeton, NJ: Princeton University Press, 2018.

Wyatt-Brown, Bertram. *Southern Honor: Ethics and Behavior in the Old South*. New York: Oxford University Press, 2007.

Yafa, Stephen. Cotton: *The Biography of a Revolutionary Fiber*. New York: Penguin Books, 2006.

INDEX

ABOUT THE AUTHOR

Tom Diaz is a retired lawyer and former journalist who lives in the Metropolitan Washington, DC, area. He has written five other non-fiction books and a number of monographs and articles about crime, terrorism, and firearms. He is a graduate of the University of Florida and of the Georgetown University Law Center.

Diaz practiced a variety of civil and criminal law in his legal career. He was assistant managing editor at *The Washington Times* newspaper from 1985 to 1991, where as a reporter he reported on national security affairs. He was Democratic counsel to the U.S. House of Representatives Subcommittee on Crime and Criminal Justice from 1993 to 1997, where his subject matter specialties included terrorism and firearms regulation. He was a senior policy analyst at a gun violence reduction organization from 1997 to 2012.